Fairly Mounted on a Hill

Bromsgrove's Church
and its people

by
Simon Henderson

Friends of
ST. JOHN'S

A Thank You to Subscribers

Simon Henderson has donated this book to the Friends of St John's as a way of raising funds to support the ongoing maintenance and restoration needs of our historic building. In order to meet the initial publishing costs the Friends put out a call for people to subscribe to the book. The Friends of St John's are thrilled with the response and are most grateful to each of the 125 subscribers, some of whom wished to remain anonymous.

Ian Angus & Anna Fairbank
James & Jenny Ashmore
Richard Aust O.B.E.
George Barrett
Ann & Alan Batchelor
Ronald & Margaret Bearman
Mrs Pauline Bennett
Neville Billington
Graham & Fiona Boyles
Shirley Brittan
Mrs Gail Brooks
Mrs Margaret Brooks
Mrs Frances E Browne
Mrs Ann Burdett
Helen Chambers
Tony M Chance
Terry Clarke
Rosalind Cooke
Miss Michelle Cooper
Bromsgrove Court Leet
Jane Cowan
Steve Cowperthwaite
Barry Davey
Jill Dolphin
Victor Dovey

Jenny Edginton
Jeff & Jules Evans
Margaret Evans
Mrs Gilly Evans
Mrs John Foster
David & Emily Godfrey
David J Grainger
Mrs J Greenhough
Pat & Geoff Grizzell
People of Gronau, Germany
Gordon Guest
Richard & Jo Hackett
John & Jo Halfpenny
Miss Jean Halfpenny
Adrienne Hall
Mrs Jean Hancox
Graham P Harris
Janine Harris - in memorium
Janet Hatton
Karl Hearne
Simon Henderson
The Henderson Family - Brenda, Alistair, Nick & Lizzie
Toby Henderson
Brenda Howard

A THANK YOU TO SUBSCRIBERS

Anstice Hughes
Rev Sue Humphries
Julian Hunt
Rob & Claire Hunter
Dr. John Jackson
Sajid Javid MP
K G Keitley
Ray Khan
Donald P Kynaston
Stephen Kyte
Giles & Sharon Lees
Beatrice Lodge
Gordon Long
Anne Maguire
David Marsh
Mary & Clive Marsh
Jennie & John McGregor-Smith
John Miller
Alastair Moseley
Shân Moule
Avoncroft Museum
Chris Nesbitt
Richard Nix
Dr. David Nokes
Elizabeth Oakley
Kenneth Parish
Betty Pickering
Nick Pinfield
Poppy & Bella Pinfield
Bob & Sally Powell
Stephen Price
Alwyn Rea
Margaret & Hilary Rice
Ann & Clive Rogers

Hans Rostrup
Hilda Roxborough
Jayne Sallis
Yvonne Scott
Jeremy & Helen Sharp
Robin & Kate Shaw
Warwick Sheffield
Cameron & Ella Slade
David & Janet Slade
Jo Slade
B J Slater
Ruth & Philip Smiglarski
The Bromsgrove Society
Bromsgrove Standard
Pat Tansell
Greg Thay
Yvette Thomas
Mrs Valda Timmis
Sean Tomlinson
Jenny Townshend
Sheila Vincent
Helen Voyle
Edward Nicholas Walsh
Malcolm Walters
Kevin Ward
Mrs Susan Elaine Waugh
John C Weston
Mrs Audrey Wheeler
Revd Alan White
Brian Williams
Hamish C Wilson
Peter & Derdra Windows
Anthony Woodward
Martyn & Therese Workman

FAIRLY MOUNTED ON A HILL

This book is a collaboration between Kissed Off Publications and Friends of St John's, Bromsgrove.

© 2015 Kissed Off Publications (design) and Simon Henderson (content)

All rights reserved. No copying, editing, publication or distribution (in whole or in part) is authorised without the express authorisation of the Publisher and the Author.

ISBN: 978-0-9928601-5-8

The Author has asserted his right to be identified as the Author of this work under the Copyright, Design and Patents Act 1988.

Author: Simon Henderson
Designer: Natalie Ballard for Kissed Off Creations Ltd

All images included herein are copyright of their original creators, and are used with permission by the Author. The Author has made every effort to contact the original copyright holders of works featured within this title. If he has been unsuccessful, we apologise and welcome correction for future editions and reprints.

Publisher details:

Kissed Off Publications is the Publishing division of Kissed Off Creations Ltd. We are a register UK publisher and our Company Number is 07875572. We can be contacted via email: info@kissedoff.co.uk

Printed and Published in the UK

Contents

INTRODUCTION	7
PART ONE: EARLY DAYS TO THE REFORMATION	11
CHAPTER 1: BEGINNINGS	12
CHAPTER 2: GROWTH	25
CHAPTER 3: EXPANSION	41
CHAPTER 4: COMPLETION	56
PART TWO: THE 17th CENTURY TO MODERN TIMES	85
CHAPTER 5: A DIVIDED HOUSE	86
CHAPTER 6: THE SLEEPING CHURCH	161
CHAPTER 7: A CHURCH RESTORED	212
CHAPTER 8: MODERN TIMES	257
BIBLIOGRAPHY	277
GENERAL INDEX	287
INDEX OF NAMES	293

FAIRLY MOUNTED ON A HILL

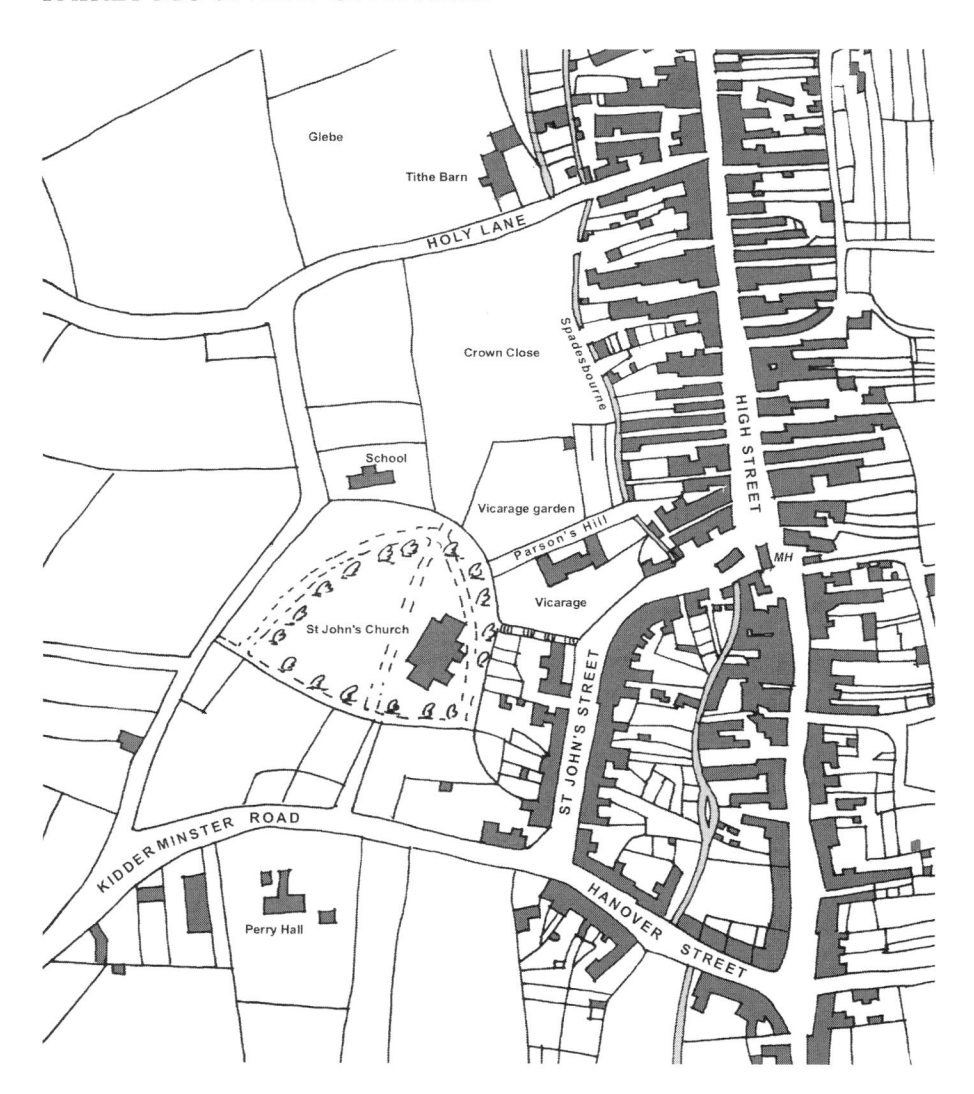

[Plan a. tithe map] St John the Baptist Parish Church and its surroundings, redrawn from the 1840 Tithe Map. The church and churchyard are much as today, but the vicarage was rebuilt in 1848 on an adjoining site, necessitating the realignment of Parson's Hill. The school still exists, albeit much extended, as offices. The Tithe Barn was demolished in 1844. Note the lack of any roadway across Crown Close, although a track was in existence from at least 1788. MH = the Market House.

INTRODUCTION

This is the story of a church and the people who used it.

The parish church of St John the Baptist has crowned its little hill in north Worcestershire for around nine hundred years. At its feet grew the market town of Bromsgrove, whose wealth once came from cloth and whose poverty from nails. Through its doors came generation upon generation of local folk, to be baptised, married and buried, to argue and debate or just to worship in the fashion of their time. Within and around its walls people played out their lives, for good or ill. Beneath its yard lie their mortal remains, under elaborate slabs, simple stones or the anonymous grass. The church has stood through all this change, cared for or neglected as time and fashion dictated, silently recording the lives of its occupants. It is the one local building that links every generation since the Norman Conquest and its fortunes reflects theirs.

The parish church was the biggest building by some margin in the average medieval town. It was possibly the only entirely stone structure and certainly the most commonly used. Only rarely the work of individuals or corporations, the main body of the church belonged of ancient right to the townspeople themselves, built, owned and maintained by them and used throughout the week for any function needing a large internal space. It was not only a market, a school, court, a meeting place, but sometimes also a party venue, newsagents, bell foundry or brew-house. The purely religious image of churches – used one day a week and locked for the remainder - is a modern falsehood, fuelled by mid-19th century notions of medieval piety and some way from the bustling reality of earlier times. In the days before parish councils acquired their present solely secular function it was also the seat of much local government, backed by powerful church courts with punitive powers equal to any lay authority. For many people the parish church was the centre of their social life, the regulator of their behaviour and their working day; and they adapted it whenever necessary to meet their changing needs and beliefs. The development of the parish is a microcosm of the development of society itself, from feudal monarchy through the oligarchies and sects of the post-Reformation period to something approaching modern democracy. The church was a sometimes unwilling catalyst for these social changes and it gives us important clues about who we now are and why we think as we do.

This story travels a long road from the uncertain light of early England to somewhere near the present day. It falls naturally into two distinct parts. Part 1 deals with the beginnings and growth of the church, from Saxon origins to the Reformation of the English Church in the 16th Century. It spans the entire period of the church's existence as a Catholic place of worship and the complex architectural development of the building fabric. Part 2 takes up the story of the newly Anglican church in the reign of Edward VI and tells a rather different tale, a very human story travelling from dissent and decay to restoration and revival.

For this is also the story of the people who used Bromsgrove's church. It is a story of important men and women, kings, lords, knights and gentry; and of ordinary folk; peasants, priests, farmers and tradesmen - some now lost, others with names that have survived the generations. This apparently immutable historical monument is really a palimpsest of individual lives, written, erased and rewritten in stone, lead, glass and wood: and in words themselves - in ledgers and record books, on gravestones and monuments, in letters and newsprint. However remote the period the people of St John's insist on behaving much as we would now: fearful or optimistic, hopeful, angry, clinging to a vision of a better England or – just occasionally - plain rude. In Latin or English, in crabbed Tudor handwriting,

INTRODUCTION

Georgian print or the letters page of the Bromsgrove Messenger, they reveal their relationship with their church through the centuries, and this story uses their own words whenever possible.

Acknowledgements

This story could not have seen the light of day without the help of many people. Amongst those who helped with specific aspects of the story, or opened doors for which I had no key, I would like to thank in particular Jenny Townshend for her enthusiastic explanation of Tudor and Stuart wills; John Weston for pointing me towards several major sources of information; Hilary Turner for putting me right on the Sheldon tapestry maps; Byron Kinney for information on John Boweter; Kevin Allen for highlighting Edward Vine Hall's musical interests; Karl Hearne for translating dense legal Latin and explaining the intricacies of post-Restoration acts of Parliament; Pat Tansell and the staff of Bromsgrove Library, Worcester Records Office and Birmingham City Library for putting up with my endless requests; Jo Slade, whose expert project-management brought this book into production; my wife, Bren, for her unfailing help and support throughout; and finally the parishioners and clergy of St John the Baptist parish church, whose encouragement was fuel to me when completion seemed a long way off, and whose patience I hope I have now rewarded.

Readers familiar with the local history of this area may wonder what could be added to William Cotton's definitive account of St John's church, published in 1881. Cotton remains an unrivalled compendium of detailed information and my inspiration to follow. But although I started my own journey with him my objective was different. William Cotton's "today" is itself now history and the late Victorian light he wrote by has gone forever. Wherever possible I have gone back to the first hand sources Cotton himself used, together with others not available to him at the time, such as the invaluable publications of the Worcestershire

Historical Society. In many cases, I have reached much the same conclusion that he did: in others, new evidence or reappraisal has cast a different light on Cotton's viewpoint. This story is not intended to supplant but to interpret for a new generation, and I readily acknowledge my debt to him.

No history can be a pure assemblage of unvarnished facts - at least not one that reaches back into a time when written records were not uppermost in peoples' minds. While this account is based firmly on the historical record where it exists, it must also interpolate, piece together or sometimes simply guess at what may have happened when the record is blank or uncertain. In the end, any history must be an interpretation and this is mine, as is the responsibility for any errors.

Simon Henderson

Bromsgrove, 2015

A note about notes

This is not an academic treatise. I have therefore not given the sources of my information as footnotes but in a general bibliography at the end. The footnotes instead comprise additional information, interesting in itself but either too detailed or too tangential to include in the general narrative. They can be ignored without disturbing the story, or they can be mined for further sidelights on people, places and events at the reader's choice.

Part 1

EARLY DAYS TO THE REFORMATION

I will first begyn in Bromesgrau because it is the Parsonage and mother churche of Kyngsnorton, and pryveleadged by the royall charter with the honor of a mercate and towe fayres, and in bothe lytell inferiour to the best of our shyre

Thomas Habington, c1640

CHAPTER 1: BEGINNINGS

Pre-conquest to the death of King John

Saxon Bromsgrove

There is little enough to begin with. A Roman road strikes northeast away from the River Severn, following the line of a much older hill-top trackway. An old cattle drove road winds slowly east from the Welsh Marches. A small, stony river runs off the Lickey Hills and meanders through a broad wooded valley. All three meet at the foot of a low, rounded hill, and together they form the nucleus around which the town of Bromsgrove and its church will grow.

The origins of Bromsgrove as a town are uncertain. There is no evidence for any long-lasting British or Roman occupation, and the first English to find this spot were the Hwicce, an independent-minded people of mixed Anglian and Saxon stock who were granted their own early diocese based on Worcester, around 680AD[1]. The junction of roads is a popular starting point for settlements, particularly a junction with the upper Saltway, a Roman arterial highway with nearly two thousand years of continuous use. You might imagine (for there is no hard evidence) a small Saxon trading post growing up around the water-splash where the drove road crossed the stream and drovers watered their cattle. You might further imagine simple timber cottages springing up around this spot and forming a basic village green, with more cottages straggling away along the main road to north and south. All this is still here - the High Street (once the A38); the

---

[1] Isolated Roman artefacts have been found in the area but there is no evidence for any permanent occupation. A supposed Roman coin was dug up in the 18th century from a sandpit near the churchyard but has now been lost.

CHAPTER 1: BEGINNINGS

Kidderminster Road heading west; the little River Spadesbourne; even the village green, now rather more prosaically the Market Street car park.

The Saxon manor of Bromsgrove was one of the biggest in Worcestershire, an enormous 23,000 acres or thereabouts, stretching northeast from Bromsgrove itself along the old Roman road for about twelve miles, well into what is now suburban Birmingham. Patches of plough-land supported the settlement at Bromsgrove and twenty-two small hamlets, including Chadwich, Wythall and Moseley; but these were really just inhabited clearings in the great swathe of woodland that covered much of the manor in a carpet around ten miles long by six wide. This was part of the Forest of Feckenham, an outlier of the great Forest of Arden that stretched in a broken wave across large swathes of the western shires. As well as providing building material and cover for game of all kind the forest supplied enormous quantities of fuel timber for the salt-making industry at Droitwich (Roman Salinae), some six miles south along the Roman road. Salt was a valuable commodity for food preservation as well as cooking, and its production was kept firmly under royal control. By the 11th century, Bromsgrove manor actually owned thirteen salt houses of its own in Droitwich, the second largest number outside Droitwich itself.

With its highly profitable salt-works, a decent hunting forest and command of several major roads through otherwise impenetrable territory, the manor of Bromsgrove was one asset that Saxon kings did not wish to part with, other than to their own kin. A settlement of some sort was certainly in existence by 804 AD, held by a Mercian nobleman, Æthelric, son of Æthelmund. Although the manor was apparently granted to the Church in the early 9th century it was restored to royal ownership after 823 AD when the Mercian King Ceolwulf recovered Bremsgrafen from Bishop Heaberht of Worcester's tenant, Wulfhærd of Inkberrow, and by the mid 11th century Saxon Bremesgriefa was held by Edwin, the very last Saxon earl of Mercia. None of these aristocratic owners actually lived anywhere near Bromsgrove, of course - even tenants like Wulfhærd had somewhere better to go. But Bromsgrove's very name hints that at least one person saw it as his own. The small wood belonging to Brem [*"an illustrious man"*], it means in Old English. No-one knows who Brem was, or even why he was illustrious. If the incoming Hwicce only knew of him by reputation, was he even older – a Briton, perhaps?

As its name suggests, the value of Bromsgrove as a manor lay largely in its natural and geographical aspects, not in the importance of its towns. The only settlement of any size at all was Bromsgrove itself, and even this would hardly qualify as a village by today's standards. But it differed in one important respect from its neighbouring hamlets. It is certain that Bremesgrave had a priest in 1086 because William the Conqueror's roving commissioners duly recorded him for the Domesday Book - and a priest implies a church of some sort, however humble. Although clergy are recorded in adjacent manors at Chaddesley to the west, Alvechurch to the east and Stoke Prior just to the south, Bromsgrove's priest sits alone in his manor, with no other church to the north for some considerable distance. But the southernmost point in the whole manor is an odd place to build its one place of worship; and the top of a steep hill is a curious place to put a church, in a town with plenty of level ground nearly. There are two possibilities that might explain this decision.

Some writers have speculated that the hill on which the church of St John the Baptist now sits was once a site of heathen worship. Early churches were sometimes planted on pre-Christian sacred sites to provide continuity of worship and St John's ancient churchyard is similar in some ways to other suspected pagan sanctuaries, their circular enclosures a magical endless chain against evil forces. Several north Worcestershire place names suggest sites of Saxon pre-Christian worship[2] and it is just possible that missionary monks from the new minster at

CHAPTER 1: BEGINNINGS

Worcester established a small chapel at an old British or Saxon temple-grove hard by the main road north late in the 7th Century. It has also been suggested that the dedication to St John the Baptist, whose Saint's Day is 24th June, merely Christianises the old British pagan summer solstice celebration. But however tempting the vision of bearded druids circling a sacred oak on the hill-top there is alas no evidence for it. The Hwicce were a Christian folk from early days, the illustrious Brem probably just kept some local woodland for hunting in, and we will have to look for a more tangible origin behind the church on the hill.[3]

In the early 10th century King Alfred's resourceful daughter, Æthelflaed, fortified key settlements across Mercia against the threat of Danish invasion, which duly came. In 910AD, The Anglo-Saxon Chronicle records that she fortified Bremesbyrig, which is otherwise unidentified. If this is Bromsgrove, it is the only recorded instance of the name with a burh-type ending, denoting a fortified settlement. The site is small by comparison with other known Æthelflaedian burhs but the location is plausible. The hill offered good protection and excellent observation of the comings and goings on both main roads, especially when a bank and ditch had been dug round it with a timber palisade on top. Even if Bromsgrove is not an Æthelflaedian site, it may still be a domestic burh. Many pre-Conquest gentry preferred hilltop sites for their residences, as much for status as defence, and the owner would build a small church for his family and retainers, or to fulfil a condition of the land grant. The owner got not only the spiritual comfort of a personal chapel and priest but also the rather more temporal benefits of his tenants' tithes and offerings, which would otherwise go to the minster.

A number of churches with Saxon origins sit within otherwise empty elevated

---

[2] Including Weoley and Arrowfield. Both name-roots imply worship sites for heathen Saxon deities. However, the "-grove" element in Bromsgrove's name has no implications of religious use.

[3] Out of around 14,000 parish churches in England, less than ten have any certain association with pre-Christian worship sites.

and embanked sites which have been shown to be the relic of these domestic burhs. Local churches were comparatively rare before the beginning of the 10th century and a manorial church owned by the local thegn would fit well with this general date. Such sites were no use to the new Norman overlords, who much preferred to rule from military castles, and the church would have been left isolated when the last Saxon owner was ejected from his wooden hall. The rather less than perfect circle of the churchyard is also more suggestive of this theory, with the church built off-centre to accommodate the main residential buildings.[4]

The real answer may be a combination of both theories. The site is an ancient one, possibly with pre-Christian significance. It was prominent, visible and defensible, all of which would naturally appeal to a Saxon noble whether or not there was a church already on the site. A small village gathered round a common green and overlooked by a lordly hall and chapel is recognisably late Saxon. This history must necessarily start with speculation, but in the absence of other evidence this is at least a feasible image of pre-Conquest Bromsgrove.

The First Church

St John's was comprehensively rebuilt in the 12th and 13th centuries and there is no certain way of knowing what the Saxon church looked like. Virtually no Saxon church fabric survives in Worcestershire which, like much of lowland England, underwent a huge programme of church building after 1066. Most smaller Saxon churches were built of wood and the complete lack of any visible pre-Conquest stonework, together with the abundance of good local timber, suggests that the first St John's was a timber building.[5] As the only church in the pre-Conquest manor, Bromsgrove had right of burial - and thus a graveyard – making it bigger

---

[4] Most churches were rebuilt on their original sites and it is unlikely that the physical location of St John's has ever changed.

[5] As were nearly all Saxon buildings, usually of oak. The Old English word for "to build" is timbrian, and Brem's woodland supplied building timber as well as game.

CHAPTER 1: BEGINNINGS

than the simple thatched sheds known to Saxon legislators as *"field-churches"*. It served the household of the local thegn and as many villagers as could make the journey, and its main-road position on the edge of Feckenham Forest may also have made the church a useful Sunday calling point for aristocratic hunting parties. But it was still a comparatively small building, smoky and ill-lit, served by a single priest who owed his job to his secular master. And although he ministered to the local populace, his patch was defined by the far-flung boundaries of the manor, for the concept of local parishes in the modern sense had yet to emerge.

It would be interesting to know the name of any of Bromsgrove's early priests but again the record is blank. In contrast to the more exalted status of later medieval clergy, Saxon priests were very much common folk, working the land with their fellow villagers and usually possessing only a rudimentary knowledge of Latin. Many were married, a practice that did not finally cease until the 13th century although it had been officially frowned on for several centuries. Some Saxon clergy were fortunate, holding land of their own from which they gained an income. Arnwin, priest at Little Witney some miles to the west, held around 100 acres of land from Worcester Priory before 1086 and made enough honey from his bees to pay part of his rent with it. Bromsgrove's unnamed priest was not nearly so well favoured. He had to plough his strips in the common field with a shared plough and live on whatever he could grow. Domesday Book simply lumps him in with the cottagers, and in truth he was not so very different from the people he ministered to.

The Great Rebuilding

The Norman kings were great hunters and several prime areas of woodland previously open to all under Saxon law were set aside for the chase. Feckenham Forest was one such area and as Bromsgrove lay within its northern limit William the Conqueror retained the manor and its church as part of the royal demesne,

FAIRLY MOUNTED ON A HILL

under the local administration of a reeve. Bromsgrove itself was therefore spared the worst attentions of the rapacious Urso d'Abetot, William's cousin and Sheriff of Worcestershire, who nonetheless acquired several outlying portions of the manor, including Grafton and Chadwich, by gift or force. William's successors also kept Bromsgrove in the family. When Hugh Bardulf, the royal tenant, died without heirs in 1204, King John promptly granted the manor to William de Longespée, 3rd Earl of Salisbury, his half-brother and until his desertion in 1215 one of his most trusted military commanders.

This royal relationship was to prove useful in other ways too. On 27th April 1200, John granted Hugh Bardulf a charter for a weekly Wednesday market in Bromsgrove.[6] Market charters were highly prized for the wealth and prestige they brought and Bromsgrove's charter was one of the earliest in Worcestershire. As the church's hilltop position was not suited for market stalls the first markets were probably held on the green at the foot of the church steps, the long and ancient stone stair that links the churchyard with the town below.[7] This general area has been the site of several later market halls and an ancient stone market cross - the *"great high cross"* - stood at the junction of the High Street and St John's Street until its removal in 1832.

It is likely that the townsfolk celebrated their new privilege in the boxy Saxon building provided for the old burh. The earliest date-able stonework in St John's is supposedly the isolated easternmost arch of the north aisle, a simple pointed arch of two orders. This arch appears to be very late 12th century work and is curiously

---

[6] Leadbetter claims that annual fairs on 24th June and 1st October were also established by this charter, but this is not supported by other writers. Edward II granted a charter for an annual fair on 29th August – the feast of the beheading of St John the Baptist – to John de Mortimer, lord of the royal manor, on 30th September 1317, but the June and October fairs are first recorded in 1792. It is however likely that a major Church Ale (a parish feast) was held on the patronal day from early times.

[7] First mentioned in a will of 1586, when money was given for their repair, but much older as an access to the churchyard. Now comprising forty-eight steps, the number has varied over time between 42 and 63.

CHAPTER 1: BEGINNINGS

separated from the rest of the arcade by a length of originally blank walling. This suggests that it may be the entrance to a long-gone north transept, or side wing. If so, there may have been a corresponding south transept and a very wide nave of the same date from which both extended. This would match the typically cruciform plan of a church of c1200 AD, a style now known as Early English. The nave and transepts in most churches were the responsibility of the parishioners[8] and such a radical improvement on the old timber chapel could only have been built with substantial civic funding. The granting of the market charter would provide the necessary impetus for a major piece of rebuilding; for this new stone church was large, not just by comparison with its Saxon predecessor but in the locality as a whole. Here was a bold statement of civic pride, a bid for recognition as a rival to Droitwich, Alvechurch and other nearby market towns. But what did this splendid new church look like?

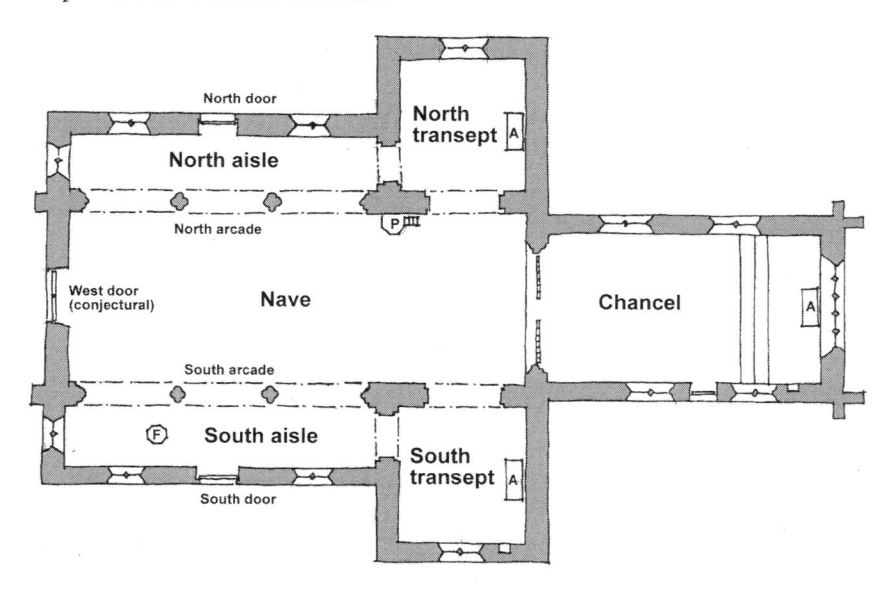

[Plan b] St John's c1250. This is the earliest likely plan form, although the north aisle and south transept are conjectural. A = altar; F = font; P = pulpit

---

[8] An ancient right, formalised by the Synod of Exeter in 1287.

19

FAIRLY MOUNTED ON A HILL

The present nave probably contains the same form, if not the fabric, of the new church. Without the later arcades, the main nave formed a rectangular stone box, pierced to north and south by plain single or doubled lancet windows containing clear glass, at least to start with. Overhead, a steeply pitched shingled or leaded roof was carried on massive oak trusses spanning clear across the very wide nave and open to the rafters. Its outline, still visible in the stonework of the present east and west nave walls, shows just what an enormous and impressive structure this lost first roof must have been. Doors on the north and south sides gave entry into the church: the present doorways may be the reused originals from this time, reset in the aisle walls when these were added. Before the later tower, there was possibly also a west door, necessary for processions in the old liturgy. Towards the east end of the nave, arches on either side opened into the two transepts, each of which contained an altar. That to the north was to Our Lady, while the south transept may have been the patronal altar to St John. There is actually evidence for an early and narrow South Aisle in the exterior stonework but no similar evidence for a northern counterpart. The presently bare stonework would have been lime-washed inside and out and perhaps decorated internally with artificial stone courses lined out in red, with more elaborate patterning surrounding the windows.

The largest opening in the nave was the chancel arch at the east end, leading into the chancel itself. This was the most sacred part of the church, with the main altar placed in the middle of the floor and not, as later, hard under the east window. While the nave was the responsibility of the parishioners, the chancel was ordinarily the responsibility of the patron, in this case King John's lay rector [9] and lord of the royal manor. The present chancel is some thirty or forty years later in date than the nave and suggests one of two possibilities.

---

[9] Literally *"one who has the right"* to exercise ecclesiastical authority, including receiving the full income from parochial tithes.

CHAPTER 1: BEGINNINGS

[Picture 2] The mid 13th century Chancel, photographed around 1920. The fabric reredos, wrought iron altar rails, chandelier, and wall panelling on the right side have all long gone

Either it is the last stage of a prolonged building campaign that started with the nave; or there might have been an earlier stone chancel, perhaps a gift of the royal patron of the time to the old wooden church. This would have been shorter than the present work, and would have been entered through a smaller chancel arch from the nave.

There is no firm evidence that the first stone church had a tower. Despite a much later story that the collapse of an early central tower necessitated the rebuilding of the church, the sheer width of the nave and the thinness of the nave walls rule out a crossing tower.[10] If there was ever an early west tower, it disappeared without trace beneath the foundations of its majestic successor.

The churchyard itself looked very different from its present appearance, which is largely the creation of the 17th and 18th centuries. With the earthen banks of the old burh still in place, it was a much more private place, isolated on its hilltop site and accessible only by narrow entries from the steep church steps and a field path from Holy Lane, now Church Street. Without the succeeding centuries of burials, the yard itself was a good two-to-three feet lower than its present level. Early medieval gravestones were generally much smaller and plainer - simple upright stones or flat slabs with plain or foliated inscribed crosses. The most prominent monument was the large stone preaching cross in the southern corner, between the chancel door and the top of the church steps. This was deliberately sited at the point of the churchyard most visible from the town as a permanent reminder of the church's presence. Preaching crosses often preceded the building of the church itself and the base and shaft of this cross survived until 1773, when it was unceremoniously replaced by a rather inept horizontal sundial. Evidence from a 14th century court case hints that at least part of the churchyard was still wooded and the whole area would have been regarded with respect, and a fair degree of superstition.

Superstition still sat uneasily alongside Christian belief in the early medieval church, when saints shared their feast days with older spirits, and trees, stones and wells still kept the vestiges of their ancient magical properties. To counter this lingering tendency the church spread its net as widely as possible across the town, creating a kind of spiritual geography with St John's and its churchyard at the centre. One feature needed particular attention. Road junctions had a

---

[10] The Early English crossing tower at Ripple, south of Worcester, shows just how massive the supporting masonry had to be, even over a narrower span. But see Ch.3 for a possible early detached tower.

CHAPTER 1: BEGINNINGS

significant function in pagan belief. They were powerful places, the meeting point of several ways where forces converged, offerings were made and things happened.[11] To the church, *"meeting the Devil at the crossroads"* was an abhorrence that had to be countered by something stronger. Wayside crosses were therefore set up at all the important road junctions in and around the town, their names sometimes preserved in later buildings. The Black Cross guarded the meeting of the Kidderminster Road and the High Street; the Golden Cross stood over the junction of St John Street and the High Street, and the Red Cross protected the crossing of the Kidderminster Road by Whitford Hall Road. These crosses exorcised the old spirits, guarded the entry points to the town and protected passing travellers, who would stop to pray by them before journeying on. Over time they came to form part of the regular route followed by church processions and their earlier, darker role faded from memory.

While we can create a convincing physical picture of St John's in 1200 it is harder to recreate the way in which it, or any early medieval church, was actually used. Processions would circle the church before services but the Masses themselves were said entirely in the chancel. The congregation meanwhile drifted in and out of the nave, kneeling for prayers on the rush-strewn floor, for there were no pews as such until the 15th century. The three standard services on a Sunday - Matins first thing in the morning, Mass mid-morning and Evensong in the afternoon – were augmented by daily masses or other services at the main or side altars. There were no congregational hymns and few if any sermons. Although much of the service was sung the Latin liturgy, poorly intoned by clergy who had often learnt it by rote, would be incomprehensible to townsfolk who valued familiar and comforting ritual far more than badly explained theology. As the single largest building in town and the responsibility of the townsfolk the nave also met any other need for covered large-scale accommodation. It could find itself

---

[11] The 12th century monk William of Malmsbury, echoing earlier writers, mentions the English dread of *"powers that reside at crossroads"*.

23

functioning as a market hall, moot hall, school or courtroom on occasion, as well as a place of refuge in times of trouble. The modern impression of churches is usually of quiet solemnity but the early medieval church was colourful, noisy and – at times - downright smelly.

As the population of the manor expanded over time, the inconvenience of travelling the length of the manor for every church service became apparent, if indeed anyone bothered. Early in the 12th century, a small stone chapel of ease was established at Kings Norton (the King's north-town), to encourage attendance by the northern parishioners. Over time, four other such chapels were established to cater for new centres of population. Two early chapels appeared at Grafton (the grove-town), just south of Bromsgrove itself, and at Chadwich, two miles to the north near an ancient holy-well: both are associated with manor houses and originated as private chapels. Later - and further afield - came Wythall and then Moseley in 1405, both subordinate to Kings Norton. Bromsgrove's church therefore became a lucrative benefice for its rector, who was entitled to receive the parish's Great Tithe on his royal patron's behalf, and he would have paid for a lesser priest to say the Daily Offices. The earliest named priest is William of Avignon in 1227, a distinctly Norman French appointment as one might expect. His immediate predecessors were probably from similarly favoured stock and we can only guess what the largely Saxon villagers thought of their new foreign clergy.

CHAPTER 2: GROWTH

The 13th Century

King and Prior

King John would never be England's favourite monarch. His clash with Pope Innocent III provoked a Papal interdict in 1208 and the suspension of all church services in England for six years. John's death in October 1216 therefore went generally unmourned as the country struggled through a vicious civil war, and it put little faith in his nine-year-old son and successor, Henry III. Yet Worcestershire remained relatively loyal to its old King, as it would be to another king four centuries later and John was buried, as he wished, in Worcester Cathedral. St John's also honoured its old benefactor. It paid ten marks a year to the cathedral for tapers to be burned at the tomb, where the king's bearded effigy, flanked by two bishop-saints, still stares blankly heavenward.

Henry III survived the upheaval of his accession and on the 21st May 1232 he conferred the presentation of the rectory of St John's on the prior and convent of Worcester Priory, to hold *"well and peaceably, freely and quietly....for the health of our soul and for, the soul of the Lord King John, our father, and for the souls of our ancestors and our heirs"*. The last rector and priest, William de Furnell, had been appointed by King John in 1204 and was allowed to remain in post until he died. Just before his own death in 1236 Bishop William de Blois appointed St John's first vicar, the comfortably local-sounding Richard of Winchcombe. Vicars did not have the freedom of rectors and Richard would have been very much the Bishop's man.[12]

FAIRLY MOUNTED ON A HILL

It is an uncomfortable fact that medieval patrons – lay or monastic – saw local churches primarily as a regular and compliant source of income rather than as a base for evangelism. The granting of parish churches to monastic patrons was a prominent feature of Norman rule, and by 1200 a quarter of all parish churches had been signed over to the great monastic houses of England or France. The monastery now kept the greater part of the church's income from endowments and tithes and left the priest with the altar offerings and any lesser tithes with which to run his parish and keep himself. Appropriation, as it was known, greatly enriched monasteries at the expense of local clergy until the Council of Westminster in 1200 decreed that vicars must be given a reasonable standard of living, literally the "living" of the church. This included the freehold of their house - the "vicarage" - a practice that remains today.

We can see appropriation at work in Bromsgrove. The Priory of Worcester was granted the Great Tithe - that is, a tenth of all the arable crops of this large agricultural parish. In addition the parish had to pay annual sums from its monetary income: ten marks to the infirmary at Worcester and a further three marks as a compulsory donation to the cathedral on the patronal day, 24th June. The new vicar, Richard, was left the lesser tithes of woods, orchards and gardens; the hay tithe from Bromsgrove only; the direct income from the churches at Bromsgrove and Kings Norton; two houses in Bromsgrove and Kings Norton (presumably the vicarages); and the donations from burials at St John's, known as mortuaries. A successor to the old Saxon soul-scot, these were propitiatory offerings of the deceased's goods, made at the graveside for the welfare of his soul.[13]

---

[12] Vicar literally means "substitute". Vicars were local representatives of the rector, in this case the prior and convent. Most clergy at this time were from monastic orders and Richard was possibly a monk from Winchcombe Abbey in Gloucestershire.

[13] Of pagan origin, mortuaries lasted until the Reformation. In a late example from 1509, Richard Astmore of Bromsgrove gives *"for my mortuari a heyfur [heifer]"*.

CHAPTER 2: GROWTH

Medieval parishes were expected to be self sustaining, producing all the resources needed to support church and priest as well as to pay their dues to the patron. Tithes were therefore imposed on almost anything that could be subdivided - livestock, produce, materials or services. Like the funeral payments, they bound the parishioner to his local church, living and dead. With such a large part of the parish still covered in woodland or intractable hill country, the income per acre from arable land was far less than more densely settled areas. Such a large parish was therefore essential if the twin demands of priory and priest were to be met and a roof kept on the church. Even collecting the tithe over this great area must have had its problems and we can sympathise with the churchwardens as they scoured every outlying hamlet for onions, garlic, honey, eggs and apples on behalf of their vicar. Any residue over and above the vicar's living expenses was to go to the priory for the support of "strangers and paupers". Although the medieval church is often criticised for growing fat at the expense of the people, it was the sole source of comfort for the poor or weak and such payments helped to run England's first national welfare system, albeit a charitable one.

The payment of tithes had been compulsory since the mid 10th century, and the importance of accurately determining the area over which they could be gathered underpinned the development of parish boundaries from the 12th century onwards. As these boundaries were marked by transient natural features and fallible human memory, rather than recorded on maps, disputes between adjacent parishes were inevitable. In December 1297, for example, the bishop's court had to adjudicate between the parishes of Bromsgrove and Tardebigge, owned by Bordesely Abbey, over rights to the tithes from a piece of land at *"Sonderic, in Sidenhale, next to the royal road [i.e. the high road] in the east that divides the two manors"*.[14] Ten years earlier the same court unpicked the boundary between Bromsgrove and Upton Warren parishes, which ran through a piece of land at the

---

[14] Possibly Sidnals (now "The Sidnalls") a farm near Blackwell, some three miles east of Bromsgrove.

now-lost *"little Callow herste"* somewhere south of town. The decision here inevitably reflected the relative importance of the two parishes: Bromsgrove retained the main tithe of crops, while rural Upton and its vicar had to make do with whatever constituted the small tithe.

Tithes were enforced equally rigorously on defaulting individuals. In 1309, Robert de Wych of Alvechurch lost a long-running dispute with the prior regarding unpaid tithes on a field in Bromsgrove parish. Summoned to pay the legal costs of the dispute in front of the altar of St Thomas at Worcester, he agreed to keep the peace and pay a hefty £20 fine *"unless the prior would be generously pleased to remit any part of it"*. No doubt the prior's generosity stopped slightly short of waiving fines and Robert probably paid up. The priory court was to deal with many more such cases in the years to come, and it usually won.

Appropriation gave Worcester Priory more than just a church. With it came land - and power. The priory now owned the rectory manor, the personal estate of the former rectors. This included the glebe, a great swathe of land to the west of the High Street supplying the immediate needs of the vicar, who farmed it himself with the churchwardens. It did not take long for the priory to realise that the manor and its tithes could be turned into hard cash, rather more useful than sacks of oats to a big church with an expensive building programme. As rector of the parish the prior and convent could sign over the right to tithes for a limited period for a suitably profitable rent. In 1256 they did just that, leasing the two churches of Bromsgrove and Kings Norton, with all their associated houses, rents and profits for five years to "Sir Sampson of Bromsgrove" rector of Herforton, for £50 a year, plus a further 10 marks to the priory infirmerer and 40s to the pittancer.[15] Oh, and could they also please have fifty quarters of oats from the

---

[15] The Infirmerer ran the priory hospital while the Pittancer was in charge of allocating funds – the pittance - to the poor. "Sir" Sampson (the title is a medieval courtesy given to priests as well as knights) was also vicar of nearby Stoke Prior from 1260 to 1274.

CHAPTER 2: GROWTH

tithe itself - a fine case of having one's cake and eating it. The priory carefully retained the appointment of both vicars, just to make sure that no matter who occupied the manor house, they kept their own men in the pulpits.

With the advent of the new rectory manor Bromsgrove became a town divided between two masters. The properties on the west (church) side of the growing High Street now belonged to the priory but the High Street itself and the land to the east remained in the royal manor. And as the priory was not slow in exploiting its assets, this unusual situation led to many clashes of interests in the coming years.

The Church

There is much evidence for a major overhaul of the church fabric in the mid 13th century and the transfer of patronage to the priory provides a good underlying reason.[16] The chancel seems to have been the first part of the church to be improved. Whatever existed before was completely demolished and a new longer chancel with an impressive 5-lancet east window was erected. Long chancels begin to appear about this time, after the 1215 Lateran Council defined and elaborated Eucharistic doctrine and placed the priest further from his congregation. These longer chancels also accommodated the choirs that were now beginning to make themselves heard in parish churches. To emphasise the importance of this sacred area, a floor of decorative encaustic tiles was laid, their shiny red and cream surface a sharp contrast to the straw matting in the nave. And to show off the whole ensemble, the junction with the nave was opened out with a fine wide chancel arch in the Early English style.

---

[16] There was little wealth in the town itself. In 1227 the royal tax was reduced from 37 to 20 marks, and later to 17½ marks on account of the town's poverty.

FAIRLY MOUNTED ON A HILL

The fashion for rebuilding seems to have gripped the parishioners too. The expanding town was putting pressure on space in the nave, for new wide aisles were added to both the north and south. This brought the overall internal width of the church to an enormous 77ft, the widest medieval parish church in Worcestershire.[17] Although the windows were later replaced with bigger lights in the Decorated style of the 14th century, the mid 13th century north aisle arcade remains, with plain chamfered arches in two orders carried on typical quatrefoil columns with rounded bases and caps.

[Picture 3] The wide North Aisle c1910 before the War Memorial displaced the Horton monuments on the north (left) wall. The organ was relocated to the South Aisle in 1950. The electric standards were replaced many years ago.

---

[17] Halesowen, which is wider overall, has an additional outer south aisle.

CHAPTER 2: GROWTH

The replacement of the south arcade in the 15th century has destroyed any evidence for what went before but perhaps the original arcade to the narrow south aisle of c1200 was retained when the aisle itself was widened. The width of both new aisles seems to have been determined by the existing transepts. While the north transept was initially kept, the south transept was apparently demolished entirely and the new wide aisle extended across it to overlap the west end of the chancel. A plain arch of three orders was then inserted in the southwest corner of the chancel to provide a visual link between the two areas. This rather odd arrangement suggests the former presence of a chantry chapel at the east end of the south aisle, possibly for the now-lost patron of the new work. The archway would then visually link the chantry with the most sacred part of the church (as does its 16th century opposite number), allowing the Mass to be concelebrated in both chantry and chancel.

Church doors were regarded as ritually significant and, in common with many other churches, the old south doorway was carefully saved and built into the new aisle. A large wooden porch, the roofline of which can still be seen above the door arch, protected the door itself. The later north doorway, leading to the graveyard, was regarded with more superstition and was therefore much plainer. North aisles, on the shady side of the church, were seen as the repose of the dead and tended to collect monuments and memorials, both inside and immediately outside. The weathered effigy of an anonymous 13th century cleric was dug up from under the north aisle floor during the 1858 restoration and now lies in the little south aisle monument bay, along with several other early monuments.

More intriguingly a cross-legged knight on a tomb chest, again probably 13th century, was still visible below one of the western pew seats in the late 18th century but has now entirely disappeared from view. Who was he? Cross-legged effigies are commonly held to signify the subject's service on crusade in

31

the Holy Land, and it is tempting to link this lost knight with the small stone heart coffin found many years ago in a local garden and now in the north aisle. The practical difficulties of bringing back the body of anyone who died abroad - soldier, merchant or pilgrim – were resolved by removing and embalming the heart, which could then be buried in their home country as the representative portion of the person's earthly existence. Body or none, the effigy of our unknown soldier may still be there below the Victorian concrete, quietly waiting for his own resurrection.

Church and Town

How did this fine church fit into the life of the 13th century town that grew at its feet? The link between the medieval church and state was strong and symbiotic. The church as a whole was a huge landowner and its vast income from taxes and endowments made it second only to the monarch in wealth; indeed, kings regularly looked to the church for financial support, willing or otherwise. We have already seen how tithes were used as the basis of ecclesiastical taxation. As medieval tithes were paid in kind, tithe barns to house them were built near the churches and in wealthy parishes these could achieve enormous size. Worcestershire's finest remaining tithe barn is by the parish church of St Giles at Bredon, but Bromsgrove had its own until 1844. Perhaps appropriately, this sat where the town centre supermarket now stands, a site later used for Bromsgrove's livestock market. There is no record of when the tithe barn was first erected but it was a timber-framed building of some size, with a single stray – or cart entrance - and a thatched roof.

CHAPTER 2: GROWTH

At the local level, the church also wielded considerable temporal power, including the dispensing of justice via the diocesan and national church courts. The rectory manor house sat in the High Street just north of the present Mill Lane Precinct and near the town mill. On the twice-yearly visits of the Court Baron (the court for civil cases) the tenant was obliged to entertain the prior's cellarer, cook and steward, at his own cost, as well as feeding the prior's horses, perhaps one recipient of all those oats. The priory claimed jurisdiction over all matters that occurred in the rectory manor. This was fine as long as everyone agreed on what belonged to whom. But, as the town grew, boundaries became blurred and greed took a hand.

The success of the weekly market had encouraged the growth of the town, which now began to stretch northwards along the old Roman road. As a result, land became increasingly scarce in the town centre itself. Part of the problem was the boundary between the two manors. This did not run down the middle of the High Street, as logic might dictate, but up against the house frontages on the western – or priory - side. For some reason this side of the street seemed to enjoy better trade than the opposite houses on the royal manor side. Perhaps it was the little River Spadesbourne, which provided not only drinking water and power for the mills but was also the town's only sewer. Or perhaps the south-eastern aspect simply drew more people to the sunny side of the street during the peak morning trading time. Whatever the cause there was rivalry between the two sides and over time rivalry turned to jealousy. In 1281 the royal manor took commercial advantage of the situation. Claiming that some new shops built by the priory encroached on the boundary, they retaliated by erecting a fence right across the shop fronts, effectively shutting off the priory tenants and seriously affecting their ability to trade. The matter went to court, of course. Here, common sense prevailed and it was held that the boundary was actually the edge of the King's Highway; that is, the old Roman road. As this was some feet back from the building line itself the fence came down and the relieved stallholders regained their front doors and

FAIRLY MOUNTED ON A HILL

their daylight.[18]

The court rolls of medieval England are filled with such often-petty squabbles over jealously guarded rights, and the church was certainly not immune where property and money were concerned. Just two years before the fence incident the priory was forced to go to court to prove its right to the patronage of St John's against the Order of the Knights Templar. It won, quite rightly. But it was promptly taken to court for holding the assize of bread in town. This was a civil trading standards court whose job it was to check that the town's bakers were selling bread of the correct weight and quality. Defaulting traders could be fined, and fines could be lucrative. The case implies that the royal manor held this right and did not at all fancy losing its little money-spinner to a rival.

The protection of privileges was not just confined to the town. The parish of Bromsgrove was predominantly rural and country dwellers easily outnumbered townsfolk in the congregation. As the population of the whole parish grew through the 13th century more people were attending the various outlying chapels of ease and keeping their donations local rather than contributing to the mother church at St John's. The little chapel of St James at Chadwich was a case in point. Although the building itself was owned by Sir Ralph de Chadwich and sat next to his manor house the priory had devolved the patronage to the preceptor and brethren of the Hospital of St Wulstan at Worcester, one of the city's several

---

[18] The boundary was marked by three large boulders at intervals down the High Street. This very ancient form of marker must predate the division of the manor in 1232 and may be the relic of a much older line, perhaps a pre-Roman trackway. One boulder was broken up in-situ in the 18th century and the other two were relocated, first to the top end of town beside the weighing machine in the Strand, and latterly either side of the Cemetery entrance in Church Lane, where they remain. It may be significant that one stone stood by the market place. Mark-stones on old trackways have been identified in a number of locations as the origins of local markets, on the basis that anyone selling by such a stone would be guaranteed passing trade.

[19] Like Grafton and Bromsgrove itself, Chadwich seems to have started life as the domestic chapel of a local manor house. A dedication to St Chad is also recorded.

CHAPTER 2: GROWTH

monastic infirmaries.[19] Inevitably the question arose of who had right to the tithes, and the two claimants, priory and hospital, went to court in March 1239 for an answer.

As it was the priory court the hospital inevitably came off worse. They were given Sir Ralph's and some other small tithes to support their priest but the remainder went to St John's. The prior still had to approve the appointment and the priest himself had to swear that he would do nothing to injure the mother church. More tellingly, no parishioners of St John's were allowed to attend St James, and even Sir Ralph had to attend St John's four times a year, at Christmas, Candlemas, Easter and the midsummer patronal festival. This ensured that everyone knew who held the purse-strings and where the money went. In return for this beneficence the Hospital had to pay 2s a year to the Priory and half a pound of frankincense a year to the vicar of St John's, which must have kept the church fragrant for a good few weeks.[20]

Some years later the same issue came up over Grafton. In July 1278 John de Grafton challenged the prior over the advowson – the right to present vicars for appointment – at Grafton chapel. Was it an independent church, he asked, or was it a chapel of Bromsgrove? If so, did his grandfather Ralph's old chaplain, John de Catteshull (Catshill), die a clergyman in his own right or a dependent of William de Furnell, the last rector of Bromsgrove, who had died back in 1236. Forty years late or not, the priory won again, taking back the advowson in exchange for Bromsgrove's old obligation to provide tapers at King John's tomb. But such rights were a valuable source of income or influence, and little Grafton was not left in peace for long. In 1289 the bishop himself pulled rank and expropriated the advowson from the prior. Church courts were little use when the judiciary were themselves protagonists and the prior had to resort to civil justice for redress.

---

[20] The right to the 2s payment was retained by the priory when it farmed out the remainder of the tithes to Sampson of Bromsgrove in 1256. Hard cash was not for leasing.

35

FAIRLY MOUNTED ON A HILL

Seven years and £200 later he emerged victorious from this unseemly scrap and clergy appointments reverted to the priory for good.

As the market grew and townspeople prospered Bromsgrove started to look like a valuable asset for whoever controlled its trade. An undated royal taxation return from the last years of the 13th century lists 256 property owners paying a total of £60 13s 4d, nearly four times that for Dudley and Kidderminster combined.[21] As well as their obvious indication of growing wealth, these figures also imply that this growth was being driven by a relatively large number of small mercantile tax-payers, rather than a wealthy clique. Compare this with Droitwich, with its long-established and lucrative salt trade controlled by a few families: its 85 taxable townsfolk (only a third of Bromsgrove's) paid £27 13s 2d between them - nearly half of its northern neighbour's tax. In later years these many tradesmen and small businessmen will have a powerful and sometimes argumentative voice in the running of their town and church, but their long journey to the bustling, industrious Bromsgrove of the 18th and 19th centuries starts here.

The Vicarage

The first vicarage sat somewhere on the west side of the High Street and was presumably one of the two houses mentioned in the 1232 charter. It occupied a large open plot of land bounded by Church Lane to the north, Parson's Hill footpath to the south and the Spadesbourne to the west, and it included the church fishpond that supplied the vicar's food on Fridays.[22] While this central location suited a village it was rather too close to the noise and dirt of the High Street - and also

---

[21] Dudley only had 41 taxpayers and Kidderminster 58.

[22] Cotton places it at the corner of Church Street, formerly Holy Lane, on the basis of the vaulted basement of a now demolished house there. However, this sounds like a later burgess plot house, tight against its street boundaries. Dyer suggests that the vicarage was actually at the south end of the High Street and was cleared to allow the development of a market hall, but this does not fit either de Belne's claim about the long walk to church or the contemporary description of the boundaries.

CHAPTER 2: GROWTH

perhaps to the parishioners - as the town grew. Robert de Belne, vicar from 1281 to 1309, fancied a rather more select location and in 1292 he exchanged this house for another property further south at the foot of the church hill. Robert claimed that the new location saved him a long walk to work but perhaps there was also a more businesslike rationale for this move. As we have just seen, space in the growing High Street was becoming increasingly valuable. Vicars, by contrast, did not need a shop-front and the old vicarage was probably sold to open up this side of the High Street for development. We may therefore be witnessing a piece of smart commercial acumen by the good monks of Worcester, especially as Robert's new vicarage was already owned by the priory and cost nothing to acquire.

The new vicarage had previously been occupied by one Nicholas de Prestford[23] and it came with a garden, itself part of a larger garden and vineyard owned and retained by the priory. This garden is circumstantial evidence for the existence of a religious establishment of some sort, possibly a guesthouse on the main road for travelling clergy. After the dissolution of the monasteries in the 16th century this building became the Crown Inn and its pleasure grounds, now Crown Close, took over the old priory-owned garden.[24] Building work to enlarge the Crown in the 18th century revealed an underlying medieval timber hall of some grandeur, suggesting more than just a domestic use. This corner of Bromsgrove has now changed beyond all recognition but it must once have been a lush and pleasant spot, well watered by the little Spadesbourne and just the place for a vicar who wanted some peace and quiet.

We have already come some way from our Saxon chapel. By the end of the century a substantial stone church of nearly the present size crowns its little hill, with

---

[23] De Prestford's name itself is suggestive – the ford (across the Spadesbourne, presumably) where the priest lived.

[24] The top path in Crown Close was once known as Nun's Path but this may be a personal name rather than a religious reference. There is no record of any monastic house in Bromsgrove.

the vicarage and tithe barn on the glebe land behind the growing High Street of a small but growing town. From the church hill, the glebe land stretches away to the north and east, bounded by what is now the Stourbridge Road, and still comprising 26 acres in 1811. As well as agricultural land and pasture it includes the town mill and millpond, and the tenter-grounds (now the Recreation Ground, but once Rack Close) where sheep's wool for the town's growing cloth industry is spread out on wooden racks to dry. The stage is set for growth.

Piety and Superstition

From our largely secular age, it is difficult to see St John's as the early medieval parishioner saw it, far less to think as he or she did. There was one Church, universal and indivisible; one God and one faith, from which there was little or no dissent. The Church had been there forever and would remain so. It was a central part of daily life: it carried equal weight with the monarchy and was a great deal nearer at hand; it affected the lives of most people and ruled the lives of many. In this great age of piety, eternal life - or damnation - hung entirely on your behaviour on earth and the church was your passport, in either direction.

And yet, for the average 13th or 14th century person, the church as a physical entity was largely a thing of mystery and, to many, superstition. Visual imagery was all the more important to an illiterate congregation and the walls of medieval churches were highly decorated with patterning and with pictures from a standard repertoire approved in the 8th century. This included the lives of the saints, St Christopher (the patron saint of travellers and therefore usually opposite the main door) and the day of judgement - or doom. All carried a lesson, usually simple and direct - live a good life or face the awful consequences. The doom painting over the chancel arch was particularly effective. Christ sat in majesty over the apex of the arch and presided over the last judgement. While the saved rose heavenward on his right hand, the damned fell into Hell on his left, tormented by demons and

CHAPTER 2: GROWTH

usually painted with a vigorous and grotesque enthusiasm. Taken together with the whitewashed and lined walls the overall effect would have completely altered the internal appearance of the church from what we see now. Although the Victorian restorers of St John's rediscovered the remains of the Doom painting over the chancel arch in 1858 it was (they said) in too poor a condition to keep and the whole thing was scraped off without being recorded. Graphic depictions of Hell were not to the Victorian taste.

While the main church walls might be painted with inspirational Christian scenes the nooks and crannies of most naves hid rather different carvings of half-remembered folk mythology, popular stories, forest beasts and comic grotesques or ruderies. St John's has fewer of these than one might expect from a church of this age but the careful observer will find a number of later medieval "green men" around the church. These leafy faces are an ancient classical motif whose original meaning we have now lost.[25] Their anthropomorphic and slightly sinister appearance hints at a much closer relationship between man and nature, especially in a land of extensive forests. They obviously appealed to the medieval mind for they stare down from roof bosses and wall-heads, inside and out.

These strange figures apart, St John's, in common with many of Worcestershire's medieval churches, is notably plain compared with the equivalent churches in, say, East Anglia. This general lack of ornament has been explained as the result of the monastic patronage of so many of the county's churches. Unlike private benefactors, who beautified churches out of piety or pride, monastic orders such as Worcester priory's Benedictines saw little virtue in ornament for its own sake. Columns and arches were generally simply moulded, and representational work was largely notable by its absence. The decorative effects of patronage will be

---

[25] The earliest English examples seem to date from the 11th century although several Romano-British depictions of native gods bear a striking resemblance. Lady Raglan coined the term "Green Man" in 1939.

evident in later centuries but for the time being the impressively large interior of Bromsgrove's church remains relatively unadorned.

CHAPTER 3: EXPANSION
The 14th Century

The Growing Church

No medieval century was quite as calamitous as the 14th. A promising start with the strong kingship of Edward I slid quickly into a succession of intermittent wars and natural disasters that lasted for much of the century. A series of plagues that swept across Europe from 1348 to 1370 (and which first hit Worcestershire in the spring of 1349) devastated towns and countryside alike and brought church building to a halt for many years. The England that emerged was changed forever, its unquestioning piety and allegiance to Church authority challenged by John Wycliffe and others in a new spirit of radicalism that would lead eventually to an English church, separated from Rome. But how is this period of change reflected in Bromsgrove's church?

Architecturally, the 14th century is relatively disparate in St John's. Various existing aisle and chancel windows were enlarged to admit more light and, perhaps, the north aisle was rebuilt. While the church's original 13th century windows were essentially single or grouped lancets, plain pointed lights with simple pierced openings in otherwise solid stonework, the new windows exploited the recent development of full-blown tracery in what we now call the Decorated style. Lines flow upwards, branching and crossing as they rise, creating complex organic shapes that were filled with increasingly elaborate stained and painted glass. The last medieval glass in St John's disappeared at the beginning of the 19th century but the windows themselves survive, albeit in restored condition.

FAIRLY MOUNTED ON A HILL

The first definite chantry chapel also appears at this time. A feature of many medieval churches, chantries were private chapels or oratories endowed by a particular person or family. The benefactor would fund any necessary building work and leave a legacy to pay for a priest to say (or "chant") daily masses in his or her memory. The most important part of a medieval church was the high altar at the east end of the chancel and it was a great honour to be buried as near as possible to this sacred spot. In 1305, Richard de la Lynde endowed a chantry at St John's worth 50s, with a priest to pray for the souls of all the faithful departed. This may just have consisted of a new altar, as there is no definite building fabric associated with it.[26] However, at some time in the mid 14th century a large chapel was added to the northeast side of the chancel, its east wall aligning with the chancel east wall and its north and west walls free-standing. Any internal fittings were stripped out some time after the Reformation to form the present vestry and the only date-able feature is its decorated east window. Originally, however, it would have had one or more table or wall tombs and a small altar, all under an open timber roof and with wall paintings like those of the nave. There seems to have been no internal link between the chapel and the rest of the church, and access was gained solely via an external door in the chapel's west wall; the present blocked archway is a later modification. This obviously made internal communication rather difficult and as masses were often said at the same time in both places, a narrow hagioscope[27] was cut through the intervening wall. This allowed both the parish priest and chantry priest to co-ordinate their movements at important parts of the service, particular the Elevation of the Host. The alignment of this peep-hole also shows the relative positions of both altars at this time.

---

[26] De La Lynde owed the priory 100 marks in 1289, to be paid off in two years, so his finances must have improved in the interim.

[27] A narrow angled opening giving a clear view through an otherwise solid wall; literally a *"holy-viewer"*. Hagioscopes are sometimes wrongly described as leper windows, allowing lepers to see the altar without entering the church.

CHAPTER 3: EXPANSION

From a later will it appears that this chapel was dedicated to St Nicholas; but who was actually buried here? There is no certain benefactor but a chapel of such size is most likely to have been funded by the big local family of this period, the Staffords of Grafton Manor. Grafton was a very old estate and was already in existence in 1066, when William the Conqueror granted it to Urso d'Abitot. Ralph Stafford acquired Grafton from John Hastings by marrying Hasting's daughter, Maud.[28] Although Grafton had its own chapel of ease, such chapels had no right of burial and St John's therefore held the family tombs. The Staffords will come to prominence in the next century but for now an early, unnamed Stafford seems the most likely occupant.

The Tower

The 14th century's biggest contribution to St John's was the tower. No written or physical evidence exists for any earlier tower, but this does not mean that one did not exist. Such a large church would surely have had somewhere to hang its early bells, and there is one possible hint. In the mid sixteenth century William Sheldon of nearby Beoley set up tapestry works at Bordesley and Barneston (Warks) to produce a series of tapestry maps for his new house, as a way of providing employment for the local poor. His original 1588 map of Worcestershire is now fragmentary, but a close copy made some sixty years later does show Bromsgrove town and its newly completed church. The thin spire of St John's rises prominently over the closely clustered cottages; but it is not alone. For just to its left is another tall, stout tower, spire-less but with what might be belfry openings in its top storey. What is it?

---

[28] So says Cotton, which would put the date at 1383. However, an earlier Sir Ralph de Stafford married Catherine Hastings, daughter of an earlier John Hastings of Grafton, in 1326. They had only one daughter, so the house may have passed out of the Stafford family for a generation.

FAIRLY MOUNTED ON A HILL

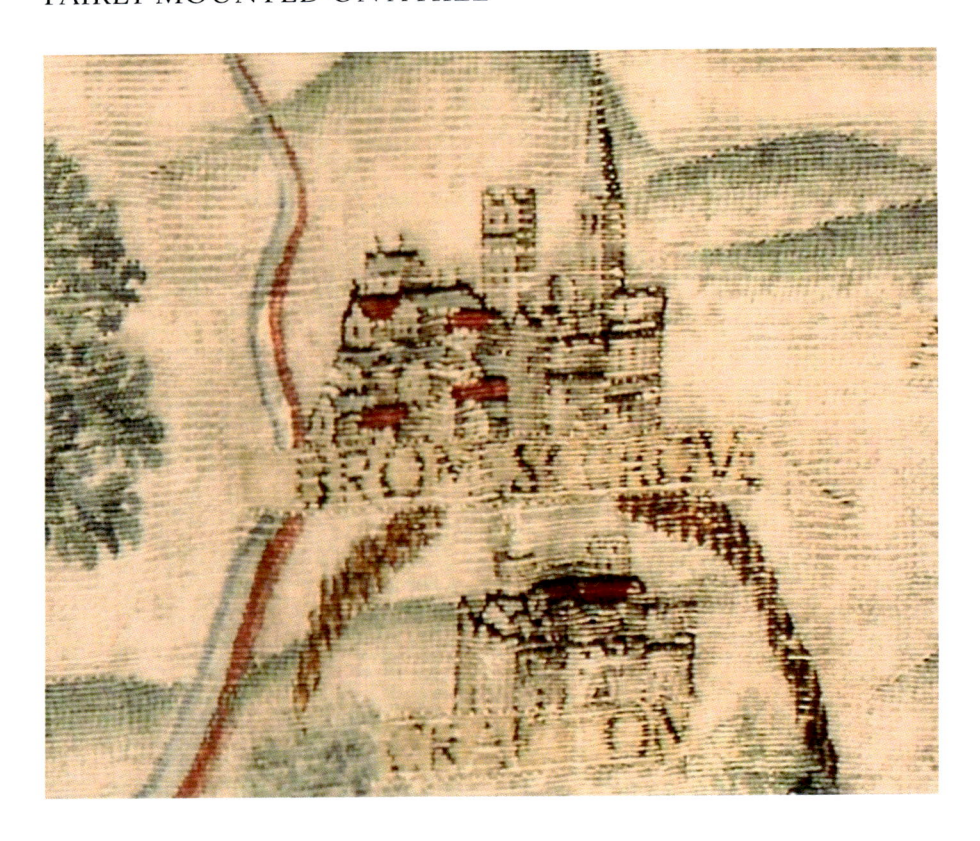

[Picture 4] Extract from the Sheldon tapestry map showing Bromsgrove, with Grafton and its park enclosure below, and the Spadesbourne to the left. The church tower and spire is unmistakeable, but the second mysterious battlemented tower looks more than mere artistic license.

Opinions differ as to the accuracy of the town representations on the Sheldon maps and our second tower could just be a picturesque flourish to indicate a larger town amidst the villages of north Worcestershire. But Bordesley is only eight miles from Bromsgrove, and that persistent legend of a collapsing tower may have a basis in fact. Just supposing there was indeed an earlier bell-tower, perhaps free-standing in the churchyard as some were. Did it gradually become unsafe over time and eventually provide the spur to build something special as a replacement? And was its final fall or demolition the source of our legend? [29]

CHAPTER 3: EXPANSION

There is no record of how long the new tower took to build, but it is generally agreed that the lower stages were started in the early 14th century, on a grand scale. Towers were enormously expensive and their building took many years. This was for constructional as well as financial reasons. The sheer weight of stonework in a large tower imposed a huge load on the relatively non-adhesive lime mortar used. Building more than a few courses at a time risked a catastrophic collapse, particularly in the upper stages. In addition, the massive stones had to be lifted one at a time by a treadmill crane and positioned off wooden scaffolding, a task that could not be rushed. Towers were therefore usually left for long periods for the mortar to bed down and set. Work stopped altogether in winter and the wall-heads were thatched with straw to prevent frost damage.

Left: [Picture 4a] The tower (from Stanton, 1881)

Did its designer-mason knew what the finished height would be, and did he foresee the enormous spire that would eventually cap it? The fine proportions certainly hint at grand ambition. Unlike the main body of the church, the tower itself is a unified architectural concept, designed to be seen from a distance. The detailing of the lower stages, in the Decorated style of the 14th century, is bold and confident. Two slim angled buttresses with now-empty statue niches rise in

---

[29] There is interesting circumstantial evidence. Richard Heeks (or Hyckes), Sheldon's master weaver at Barneston, was a friend of Robert Avys, vicar of St John's to 1581. Heeks designed and signed the 1588 Worcestershire tapestry map, and he would certainly have known of any local stories about the church. Thomas Chance, Sheldon's master weaver at Bordesley (where the Worcestershire map was actually woven) also had friends and family in Bromsgrove. We shall meet more members of both families later in this story.

five stages from the western corners. Their third offset coincides with a moulded stringcourse running round the whole perimeter of the tower. This projecting stone band had both the practical function of throwing rainwater off the wall-face, and a decorative function as a horizontal counterpoint to the strong vertical emphasis of the tower.

This stringcourse also acted as the visual anchor for a row of three life-size statues, set in niches and capped with ornate stone canopies topped with ogee arches. A wild-haired St John the Baptist, flanked by Saints Peter and Paul and holding the remains of a paschal lamb, stares down at all comers, the only genuine medieval figure carvings left at St John's. These rare pre-Reformation statues unaccountably survived the iconoclasts of the mid 17th century, although well within range of musket shot. Perhaps they were just too well regarded to spoil.

Below the statues, the off-centre position of the great west window looks curiously asymmetrical to modern eyes. The medieval mind saw things differently and was not offended by a lack of symmetry, as the interior of the nave amply demonstrates. Although the present restored tracery is early 15th century in pattern, it is possible that the window itself is actually the old nave west window, reset and squeezed sideways in its new position to make room for the spiral tower staircase in the southwest corner. Such a size of window - and the glass in it - would be too valuable to cast aside and its reuse enabled this stage of the new tower to be made weather tight that much sooner. The door below was certainly salvaged from the west wall of the nave as the stones of its arch are numbered in two different styles of Roman numeral on the underside, allowing the mason to reset them in the correct order.

Towers were usually built as structurally independent elements. They took little or no support from the rest of the church, not least because their sheer massiveness could easily overwhelm the limited foundations of ancient naves and

CHAPTER 3: EXPANSION

arcades. This is the case here. The east face of the tower forms the west face of the nave, its massive regular stonework contrasting with the much smaller stones of the north aisle. The buttresses to this face of the tower are flat, rather than angled, to widen the wall surface and avoid intrusion into the aisles. To build it in this way must have involved the wholesale demolition of the old west wall and St John's 14th century parishioners probably occupied a rather draughty church for some years.

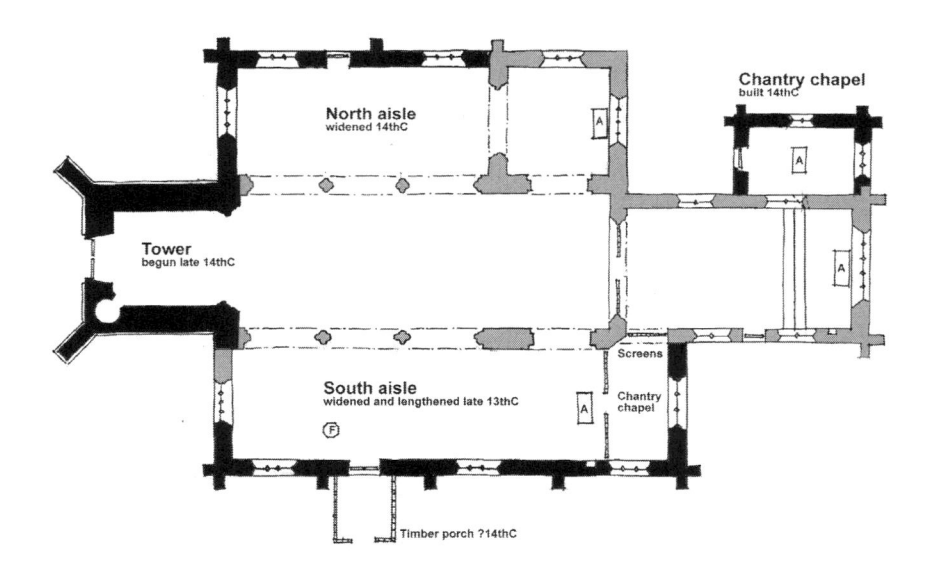

[Plan c] St John's c1380. Changes since 1250 are shown in black. The tower has been started but is still some way from completion. A = altar; F = font; P = pulpit]

What does the inside of Bromsgrove's church look like by the middle of the 14th Century? Well, the brightly painted nave still carries its old steeply pitched roof, now dark with many years of candle soot. Beyond the chancel arch the new windows make the east end and the widened aisles much lighter. Both aisles also carry steep pitched roofs open to the rafters, although the north aisle still stops short in a transept. There are altars at the east ends of both aisles as well as the chancel, and simple oak benches with poppy-head ends fill the once clear floor space. But the biggest change is at the west end of the nave. Replacing the old west window is an enormous dark opening, a bold and elegant arch rising forty feet in a single leap without break or capital. Externally the tower is already beginning to dwarf the church, incomplete as it is and capped with a temporary thatched roof just above the nave ridgeline. Inside, it is the tallest internal space that most Bromsgrove folk have ever seen.

There is no benefactor recorded for this work, the cost of which must have been enormous. Evidence from elsewhere shows that towers were often funded by a mixture of large bequests and smaller donations, the latter often in the form of legacies. Indeed, the wording of some legacies clearly implies the impatience of the donor in wanting to see their tower finished. Perhaps the two small niches on the tower buttresses - and similar niches either side of the main statues - were intended to take donors' statues. In all probability the work just went on slowly as funds came in, a few courses at a time, over the century. There is no obvious break in the visible stonework, although the coursing does reduce and coarsen a little just below the top stage, as if money was less forthcoming or masons were scarce after the mid-century plagues.

Priest And Parishioners

As the church was changing so were the townspeople, and this increasingly elaborate church sat in the middle of an increasingly argumentative town. An odd case came to the prior's notice during his visitation at Bromsgrove early in 1338. A number of parishioners from St John's and other churches in the Wyche deanery[30] had claimed that they alone had the right to cut down trees in their churchyards. Roger, the vicar of St John's, complained to the prior that the parishioners *"did not*

---

[30] The old name for Droitwich, literally *"dirty Wyche"*. Bromsgrove only gained its own Deanery on 5th August 1892.

CHAPTER 3: EXPANSION

permit, nay even openly prohibited their rectors and vicars to meddle with such trees... unless the consent of the parishioners be given." These trees were important. Although the ownership of churchyards was routinely vested in the vicar a law of Edward I in 1306 forbad the felling of churchyard trees other than for repairing the chancel, the upkeep of which was normally the vicar's responsibility. By claiming this right for themselves the parishioners were effectively removing the vicar's main resource for repairs and alterations, as well as imposing a costly penalty on him. They apparently believed that they had some ancient right, perhaps a half-remembered Saxon privilege of lopping or felling for their personal use when so much of the surrounding Feckenham Forest was now out of bounds.

No matter what the parishioners believed the prior's answer on the 13th February 1338 was unequivocal. Pointing out that the churchyard and everything growing in it was dedicated to God and was therefore ecclesiastical property he ordered Roger *"openly and publicly in his church and other churches of the Deanery of Wyche on Sundays and festivals....to admonish and persuade the said parishioners to abstain from all vain and damnable presumption"*. If they did not withdraw and apologise within fifteen days Roger was instructed to excommunicate them. As this involved the withdrawal of all sacraments - and therefore eternal damnation should anyone die while excommunicated - no doubt the parishioners backed off smartly.

Priest and parishioners might sometimes have rather too much contact, and the temptations of the flesh could prove irresistible for a clergy now sworn to celibacy. It certainly proved irresistible to John Sekesteinn (Sexton), one of the chaplains at St John's. When his lover Agnes Hucheinn inconveniently presented him with a child in 1325, the secret was out and he quickly found himself up in front of the bishop. If the eight shilling fine sounds fairly lenient it was certainly more than Sekesteinn could afford, as he was allowed to pay it in five instalments over a number of months. It probably did his career prospects as a priest no good either.

Despite the occasional dispute St John's remained a strong influence on its parishioners and a steady stream of local men sought a role in church life, either as monks at Worcester or as minor clergy in various churches around the diocese. Their names litter the lists of ordinands in the bishops' registers of this period, as acolytes – the lowest rung on the ladder - sub-deacons, deacons and, just occasionally, priests. Those in earlier years were rough yeoman folk with just a single, baptismal name or an added descriptive nickname: Robert of Bromsgrove in 1284, Richard of Bromsgrove in 1285, Henry Goodsoul in 1294, Richard Simple in 1295. The 14th century saw some improvement in personal status if not the position attained. In 1302 John, the Bishop of Llandaff standing in during a vacancy, ordained Richard Pencrich[31] as sub-deacon and John de Southwood as deacon. It is not recorded where they served but minor clergy such as these often had to fill in for vicars absent through illness or secondment, and the medieval incumbents of St John's would have headed a small team of less qualified clerics. Some men achieved rapid promotion. Henry Hall of Bromsgrove was appointed acolyte in 1373 and confirmed as prior of Dodford, a small Augustinian monastery three miles west of Bromsgrove, only two years later. But even vicars were still relatively low in the social scale, as the prior of Worcester demonstrated in 1302 by directing the vicar of another parish to appoint *"any literate and honest man"* as a locum priest while he was away on a 3-year academic sabbatical.

One man at least went on to a wider fame. John de Bromsgrove, a monk at Worcester Priory, was ordained Deacon in 1287 and priest in 1294. He showed enough promise to be appointed proctor – a legal representative of the prior – in January 1302, and was sent on various diplomatic missions to the Archbishop of

---

[31] An older Richard de Pencrich bequeathed a tenement at the foot of the church hill to his son – possibly sub-deacon Richard – by a undated late 13th century deed in the cathedral library. In the same bequest are other tenements at Bordesley held by Robert de Belne, the vicar with the new vicarage, who apparently augmented his stipend with a small property portfolio.

CHAPTER 3: EXPANSION

Canterbury. In February the same year he was commended to the prior by Edward I and was granted *"one monk's loaf and one draught of good ale daily"* for his valuable and faithful service to the king on an unspecified but delicate political matter. He also attended parliament, armed with the enormous sum of £90, to bankroll the prior's claim to the patronage of Dodderhill church in Droitwich - all in all, not bad going for a local lad.[32]

By contrast, someone else however was not who he claimed to be. William de Hampton was legitimately admitted as vicar of St John's by Bishop Simon de Montacute on 1st June 1335. He barely had time to unpack before Philip le Yonge, a priest from Bromyard (Herefordshire) claimed that he was the rightful occupant of the vicarage. Was le Yonge just a mischief-maker, or had he been put forward by a rival claimant to the patronage? Afraid that he might attract *"severe prejudice"* by being caught between two putative patrons, de Hampton went straight to the Court of Canterbury, the high ecclesiastical court in London, for a ruling. They wrote back to the bishop on the 20th June with an instruction that le Yonge should not attempt anything prejudicial while judgement was pending, and that he should appear before the court on the 7th July to receive its verdict. Bearing in mind that it took at around five days to travel from Bromsgrove to London one wonders whether he made it in time.

Although de Hampton retained the incumbency the problem of Philip le Yonge did not go away. In 1339 Bishop Wulstan de Bransford appointed le Yonge as one of two diocesan proctors to the Curia, the Papal court in Rome. This was something of an honour, as well as involving a lengthy and hazardous journey, and those sent were chosen with some care. Someone certainly liked le Yonge, and perhaps the appointment was in compensation for his failure to secure St John's. If so it was a mistake. Just a year later a third proctor was sent hurriedly

---

[32] Richard de Bromsgrove, possible the same Richard who was ordained in 1285, was one of several people granted passage to foreign parts on 14th November 1307 as servants of the new King, Edward II.

51

in pursuit with a remit to prosecute a case in the Curia against le Yonge, who was once again *"calling himself vicar of Bromsgrove"*. The allegation is curiously worded, as if delicacy prevented an overt statement: *"certain processes touching the bishop and his church involving suspension, interdict and excommunication, which at the instance of Philip have been effected on apostolic authority"*. The inference is clear: le Yonge had used the opportunity of an influential new audience to re-open his case and had demanded a papal interdict against the bishop. Perhaps he had actually succeeded, for the speeding messenger and veiled wording of the record hint at a high degree of diocesan embarrassment.

And this was no isolated incident. Eighteen years later no less than three priests each laid claim to the vicarage of St John's. Edward Brigge was appointed on the 6th October 1357 and his rival, John de Oxford, only two days later. While they were arguing about who was right a third claimant, Henry de Raggele, took possession of the vicarage by (he said) the power of the Apostolic See; that is, papal direction. It took eighteen months to sort the mess out but John de Oxford eventually prevailed and was formally admitted on 23rd May 1359. In a town with two masters these incidents were almost certainly an attempt by the royal manor to force the priory's hand by inserting their own man into the vicarage. Such underhand tactics were becoming increasing common under the royal manor's forceful new tenants.

Church Against Town

Down in the town, the division of responsibilities between priory and royal ownership was causing similar problems. By the 13th century, the royal manor of Bromsgrove and Norton was held by the Mortimers, powerful and independent-minded Earls of March. In 1319 John de Mortimer was paying £12 a year to the King's Exchequer for this privilege but, by 1330, the manor was back with the king after Roger de Mortimer ran off with Edward II's rebellious wife Isabella and

CHAPTER 3: EXPANSION

was beheaded for his treason by Edward III. Joan, Roger's long-suffering widow, regained the manor in 1350 and was paying nothing at all at the time she died six years later, holding the manor by an oath of fealty only. Her grandson and his successors then held the manor for the rest of the century.

The Mortimers took every advantage of their position to acquire land and influence by fair means and foul. Several examples survive from no doubt many complaints from the priory to the king about *"the crafty indevoures and suttell procvrementes of theyse malignant chyldren"*, as the 17th century Worcestershire historian Thomas Habington noted. In 1349 the whole parish complained that matters relating to St John's were being decided in the royal manor court, not the prior's rectory court, and that the Mortimers' local officers, *"suttelly, secreatly and maliciously"* were working to deprive the church of its ancient rights and liberties, ignoring the fact that Henry III had given the church to the priory over a century before. This time the parish won. The property rights of the priory had been reconfirmed by an Inquiry thirty years previously and John, the president of the priory's consistory court, wrote to the rural dean and the vicar of St John's, telling them to excommunicate the guilty parties. What effect this had is not recorded but it was not the last time that the Mortimers *"intruded themsealfes...without warrant"* into the life of the town.

The line between lay and ecclesiastical misdemeanours was sometimes a fine one, but in matters of the heart the church claimed a certain moral authority. So, when Adam le Coke's long-running affair with the married Juliana Melewarde came to light in the little hamlet of Woodcote in 1325 the case went straight to the bishop's court. The adulterous pair had to renounce their sin and Juliana had to promise to keep her cuckolded and no-doubt furious husband Thomas in bed and board. That was the easy part. Rather more painfully, both then had to walk round St John's church three times while receiving the *"customary discipline"*, in this case a thorough thrashing from the assembled townsfolk. And they then had to repeat the same humiliation round the market place, in full view of every passer-by in town. Showing not too much clemency the judge let the unfortunate pair off two out of three thrashings – but only until Bishop Cobham returned from a trip to London.

Increasing Wealth

People only fight over money if there is money to fight over. Despite the depredations of plague and war, wealth was increasing - for some at least - and this wealth came from the land. The Bromsgrove of the Domesday Book was an arable farming district. Despite its extensive woodland it possessed the seemingly enormous number of 77 ploughs, and every acre that was not heath or forest was cultivated. Indeed, so inefficient was the agricultural practice of the time that every inch had to be ploughed, just to support the local populace and pay the tithes. Little or no surplus was left for trading. Even after half a millennium the marks of the distinctive medieval ridge and furrow ploughing system can still be seen around Bromsgrove, running up impossibly steep banks where the standard ploughing team of eight oxen must have laboured over every step.

But the fact that these old plough marks are still visible indicates a change in agriculture that began to sweep over lowland England during this period, as arable land gave way to pasture. Sheep were the great wealth creators of the later medieval period. They needed less labour than arable crops, and of course the plagues of the period ensured that less labour was available. But, most importantly their produce was easily transportable and could be sold for profit. Here too in Bromsgrove sheep were gaining ground, not least to supply wool for the growing cloth trade for which Bromsgrove was becoming known - remember those tenter-racks in the Glebe fields?

CHAPTER 3: EXPANSION

In 1341, Edward III's administrators carried out a wide-ranging enquiry into the value of ecclesiastical property for taxation purposes, called the "Nonarum Inquisitiones". The return for Bromsgrove was made by nine of the town's leading landowners and, as one might expect, claimed that the parish was being over-taxed. While *"the church of Bromsgrove with the chapels of Norton and Grafton"* was valued at 62 marks (that is, £20 13s 4d), the value of its produce was only 40 marks (£13 6s 8d). But this produce was no longer merely arable. Alongside the usual corn the assessors also listed wool and lambs, two new sources of wealth that would transform the town economy in years to come.

As ever the landowners were first to profit. An Inquiry was held in 1380 at Hartlebury before Bishop Wakefield to reassess the apportionment of tithes between the priory and the vicar, Richard atte Lake. It held that not only did the priory have the right to the main arable tithe but also to the tithe on any land in Bromsgrove and Kings Norton which had been converted to sheep pasture more than 20 years ago, even if that land produced hay (the vicar's tithe) as a result. Richard had apparently objected to this sneaky manoeuvre by the priory - but he lost. Sheep were simply too valuable to leave to a local priest. And this same inquiry produced another unpleasant surprise for our Richard. Chancel repairs were traditionally the responsibility of the patron. Because the parish had two growing churches however, the priory now decided that this was one burden it was not prepared to shoulder alone. It therefore agreed only to cover repairs at Kings Norton and dumped the responsibility for Bromsgrove - the larger church - firmly on the vicar. This apportionment caused considerable trouble for later Incumbents and it was still being argued over in 1882. [33]

---

[33] While rectors indeed had the obligation for chancel repairs, they also had the income from the parish's great tithe to help them. Vicars such as Richard only had the lesser tithe, which was hardly adequate to fund major building work.

CHAPTER 4: COMPLETION

The 15th and 16th Centuries

Tower and Spire

The building of the tower must have absorbed all the townsfolk's energies and money, for we can find no evidence of any other alterations to the church until the middle of the 15th century. But then, what improvements there are! By the end of the century St Johns' was transformed from its early medieval roots to something approaching fashionable. Its disparate parts - at least those owned by the parishioners - were brought together under a unifying architectural cloak to form one of the most impressive parish church exteriors in the West Midlands and a landmark for the entire district.

To trace the story in stone we must first complete the tower. There is no obvious sign of a break in construction, and work probably continued intermittently as funds permitted into the early part of the new century. While the bell openings in the top stage could be as early as the 1380s the fine ogee-headed blank arcading either side, and the panelled battlements and crocketted finials above, look like early-to-mid 15th century work in the new Perpendicular style. By itself this tower top would be impressive enough. Almost doubling the total height with a slender octagonal spire created not only the tallest combination in Worcestershire but also a beautifully proportioned composition in itself. The spire itself is kept quite plain, enlivened with four lucarnes (miniature windows) at the base and top, and with an unusual garter of quatrefoil panelling two-thirds of the way up, perhaps reflecting a break in construction. Each of the eight edges of the spire is emphasised with a roll moulding, increasing the illusion of slenderness and

CHAPTER 4: COMPLETION

perspective. Despite St John's hilltop position, Bromsgrove itself sits in a bowl of land, and such a height of spire was a practical necessity in order to be seen from the surrounding countryside.

It is no coincidence that the main daughter-church of St John's, St Nicholas' at Kings Norton, has a slightly smaller but otherwise very similar tower. Again the top stage is enlivened with battlemented blank arcading; there are again three statue niches, this time stepped on the more visible south face of the tower, and the spire rises equally slenderly, its edges decorated this time with curling crockets. There is another very similar tower and spire at Coleshill and four smaller towers with stylistic similarities at Yardley, Romsley, Beaudesert and Sheldon, the latter three without spires. All date from the around the mid 15th century and were apparently designed by the same master mason, showing how the role of this essential craftsman was beginning to transform from highly skilled artisan to something more akin to architect as the Middle Ages reached their zenith.

And we may just know who he was, for Sheldon's tower carries a rare dated inscription of 1461 recording its builder's name - Henry Ulm. Surviving building contracts for medieval towers often ask the mason to copy a nearby church, with or without adaptations. If Ulm is indeed our man, we can imagine him and his itinerant masons' lodge travelling from parish to parish, adding splendid and fashionable tower-heads and spires to churches across north Worcestershire and Warwickshire, each of whom wanted something a little bigger or better than the last and now had the money to pay for it.

FAIRLY MOUNTED ON A HILL

[Picture 5] The choir singing from the tower on Ascension Day, c1908. The ornate mid 15th century panelling, gargoyles and lucarnes on the spire are clearly visible

CHAPTER 4: COMPLETION

Bells

Towers of this date had one purpose - to house bells. Churches had bells from the earliest times, single untuned instruments which were tolled to summon the congregation, to emphasise significant points in the service and to mark the passing times of day and night. They were, in effect, the clocks of the Middle Ages, rousing the town at 4am (later 5am) and confining it indoors - the curfew - at 8pm. St John's certainly had a small Sanctus bell in the 13th Century, carried in a pierced finial above the chancel arch on the east gable of the nave. Before the present tower was completed, any other bells must have been hung either in a bellcote over the west gable, in a separate timber bell-frame or, just possibly, our mysterious second tower.

These simple bells on plain yokes were restricted to tolling and could not be used to play music as such. From the beginning of the 14th century however, improvements were made to the way in which they were hung, to increase the control of the ringer. Although the change ringing method used today was not codified until 1668, churches now began to acquire collections of bells, hung in frames on wooden bell-wheels and rung in regular rhythms. The first reference to bells at St John's occurs in 1483, when four bells are mentioned, rising to five in 1524. This accords well with the likely completion date of the tower.

Curfews apart, there was one other way of telling the time. The sunny south wall of the church was an ideal location for sundials and in later years a large dial sat over the south door, emblazoned with a typically morbid Georgian pun. "We shall..." it read, leaving the reader to infer the last word from the instrument itself (dial, i.e. "die-all"). But long before this relatively sophisticated clock the churchwardens made their own basic time-piece to gauge the correct times for services. Scratch dials are relatively common in medieval churches and St John's had two, crudely etched into the south aisle wall at low level east of the porch.

Lines marking the times of the main services radiate out from a shallow hole, into which the user inserted a stick as a basic gnomon to cast the necessary shadow.

The People's Church

With the tower complete the rest of the church looked distinctly old-fashioned by comparison, not to say dwarfed. The old steeply pitched nave roof barely rose to the top of the first tower stage and the good burghers of Bromsgrove must have felt increasingly that the church was no advertisement for their town's albeit modest prosperity - nor their own. In the cities, wealthy individuals and trade guilds were pouring money into the major churches, creating new aisles and chapels and generally overhauling the ancient fabric in the latest fashionable styles, often at considerable expense. These guilds were evidence of a growing new class of people - well-to-do self-made merchants with money to spare and little obligation to the old aristocracy. While the great families were subject to the whims of royal favour this new "middle" class used its steadily growing wealth to buy influence and status. Richard Penne was typical. A prominent merchant and the richest man in town, he gave twenty acres of land in 1389 to endow a chantry light at one of the church altars. Bromsgrove also had its own guild (and guildhall) in 1275, although this seems to have lapsed by the 14th century. Whether or not they sponsored any work at St John's, the sheer amount of new building at this time was more than noble patronage alone could fund, and the resources of the whole town would have been put to the task for a good few years, both in labour and money.

And every parish knew that the best way of raising money was through beer. The festivals known as Church Ales were an ancient practice whose origins may even predate Christianity itself, when beer was used as a ritual drink. By late medieval times the Church Ale had become a huge money-spinner for the average church, and parish accounts throughout the country attest both to its effectiveness

CHAPTER 4: COMPLETION

as a fundraiser and its popularity with the parishioners. Beer, brewed by the churchwardens and sometimes in the church itself, was sold to raise money as the centrepiece of a huge party, usually held on one of the hundred or more saint's days in the medieval calendar. Food, games, and sports such as archery and bowling were laid on, dances organised and travelling players and musicians entertained large crowds through the day.

In the days before fixed seating the church itself formed the main indoor venue. But with the advent of pews in the 15th century, clear floor space became scarce and special buildings – church houses - were constructed in the churchyards for these festivities. These were usually of two storeys, a secure undercroft for brewing and storage under an open upper floor. The lack of pre-Reformation parish records robs us of any specific account of church ales in Bromsgrove but we know from several wills that a church house was built in 1542-3. As well as keeping the festivities dry, church houses were used for parish meetings of all sorts and often functioned as schoolhouses during the week. The presence of a church house at St John's, even at this late date, indicates that the parish was still very much involved in fundraising for their now enormous and costly church.

Church houses were usually placed just outside the consecrated area of the churchyard, convenient for both church and town. This is certainly the case with Worcestershire's two surviving medieval church houses at Arley Kings, near Stourport, and Claines, to the north of Worcester. Bromsgrove's steeply sloping church hill therefore presented something of a problem, offering almost no level ground around the yard itself and leaving little clue as to where this long-lost building once sat. The gentler slope of Crown Close may be one location, perhaps the site of the Dipple family vault in the north-west corner of the churchyard which was apparently converted out of two old vaulted undercrofts after this area was incorporated into the churchyard in the 18th century. But there is another intriguing possibility. The churchyard came nearest to the town on St John's Street, linked from an early date by the church steps. This is also the steepest side of the hill, and the building owners along the street dug back into the soft red sandstone of the hill to maximise the space available to them. The back yard of the Shoulder of Mutton public house (later the Wishing Well) contains a particularly interesting set of recesses suggestive of former outbuildings and storerooms, all carved from the living rock. The presence of a rock-cut baking oven at one end points to a catering function for at least part of the range. But most revealing of all is the carefully cut flight of steps that rise through the rock from this level directly towards the west end of the church above. Whatever these buildings' original use, it was somehow related to the church.

The Victorian frontage of the Shoulder of Mutton conceals an older building within, listed as an inn in 1610. Could its medieval predecessor be our church house? The location is good - reasonably close to the church and opening onto what may still have been an open green in the 16th century. Many church houses were sold out of church use after 1600, and conversion to an inn perpetuated the tradition of feasting and drinking. This close relationship between church and inn still exists in many towns throughout England and offers one as yet unproven explanation for some otherwise mystifying features.[34]

---

[34] The fact that the inn was being used as the base for diocesan visitations in the mid-19th century suggests more than a casual link with the church. The range of outhouses came to a rather dramatic end when they were demolished by a large fall of rock from just below the churchyard wall in the early hours of Saturday 25th January 1862. The shock, *"resembling that of an earthquake"*, rattled the whole row of houses on that side of the street. My thanks to Tom Ayres, erstwhile landlord of the Wishing Well, for his ready agreement to let me explore this most interesting area. The inferences I have drawn are entirely speculative but would repay further investigation.

CHAPTER 4: COMPLETION

The Chantry Chapels

We have already met the Staffords of Grafton Manor as putative patrons of our 14th century chantry chapel. They now re-enter the stage in dramatic fashion. Sir Humphrey Stafford obtained a royal licence in 1447 to found a perpetual chantry of two chaplains in St John's *"at the altar of St Mary"*. This was probably at the east end of the north aisle, a common site for this dedication.

[Picture 6] The Chantry Chapel, from an 1857 engraving

The chantry was to be founded for the good estate of the king and queen, and of himself and his wife Alianora Burdet; and it was to be named, not surprisingly, *"The Chantry of Sir Humphrey Stafford of Grafton"*. The King and Queen in question were the weak and beleaguered Henry VI and his fierce young French wife, Margaret of Anjou. As Henry was busy losing France with Margaret's help at the time, and London was in an uproar, this dedication may well have been a piece of royal toadying.

If so, it had tragic consequences. Sir Humphrey had barely started to plan his new chapel when he was killed at Blackheath on 11th June 1450, leading the King's forces against a popular uprising of Kentishmen under an Irish adventurer named Jack Cade. Cade's Rebellion, as it became known, was a protest against the wretched state of the country under Henry and the false counsel of his treacherous advisors. It seems that Cade killed Sir Humphrey himself, for he was observed after the battle wearing his victim's armour as spoils of war. Stafford's retainers brought his body home and the grieving Alianora had him buried with honours, under a splendid alabaster monument carved by the workshop of Thomas Prentys and Robert Sutton in Chellaston (Derbys). And there he lies today, his plate armour restored to him in every authentic detail, his head resting on his jousting helm with its boar's crest, his hands clasped in prayer and his feet on one of his beloved hunting hounds.

Many years later, Alianora, now an old woman *"in pure widowhood"*, re-founded the chantry that her husband had started. In 1478, she declared that a single chaplain should say daily masses for the repose of her husband's soul, her children's and her own, at a cost of £6 13s 4d a year. The chantry was to be paid out of the income from the family's Northamptonshire estate of Dodford, rather than Grafton, and Thomas Harding was duly appointed as the first chantry priest. Around the monument of her late husband now rose a beautiful new chapel, its north wall lit by three fashionable square-headed windows with Perpendicular tracery, its parapet decorated with gargoyles and its flat lead roof underdrawn with an ornate timber ceiling with curved brackets supported on carved stone angels. The line of this ceiling can still be seen in the surviving stone moulding on the chapel's east wall, together with one mutilated angel. As well as replacing the old north transept, whose stones it re-used, this chapel also filled up the gap to the existing chantry chapel, and a high opening was formed through the dividing wall to link the two family mausoleums. Her work complete Alianora joined her husband on the cold alabaster table, her close-fitting low-bodied gown covered with an open-fronted mantle and her hair fashionably gathered into a mitre shape under a net. She was obviously a proud, strong woman: what would she have thought of her fine roof being sold for firewood by the churchwardens in 1814?

But the Stafford star was waning. Sir Humphrey's nephew, also a Sir Humphrey, remained faithful to the new Yorkist monarchy and, like King Richard III, found himself on the losing side at the Battle of Bosworth in August 1485. Unlike the King, Stafford survived the battle itself and fled south, where he tried with his brother to raise a rebellion against the victorious new Tudor King, Henry VII. The attempt failed. Stafford was captured, executed without delay in November the same year and his estates were confiscated. Sir Humphrey's son, yet another Sir Humphrey, eventually had some lands restored to him but Grafton had gone forever, given to new royal favourites.

The Church Ascendant

While Alianora's chantry chapel was the only alteration to the north aisle, the rest of St John's underwent a radical transformation at about the same time. The widening of both aisles back in the 13th century and the increasing amount of stained glass had left the old nave very dark beneath its soot-stained roof. For a major town-centre church, this was sadly out of keeping with the new fashion for light airy spaces that had been made possible by the advanced building technology of the Perpendicular style. Windows could now be made much larger, columns and mullions slenderer, arches and roofs flatter, and wall surfaces reduced to the minimum necessary for support.

FAIRLY MOUNTED ON A HILL

So, off came the old roof and down came the old south aisle arcade. In its place rose a new row of four slender piers, topped with shallow two-centred arches that continued the column mouldings, interrupted only by vestigial capitals more akin to stringcourses. The nave walls were extended upwards from the now-exposed wall-heads to form a high clerestory, pierced by five arched lights on each side that flooded the nave with unaccustomed light. To top it all, a huge flat lead roof, supported on oak beams spanned the 32ft width of the nave. Each 1½ ton beam was linked by moulded purlins carrying rafters, and was decorated with carved centre bosses and decorative brackets at each end. Beams and ceiling were both splendidly painted, the former with a formalised foliage motif that was still evident when the old roof was exposed in 1858 and was reproduced by the restorers. The nave east wall was raised over the chancel arch to the new roof level, although there seems to have been some concern about the ability of the arch to carry the greater weight as the wall itself was thinned over its middle section, inside and out.

At the same time, it seems, all but the easternmost windows in the south aisle were replaced by huge square-headed lights with Perpendicular tracery similar to those in the chantry chapel. A smaller matching window sat over the old south door. And, most unusually, a pretty little stone bay was cut through the aisle wall towards the east end, lit by traceried square-headed lights on three sides. A similar bay at Spetchley, east of Worcester, holds a funerary monument behind an iron railing. Did this bay also hold a monument and, if so, to whom? The record is largely silent, but there is one clue. The 17th century antiquarian Thomas Habington noted in the south aisle *"a tombe equallyinge any here in contynuance of tyme, though inferior for cost and curiosity"*. This raised monument contained a brass to an Edward Blundell, lying in his armour with his wife, Margery, on his right-hand side. Little is known of the Blundells, save that they accompanied William the Conqueror in 1066 and seem to have held land near Stoke Prior. There

CHAPTER 4: COMPLETION

is no way of knowing whether this tomb sat in the bay, for it has disappeared without trace since - but it is a possibility.

The easternmost southern window and the aisle east window itself were not replaced. This is further indication that the east end of the aisle was regarded as a distinct space, most likely a chantry chapel. If so, it was probably separated from the rest of the aisle by a traceried oak screen similar to that in the Stafford chantry. This chantry was now one of at least four altars, each with its own priest. The high altar at the east end of the chancel was the most important, followed by the altars of St Mary in the north aisle, St John in the south aisle and St Nicholas in the 14th century chantry, north of the chancel and overseen by the Staffords' chantry priest.

The proliferation of altars was matched by the increasing subdivision of space within the church, as private and corporate benefactors expressed their beneficence in timber and gold paint. But the screening of chantry chapels and private pews was more than matched by the creation of the single biggest division in the whole building, one that purposely separated priest from people, sacred from profane, God from the world. Late medieval notions of piety and the availability of private money came together in the rood screen, a huge ornate timber partition that filled the chancel arch, its arcaded and panelled frame covered with finely carved and painted decorations. Central gates led into the chancel, at once an access and a separation. The mystery of the mass was now given tangible form, awesome and remote, a rite performed behind a veil, something to be imagined as much as seen or heard.

Rood screens derived their name from the rood, an old name for the large and elaborate crucifix which was mounted centrally over the screen itself. Flanked by near life-size statues of the Virgin and St John this powerful ensemble was visible to all worshippers as a reminder of the central focus for their faith. And to emphasise that focus the screen itself was topped by a narrow gallery – the rood loft – cantilevered out on richly carved timber vaulting and with a solid balustrade to match the screen panelling. Elevated above the nave, this loft acted as a musicians' gallery, a stage for religious plays and a mount for the small medieval organ, its reedy polyphony drifting over the congregation like a voice from heaven.

Access to the loft was via a tight stone spiral stair tunnelled into the north-east corner of the nave wall that emerged via a stone archway halfway up the wall-face. This is now the only relic of what was once the pride of the church, a tangible, awe-inspiring metaphor for medieval man's relationship with God - but we must mourn its loss later.

More money was poured into the outside of St John's – this was, after all, partly an exercise in civic pride. Like the nave, both aisles had now acquired flat lead roofs, replacing the old steep pitches and probably with beamed oak ceilings to match. Lead roofs themselves were an indication of a parish with money to spend and the hint would not have been lost on visitors. These flat roofs not only allowed the construction of the clerestory – literally a clear storey - but also followed the new fashion for hiding roofs behind an ornate parapet. The hill-top location of the church lent itself to a bold silhouette and the master mason duly obliged with a filigree crown of battlements and pinnacles around the clerestory and aisle wall-heads, matching the tower. Its proportions restored, the outside of St John's looked little different in the late 15th century from its appearance today, riding majestically against the skyline from every direction.

As a final gesture, the old timber porch was replaced in stone with a boldly modelled church-in-miniature, complete with its own overhanging battlements, stained glass and bestial gargoyles.

CHAPTER 4: COMPLETION

[Picture 7] The South Porch, c1900

Two opposing niches within held, to the left a statue and, to the right a holy water stoop, placed high off the ground to discourage pilfering. Porches, like doors, were ritually important: baptism and marriage services started here, schools were run and meetings held. To fit this porch onto the battered old stonework of the South aisle, it was necessary to alter the south door by narrowing the opening. This is the only logical explanation for the present curiously disjointed appearance of the doorway, its partly segmental arch truncated at each end over oddly plain jambs in a different stone. Perhaps it mattered less now, hidden behind such a splendid canopy.

Embellishment was not confirmed to the bricks and mortar. To accompany all the architectural finery, William Moore, prior of Worcester, presented the church in 1521 with a beautiful *"Missale ad Usam Ecclesiae Wygorniensis cum calendario"*, a combined service book and lectionary suitable for use in churches across Worcestershire.[35]

One part of St John's did not participate in the general beautification. The chancel, alone, retained its steep roof and early windows, its plain domestic outline a curious counterpoint to the ornate fripperies of the nave. The difference is still obvious today, especially outside, although the rood screen would have blocked much of the internal view in medieval times. This, more than anything else, highlighted the continuing divergence between town and priory, between St John's austere Benedictine patrons and the increasingly prosperous townsfolk, keen to flaunt their newfound status in front of their old masters.

Perhaps the old chancel did have a moment of glory though. The main body of the church must have been unusable for many months while its roof and south walls were dismantled in a forest of wooden scaffolding, its floor littered with sawn timber and stone-dust, masons' benches and the perennial clutter of builders through the centuries. As the only roofed portion of the church the chancel must have been a welcome refuge, as well as a rather crowded venue for services. Indeed, there was no other suitably large space in town.

---

[35] This disappeared after the reformation and only surfaced in the 19th century, when it was purchased privately at auction.

CHAPTER 4: COMPLETION

Outside, the graveyard was filling up and earlier stones were being displaced to accommodate the growing town.[36] Peter Prattinton, the Bewdley antiquary, found a medieval child's coffin, hewn from a single stone, lying abandoned in the churchyard in the early 19th century, and the 13th century sandstone coffin lid with a foliated cross which now sits in the south aisle had at some time been dug up and used to support one of the raised grass banks at the top of the church steps. At some point before 1600, the whole 248 yard circumference of the churchyard was walled in stone, the repair of which was shared between the various tithe districts – or yields – of the parish. All the lengths were measured from *"the stayers"*, that is, the church steps. This was one of only two points of access recorded in the yield list. The other, eighty yards further along the wall, was a "lydiate", a swing-gate for carts at the top of the footpath across Crown Close. Like church doors, gates into the churchyard had a ritual function as penetrations of the otherwise unbroken sacred boundary, and some services had specific portions conducted at the gate to sanctify those entering. During burials, for example, the cortege stopped at the churchyard gate to await the priest's arrival. While the opening sentences of the old burial service were read over it, the coffin was kept dry by a roof over the whole structure. These lych gates[37] are a feature of most historic churchyards, although 17th century examples like that at the head of the church steps are comparatively uncommon.

From these gates, a series of narrow footways fanned out across the town and surrounding fields like the irregular spokes of a giant wheel. These so-called "church paths" were created time out of mind by generations of parishioners all taking the shortest route to church from their particular part of the parish. In the days when much more land was held in common and ancient rights of access still held some sway footpaths were established by precedent and need, for only

---

[36] Cotton states that the earliest remaining gravestone was that of Abel Wannerton, dated 1567. This is a misreading, as Wannerton died in 1657. There are no known dated stones before the 17th century.

[37] Literally "corpse gate". See also *Chapter 5: the 17th century church*.

the well off could afford a horse. Some church paths still survive, either as field paths in the countryside or alleyways in the town. The church steps, for example, continued across what is now the Market Street car park as Little Lane before crossing Worcester Street and running uphill as Old Station Road on its way to Finstall. From the chancel door another church path left the northeast corner of the churchyard, dropped down behind the old vicarage as Parsons Hill then Huxley's Entry before crossing the High Street, then slipped beside what is now the Prezzo restaurant on its way up to Ednall Lane.

New Faces

The Stafford's old home at Grafton did not remain empty for long. The victorious Henry VII was quick to reward his own supporters and the estate passed immediately to the Talbots, Earls of Shrewsbury and one of the foremost families in the land. Gilbert Talbot, High Sheriff of Shropshire, had defied Richard III's orders in 1485 and, seeing where the future lay, had marched his two thousand men down to Newport to join the rebellious Henry Tudor's army. He thus found himself on the opposing side to Sir Humphrey Stafford at Bosworth. Henry Tudor's smaller forces carried the day and, as the hero of the battle, Talbot was knighted by the future King on the field. Granting him the Stafford estates was therefore a pointed demonstration of loyalty rewarded – to the victor went the spoils of the vanquished. Governor of Calais, Knight of the Garter, Privy Counsellor, Knight of the King's Bodyguard, Knight Banneret, Steward of the Lordship of Feckenham and of the Bishop's deer park at Alvechurch all followed. Talbot was loaded with honours over his lifetime, a testimony not just to his *"martial valour and singular wisdom"* but his astute political sense in backing the right man at the right time.

Sir Gilbert was a great benefactor to the Church in general but could some of his largesse have also come to St John's? His star rose at just the right date for much of the major overhaul and he may well have seen such an investment as both a

CHAPTER 4: COMPLETION

pious act of gratitude and an opportunity to supplant his predecessor in good works. So, when his first wife, Elizabeth (neé Greystock), died in 1490, she was buried under an alabaster table monument every bit as ornate as her contemporary, Alianora Stafford, a comparison which may well have been deliberate. Now resting in the northeast corner of the chancel, Elizabeth's tomb shows evidence of having been moved at least once. More intriguingly, her effigy does not match the base on which it sits, suggesting that she may have displaced an older occupant – another Stafford perhaps? Be that as it may, she lies alone. Sir Gilbert married again and on his death in 1517 his body was carried north in a torch-lit procession to lie with Awdrey (neé Cotton), his second, more favoured wife, in another of the family's chapels at Whitchurch, Shropshire.[38]

[Picture 8] The remains of Grafton Manor in the late 18th Century, after the fire of 1710 (from Nash)

---

[38] Awdrey is also recorded as Anne and Ethelreda. The now-lost east window at Grafton chapel depicted Sir Gilbert in full armour, bare-headed and robed in a blue cloak, between his two wives and three sons, Gilbert, Humphrey and John.

73

FAIRLY MOUNTED ON A HILL

Talbots now dominate the last medieval phase of St John's and history promptly repeats itself. Sir Gilbert's son by his first marriage, another Gilbert, married another Elizabeth, herself the widow of a Mr Winter.[39] On his death in 1542 Gilbert, like his father, was buried at Whitchurch. And like her mother-in-law, Elizabeth preferred to be buried alone *"in the chauncell of the church of St John the Baptist in Bromsgraue"* on her own death at the end of 1547. Although her tomb is now lost she certainly had an affection for the church.[40] Like many pre-Reformation donors Elizabeth gave money as an act of piety to maintain the church fabric. 13s 8d – two marks - does not sound much now but it was her single largest monetary gift, at a time when married women had little hard currency of their own and could usually only pass on domestic furniture and plate. She did that as well, bequeathing a set of red and yellow bed curtains to the church, the money from which was to maintain the "sepulchre", the burial vault under the chantry chapel. Five shillings also went to the high altar, while the *"v [five] pristes now singinge in the said church of Bromsgraue"* got a shilling apiece to pray for her soul. One hopes they sang well.

Sir John Talbot, Sir Gilbert's son by his second wife, also rests in Bromsgrove. At his death on 10th September 1549[41] after only seven years at Grafton, he was immortalised in alabaster, lying between his two successive wives, Margaret Troutbeck and Elizabeth Wrottesley. Like Humphrey Stafford, Sir John is clad in the plate armour of his day, now more for show than protection, his feet again resting on a stylised dog and his head on his helm with its rather more realistic talbot hound crest. To his right Margaret wears a typically Tudor diamond-shaped

---

[39] Elizabeth was Gilbert's second wife. His first, Anna Paston, produced three daughters. The Winters or Wintours were a prominent local family who intermarried with the Talbots and were later prime movers in the Gunpowder Plot of 1605.

[40] The style of clothing on the monument in the chancel dates it to the earlier Elizabeth.

[41] His will was proved on 11th October 1549. The monument was probably carved some years later, when the date was wrongly attributed to 1550. Such mistakes are not uncommon on funerary monuments of this age.

CHAPTER 4: COMPLETION

headdress, her slim body cased in a close-fitted gown, gathered up at the front to show off her petticoats. Elizabeth's clothes are plain by contrast, a simple gown overlain with a mantle. All three have no doubt about their ultimate destiny. Whatever their mistakes in life, they stare upwards, hands joined in prayer, in confident hope of their heavenly reward. Rich as they were, the Talbots had the same fears of eternal damnation as their humbler tenants. The great advantage of their position was, at least in their own minds, the ability to secure their place in Paradise. Sir John was content to leave his place of burial to his family, and this great monument originally sat at the east end of the chancel, to the right of the high altar.

The very late 15th century panelled archway in the north wall of the chancel was probably the Talbot family oratory, perhaps built for Sir Gilbert. Now open to the chancel, it would originally have been enclosed on both sides by ornate openwork oak screens, with a small altar against its east wall and a desk for private prayer. The four-centred arch itself, the only stone vaulting in the church, probably replaced an older opening into the Stafford chantry. Its underside is divided into regular panels by boldly moulded ribs, with large, rather incoherent bosses at the intersections. Three bosses are more recognisable as green men, thick leafy foliage curling from their mouths. The rood loft door, now within the oratory, was given a Tudor-headed doorway at the same time. From the chancel this work looks decidedly curious. No attempt was made to match the stonework, whose large blocks are a much creamier shade than the red sandstone all around it. The mason also seems to have changed his mind while setting out the arch, as the faint line of a higher arch can be seen in the stonework above, following the line of the original window opening. This botching was originally covered up by plaster and paint but time - and Sir George Gilbert Scott in 1858 - has laid it bare.

Over time other Talbots joined Sir John and his mother. Two of Sir John's daughters, Margaret and Bridget, were buried near their father in 1612 and 1632 respectively. Although both married, they did not merit an alabaster monument to themselves and rest alone under simple bronze plaques, one beaten, the other rather naively incised and both originally set in the chancel floor under their father's monument.[42] Their cousin Humphrey Talbot, Elizabeth's grandson, did little better. He died late in 1571, leaving his pregnant wife Anne and three children to bury his body at St John's in the chapel of St Nicholas.[43] But whatever monument he may have had was unceremoniously cleared out when this chapel was converted into a vestry in the 18th century and his remains in the vault below made way for a boiler room in 1858.

An Anglican Church

With the mid 16th century Talbot monuments the medieval development of this great church comes to completion. We have come a long way from our simple Saxon timber box, as has the prosperous market town that now lies at the bottom of the church steps, including no less than a thousand registered communicants at the time of Sir John's death.[44] But as ecclesiastical architecture reached its apogee, the England that spawned it was about to change forever. A combination of radical clergy and intransigent monarch challenged the formerly unassailable position of the church, driven respectively by Protestant reform abroad and – less nobly – by Henry VIII's frustrated desire for a male heir. Henry's increasing irritation with an uncooperative papacy reached its peak in 1534 when, with Thomas Cromwell's help, he finally tore the English Church away from the

---

[42] They were discovered when the Talbot monument was moved out of the chancel in the mid 18th Century and were then fixed onto the east wall of the Chantry Chapel, next to the relocated monument.

[43] His will is dated 14th September 1556 but curiously was not proved until 15th November 1571, for reasons unknown.

[44] This was the second highest in the county after Evesham. King Norton, counted separately, had a further 910.

CHAPTER 4: COMPLETION

influence of Rome, declared himself supreme head of the Church in England, claimed the right to appoint bishops and appropriated the papal taxes of *"first fruits and tenths"* as his own.[45]

The first complete bible printed in English, Coverdale's version, was published the following year. English bibles appeared in churches by order of Thomas Cromwell's Second Injunction in September 1538 and the first English Prayer Book followed in 1549. To avoid any distractions from the newly accessible Word of God, Cromwell also ordered local clergy to remove all sacred images, wall paintings and statues in 1538. Stone altars, with their implication of ritual sacrifice, were removed two years later and replaced by wooden communion tables set away from the east wall. Sir John Talbot was therefore buried in a newly Anglican church, still outwardly Catholic in much of its doctrine but increasingly conscious of the conflicting pressures within its newfound independence from Rome.

Unlike Alianora Stafford seventy years before, the Talbots could not found a chantry chapel, for the simple reason that Edward VI had completed his father's work and abolished them in 1548.[46] No charity therefore lies behind Sir John Talbot's tomb; it is a purely personal monument to a noble family, an advertisement of secular power and status. The same act closed down the Stafford chantry and put Thomas James, its priest, out of work after a royal commission had assessed its value. Some chantry priests found new jobs as schoolmasters but Bromsgrove already had a small grammar school, run by William Fownes, another of the assistant priests at St John's. The 30 year old Fownes was *"learnyd and of honeste conuersacion"*, according to the investigating Commissioners, and his salary of

---

[45] Henry's national survey of parish taxable wealth, the Valor Ecclesiasticus of 1535, valued Bromsgrove at a wealthy £40 18s 6½d. Compare this with Alvechurch at £19 16 8d, Tardebigge at £7 18s or Dodderhill (Droitwich) at £12 11 6½d.

[46] Although the young Edward was merely a cipher for his Calvinist minder, The Duke of Somerset, Lord Protector of England.

£7 was provided by part of the income from local properties endowed for that purpose by various parishioners. Independent of chantry funding, the school survived its investigation and Fownes kept his job, although the endowment lands were seized and sold off by the Crown and Fownes's salary now came from the Auditor and Receiver of Land Revenue for Worcestershire. The remainder of the income from these properties, some £4 4s, had been used to fund various *"charitable dedes within the said parish"* including poor relief, church repairs, the upkeep of highways and bridges, and pay for the local militia. This modest sum was managed by the churchwardens, men whose importance had been steadily growing through the preceding century as ordinary people took an ever-greater part in the care and running of their church. Their reaction to having this useful income snatched from them is not recorded.

As part of this great upheaval, St John's gained if not a new patron then one in new clothes. The great monasteries, those giant repositories of parish tithes, aristocratic endowments and naked commercial profit, were dismantled one by one from 1536 by Thomas Cromwell, Henry's vicar general and so-called "hammer of the monks". The priory of Worcester was dissolved in 1542 and the dean and chapter replaced its prior and monks, although the buildings themselves escaped the fate of demolition that befell so many monasteries. The dean and chapter took over as patron of St John's and they remain so today.

With this change of employer came a change in status for their vicars. Now effectively ecclesiastical representatives of the monarch, they were expected to be men of good education and conformable politics. Given a quick wit and the right contacts, a man might go far. Take Henry Holbeach, vicar from 1544 to 1547. As the last prior of Worcester in 1536 he was canny enough to survive the Dissolution in 1542 and be appointed its first post-Reformation dean. In 1538 he was also appointed Suffragen Bishop[47] of Bristol, then still part of the great medieval

CHAPTER 4: COMPLETION

diocese of Worcester. Gaining the curacy of Bromsgrove in June 1544 might therefore sound like something of a comedown (as well as a fine piece of nepotism) if it wasn't accompanied by his simultaneous appointment by special licence as bishop of Rochester. Although this was the poorest - and one of the smallest - dioceses in England, it was a stepping stone to greater things. In Holbeach's case, it led in 1547 to the bishopric of Lincoln, anything but poor and laden with manors, abbeys and the odd castle. Henry Holbeach left Bromsgrove the same year, although it is doubtful how much time he actually spent here and most of his work would have been left to his assistant priests, William Horwood, Thomas Hill and William Clare.[48]

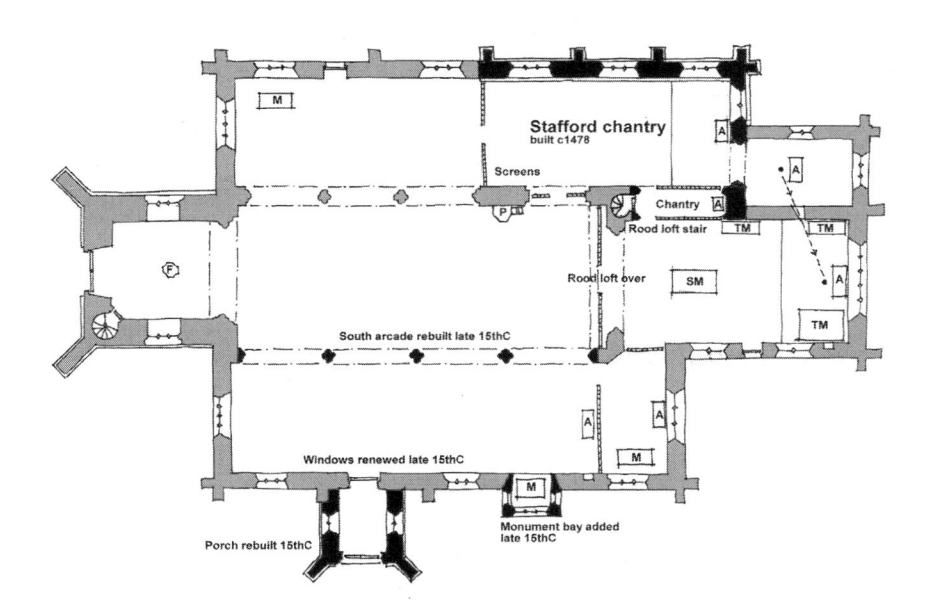

[Plan d] St John's c1500. Changes since 1380 are shown in black. Note particularly the far greater area now screened off for private or family chapels. A = altar; F = font; M = known monument (T(albot), S(tafford); P = pulpit

---

[47] A subordinate Bishop with delegated authority over a discrete area within a larger diocese.

[48] Their names appear as witnesses to several wills of this date and in requests to say masses for the soul of the deceased.

FAIRLY MOUNTED ON A HILL

When Holbeach was in town, however, he lived in a new vicarage. Robert de Belne's vicarage had apparently been built in stone, as it was rebuilt in 1513 and the old stonework gifted by the prior of Worcester (courtesy of the churchwardens) to the daughter church of Moseley, to build its tower. Nothing was wasted, even if it meant that every one of the forty-eight loads had to be carried by creaking cart twelve miles up the rutted, dirty and narrow track that passed for a main road.

Thomas Cromwell initiated another important and lasting innovation. His Second Injunction of 1538 also instructed parish clergy to keep a written register of all baptisms, marriages and burials, with a penalty of ¾d for every default. These records had to be kept in a "sure coffer" with two locks, one for the vicar and the other for the churchwardens, to ensure equal access. Written parish records did not exist before the Reformation and local inquisitions had to rely on the collective memory of the parishioners. For the first time the church became a vehicle for recording the civil status of the local population, and parish registers have been maintained in English churches continuously ever since. These handwritten documents provide an unparalleled view of every stratum in English society. Before this time, the common man or woman had generally appeared in person only when they were aggrieved, that is, through court cases; or through their will when they died. Now every single man and woman had at least two - and sometimes three - official records of their life on earth. At last the people of Bromsgrove march into view by name, and these names will increasingly take their place in this story.

Parish Records were initially suspected of being a covert method of improving the efficiency of tax gathering, but after some hesitation they were generally accepted. The earliest registers were often kept on single sheets of paper that were easily lost. This may explain why St John's registers only start in 1590, when Gervas Carington became vicar. Until separate registers were authorised by law in 1783,

CHAPTER 4: COMPLETION

all entries at St John's were made in a general register, covering baptisms, marriages and burials in one bound parchment volume. St John's registers were written in English until 1st July 1617, when they change to Latin in the middle of John Archbold's incumbency with the advent of a new, classically minded assistant curate. These irreplaceable records once lay in the parish chest, which dates from around 1600. St John's "sure coffer" actually has three locks, rather than the two stipulated; one for the vicar and two between the four churchwardens, implying a certain degree of mistrust on somebody's part. As it held all the important documents in the parish, civil and ecclesiastical, the chest was kept in the most secure and fireproof part of the church - the tower.[49] The ancient parish documents are now safely lodged in the County Records Office and the now-empty parish chest rests in the chantry Chapel, its three locks long since forced open. But that is a later story.

On The Eve Of Change: 1552

The next stage of this story does not make comfortable reading. So, before the storm breaks, let us take a last, imaginary, look inside St John's at the very end of its medieval incarnation. But we must be quiet, for a service is in progress.

After the shade of the porch, strong early August sunlight pours into the church, filtered into a rainbow of colours by the remaining painted and stained glass windows. The sun is just moving off the great east window now, leaving its image of St Wulstan and its heraldic shields in shade; but the whitewashed nave walls are beginning to glow with southern light from the high clerestory. The church is packed with town and country folk of all backgrounds, dressed accordingly in everything from finery to rags and strictly segregated by social standing and locality. The well-to-do sit upright on oak pews in the stone-floored nave and

---

[49] In 1625, Sir Thomas Cockes of Bromsgrove, answering an Exchequer deposition in a case against a Mr Middlemore, stated that he had searched through the Bromsgrove and Kings Norton manorial records "in the steeple", where they were kept.

aisles, paid for by letting the best seats to those able to afford the annual rent of around 6d. The poor sit where they can or stand against the walls and monuments in the various recesses.

Apart from the congregation, however, this is a very stark place now for anyone who can remember it a decade or so back. All those bright wall paintings now hide under a thick coat of whitewash, and the stone plinths and niches are bare of their painted and glided statues (perhaps not without a fight – were they spirited away and quietly buried before they were smashed by official order?). The small organ with its twin bellows sits unused in the chancel. The side altars with their candlesticks, statues and altar hangings have all been stripped out. Most of the silverware and all the missals are gone. The holy water stoup in the south porch is dry, its stone bowl smashed off four years previously. Four bells are still in place but they hang silent, and the sanctus bell has been removed by royal order to prevent its idolatrous use during the service. And, to make sure that every member of the congregation is fully aware of their new allegiance, a large painted board displaying the royal arms hangs prominently over the chancel arch where the doom painting once scared the young and old.

We can hear but not yet see the service, hidden as it is by the huge oak rood screen. This still stretches across the entire width of the nave and both aisles in line with the chancel arch, although the statues have been removed and the great cross has been crudely sawn off the rood loft. While the balustraded gates to the aisle chapels remain shut, those into the chancel stand open, allowing us a glimpse of the vicar, Richard Harforde in his everyday white vestments by the plain timber table that replaced the old stone altar two years ago.

Our view may be imperfect but at least we can now understand what is being said. As yet, only the vicar has one of the new English prayer books, introduced by Archbishop Cranmer on Whitsunday three years back, and the congregation

CHAPTER 4: COMPLETION

must strain to catch the still unfamiliar rubric of prayers and psalms that replace the familiar Latin chants of the old Sarum rite. After the lessons have been read, Harforde will come out to the wooden pulpit fixed against the nave north wall west of the first arch, and preach one of the twelve standard sermons from the new Book of Homilies. Perhaps he chooses "Against Strife and Contention". He will soon need its advice.

When everyone has departed Harforde takes a last look around his sunny, bare church before locking up. He has a difficult week ahead. Three of Edward VI's unsmiling commissioners are due to visit on the 9th August to take an inventory of the church's possessions and to see that St John's now accords with the King's stern view of protestant worship. Harforde has heard alarming stories of further deprivations – bells removed, church plate melted down. What else might these men demand? But his world is about to change even more than he can imagine and he wonders, with some apprehension, just what is in store for this new Church of England.

FAIRLY MOUNTED ON A HILL

[Picture 9] Harforde's view of his newly Anglican church. A photograph from around 1910, looking west to the tower arch.

Part 2

THE 17th CENTURY TO MODERN TIMES

And as the Temple of old towered above all synagogues, so the ancient parish church of Bromsgrove towers above all the multitude of meeting houses in its immediate locality. Yet the Lord who worshipped in the Temple taught in the synagogue; and I would fain believe that all Bromsgrovians think of this, and though they do not all worship within the old church, yet they reverence the sacred pile.

George Stanton, 1884

CHAPTER 5: A DIVIDED HOUSE
1550 to 1700

The World Turned Upside-Down

George Lyttleton, Sergeant at Law, lies pensively in his painted alabaster monument of 1600, his weary head propped on one hand and his other clutching the remains of a scroll. His voluminous legal robes and starched white ruff visibly proclaim his worldly success; but everything else about him speaks of the profound pessimism underlying much of early 17th religion. Whatever Lyttleton has achieved in life his inscription makes it quite clear that death has cut short all his worldly aspirations. The hourglass, skull and gravediggers' tools amongst the strap-work of the typically Elizabethan canopy reinforce his mortality and emphasise the futility of transient success. This is, if anything, a monument to death, not eternal life. Where is the confident expectation of his Talbot ancestors in the chantry chapel, their eyes steadfastly heavenward and their hands clasped in pious prayer? Where indeed is any overt religious expression at all?

To understand this profound change we have to leave the safety of St John's church for a while and step out into the turbulent waters of Tudor and Stuart England. The hundred years between 1560 and 1660 were perhaps the most difficult that the English church ever had to face, as a succession of monarchs forcibly imposed their own differing religious convictions on an increasingly factious populace. It was a century that pitted town against town, neighbour against neighbour, family against family. It changed the relationship between ruler and subject forever. It provoked the execution of an English monarch and ushered in England's only military dictatorship after a bloody civil war. It took apart the structure of

CHAPTER 5: A DIVIDED HOUSE

the Established Church and reassembled it to serve the emerging needs of an increasingly secular democracy. It touched every parish in the land. And it was all done in the name of God.

The St John's of 1600 was a rather different church to the building Lyttleton's great-great grandfather Sir John Talbot knew. We have already seen the statues, altars and great rood thrown out, the walls whitewashed. By the time John Russell, William Sheldon and George Wall had finished inspecting the church's valuables on their King's behalf that August day in 1552 the various vestments and copes, the copper and tin crucifix, the altar silverware and the organ were also slated for removal, leaving the distraught Parson Harforde with just a single chalice and paten for the one remaining altar. Unable to face the ordeal himself, he left his Welsh curate, Robert ap Davis and the four churchwardens to hand everything over to the commissioners. It could have been much worse. The author of a sermon in the Second Book of Homilies[50] lamented the fate that befell some officially ransacked churches:

"It is sin and shame to see so many churches so ruinous and so foully decayed, almost in every corner....Suffer them not to be defiled with rain and weather, with dung of doves and owls, stares [starlings] and choughs, and other filthiness, and as it is foul and lamentable to behold in many places of this country"

St John's got off comparatively lightly. But it was still a shadow of its former self, at least to anyone who remembered the church before the Reformation. Thomas Habington visited Bromsgrove one dark day in the early 1600s, trying to make

---

[50] Sanctioned under Elizabeth I in 1562 to ensure orthodoxy in teaching, as a complement to the first Book of Homilies (1547). Elizabeth had a strong aversion to unregulated preaching, which she rightly saw as a license to challenge the authority of the monarch. Set homilies also provided ill-educated clergy with something worthwhile to say to their congregations. A survey the previous year found that three-quarters of Worcestershire clergy could not preach, and even this was better than some other counties. Such clergy were known as "reading parsons" or rather more derisively as "dumb dogs".

sense of the church that had been the home of his own Catholic faith but was now in the unyielding hands of others. Once the proud owner of Hindlip Hall he had been implicated in the Gunpowder Plot of 1605 and escaped execution only at the cost of his personal freedom. Forbidden from ever leaving Worcestershire Habington spent his remaining years visiting every corner of the county, recording its towns, churches and great houses, and laboriously committing to paper its very first detailed history. *"Bromesgraue's Churche fayrely mounted on a hyll is bewtified with Arms and Monumentes"*, he duly noted. But all he could find inside were ghosts:

"In the Northe syde of the Churche are in the lofty windowes sundry Benefactors whose soules I hope are mounted to heaven thoughe theyre names are heer hard to be discovered… Theare lyeth near neer thys on the ground an auncyent monument which beeinge of softe stone is so mouldred awaye as scarcely it can bee discerned of what sex or degree the party theare portrayed was".

Habington struggled to identify the great and good of former ages, now quietly mouldering in the shadowed aisles. *"In the myddell Alley"*, he lamented, *"lyethe one of the aucient family of Barnesley of Barnesley Hall, a Gentellman of principall note in thys parish; but whosoever hathe robbed the tombe of the Bras hathe sylenced mee who coulde see nothine but a despoyled stone"*. The great medieval church and its silent inhabitants were already fading from memory.

Although the basic fabric of St John's was still recognisably medieval its layout and furniture now reflected a very Protestant view of worship. But what turned a Catholic church into a Protestant one? Hitherto, we have had to rely on the records of civil or ecclesiastical justice to know what the people of Bromsgrove thought. Now they have a new way of telling us their feelings about St John's through the directions they leave in their wills; and these brief snippets of personal belief show the world turning steadily upside down.

CHAPTER 5: A DIVIDED HOUSE

The world turns slowly at first. Apart from its split with Rome the church under Henry VIII is recognisably Catholic. Through the 1540s Bromsgrove folk still give money to the High Altar and other altars or altar lights, pay the curate to say Obits,[51] send gifts to the Cathedral at Worcester and commend their souls to Saint Mary, the Mother of God, alongside the usual gifts to the poor and the repair of the church. James Lynall in 1543 is typical, bequeathing *"to the hyghe lyght xii^d... to every altare in the said churche ii^d... to Sir Thomas Hyll to saye a trigintall of masses for my sole and all crysten soles x^s"*. But King Henry dies in 1547 and within a year everything changes. Under the uncompromisingly Protestant Edward VI, altar gifts and commendations to Our Blessed Lady disappear completely. Now, for the first time, men like Edward Bache, Roger Crowe and Richard Chaunce leave absolutely nothing at all to the church, a church they perhaps no longer recognise.

Then, in 1553, the world reverses sharply on its axis under the Catholic Mary Tudor and begins to turn the other way. Back come the altar gifts, the chantry lights,[52] the Obits and the commendations to Mary, as if the Reformation had never happened. Thomas James, the last chantry priest, is unsurprisingly one of the old school, commending his soul in 1557 to "Almighty God and to ye blessed ladye Sainte Marye and to all the blessed company of heaven". Well, some folk feel that way. More now leave nothing to this oscillating church, including eight in 1558, the last year of Mary's blood-stained reign. The once indivisible church is splitting, dividing those who hanker after the old certainties of reformed Catholicism and those who want a distinctive Protestant religion, untainted by Romish practice - and it will never be whole again.

---

[51] A commemorative mass on the deceased's behalf. A Trental was a series of masses celebrated for 30 days after the person's death. The "trigintall" in the next example, said by Thomas Hill, one of the assistant priests at St John's, is the same thing.

[52] The will of Henry Fowke in 1556 gives 2d to *"the lyghte afore the Rode"*, indicating that the great cross had been temporarily reinstated together with a nave altar during Mary's reign, as it was in a number of churches.

FAIRLY MOUNTED ON A HILL

Elizabeth I restores a moderate Anglican order for a while with her Protestant Settlement of 1559, and the few remaining gifts to the altars and cathedral cease within four years of her accession. But the force for radical change is unstoppable, and from the early 1570s a strange new note creeps into wills. Instead of simply commending their souls to Almighty God the people of Bromsgrove begin to set out increasingly elaborate declarations of their belief in redemption by grace through the sacrifice of Christ on the cross. Thomas Shuard in 1571 is typical, commending his soul to *"my maker savvyer and Redemer Trustynge in hym onelie and bye the passion of hys sonne oure Lorde Jesus Chryste toe be saved"*. William Bodle goes one better in 1598:

"nothinge doubtinge but most confidently trusting that by the deathe and passion of my sweete saviour and Redeemer Jesus Christe to have remission of all my synnes and by his glorious resurrection and assentyon to be partakers of his heavenly kingdom".

But he leaves nothing to the church, for a man so assured of his own salvation has no need of intercession. Such unswerving confidence characterises a new radical mindset that emerges in the late 1560s, dissatisfied with Elizabeth's middle-of-the-road Anglicanism. These people are mockingly called "precisionists" or "puritans", but it is the latter nickname that sticks. Reforming Anglicans, they want literally to purify the Church of its lingering Catholic taint and restore it to Edward VI's protestant ideal.

Moderate puritans can soon be found in all strata of society, including bishops and aristocracy. More radical puritans, known as Presbyterians, go one step further. They want to bring the English Church nearer the continental model pioneered by John Calvin, whose theology of predestination only guarantees salvation to an elect few and considers most people unredeemable reprobates. Bishops will be abolished and a system of locally governed parishes - or presbyteries - established, regulated by regional religious assemblies known as classes. This gloomy and

CHAPTER 5: A DIVIDED HOUSE

divisive world-view creates an atmosphere of religious melancholy in which many ordinary people feel deprived of hope and at its most extreme, driven to despair or even suicide. Little wonder that George Lyttleton looks so pensive.

Presbyterians are officially suppressed for a while in the 1580s but it is a movement that will not go away. Edward Brooke in 1599 has certainly caught the Presbyterian bug, for he trusts *"onlie in Christes merites to have remission of all my sins and to be received as one of his elect children into eternal lyfe there to remayne in joye for ever"*. He leaves nothing to St John's either. Indeed, by Elizabeth's death in 1603, gifts to the church are entirely limited to the poor (by and large generous) and to church repairs (by and large miserly). Mainstream Anglicanism is re-established by the end of the century, but it is an uneasy peace and it will not last. St John's has become for many a merely physical place, a whitewashed preaching box of wood and stone. They may feel affection for its venerable walls but it is no longer the primary focus of their religious lives.

For some people Presbyterianism is no answer. Bishops or no, it still preserves a structural hierarchy, unaccountable to the State and a law unto itself. A middle way is needed, and the rise of the Independents in the 1620s provides it. Independents want to strip out all higher church governance, leaving local churches as self-regulating entities under the overall legal jurisdiction of the civil magistrates, who would have power to rule in religious matters. The parish structure will be retained, tithes paid, and a degree of communion retained with Anglicans – for the moment, at least. Independents claim to respect religious freedom, but it is within fairly narrow limits. Radicals and Catholics are already beyond the pale, Anglicans will be soon and even Presbyterians are frowned on for seeking to separate Church and State governance. Presbyterians in turn fear the anarchy that would follow religious toleration and see the lack of any Independent liturgy or Creed as evidence that it is merely a new State monopoly on religion. Essentially similar in doctrine but opposed in terms of governance, the two main competitors to the Church of England wrangle their way through the early decades of this argumentative new century.

The Old Religion

Persecuted and purged as they are, Catholics maintain a strong foothold in Worcestershire, particularly amongst the local royalist landowners. Meeting and worshipping in secret in several local houses they risk truly horrifying penalties for practicing their faith. The Talbots' house, Grafton Manor, serves as the chief Catholic mission centre in the east of the county. Like nearby Harvington, the old building has several hideaways for its Mission Head, Father Edward Oldcorne, and the other fugitive priests who celebrate Mass in secret in the house.[53] Although Grafton is searched and looted after the failed Gunpowder Plot of 1605 Catholic worship continues there almost uninterrupted until 1860, when services transfer to St Peter's, the new Catholic church in Bromsgrove town.

Non-attendance at the parish church carries heavy penalties. Edward VI is the first to supplant the threat of eternal damnation in 1547 with the rather more worldly coercion of a fine and imprisonment for anyone who misses church on a Sunday, a punishment that exactly captures the earthly nature of the church's new authority. Elizabeth I restores her half-brother's Act of Uniformity in 1559, empowering churchwardens to collect 12d from all adult recusants (as non-attenders are called) for each offence, the money going towards the town's poor. The Conformity Law of 1581 increases the penalty to a hefty £20 per month, a sum that even reasonably well-to-do landowners find difficult to sustain for long. Defaulters are imprisoned until they have paid and those brave souls who stay

---

[53] Using Grafton Chapel itself would have been too hazardous, and the building was probably kept as a "cover" for the family's real place of Devotions. Habington saw it still roofed but the chapel was certainly ruined by the late 18th century; whether through neglect, fire or the depredations of the Civil War is not known.

CHAPTER 5: A DIVIDED HOUSE

away for more than a year have to sign over a £200 bond to ensure their good behaviour. Further such offences are dealt with, respectively, by imprisonment without bail, banishment and - should any attempt be made to sneak back into the country without Royal permission - death. Bishop Whitgift takes a particularly hard-line view of recusancy. Complaining that Worcestershire is *"much warped towards Popery"*, he obtains special powers from the Privy Council to root them out. His first list, sent to the Council in 1577, contains 39 names, including John Talbot of Grafton. While seventeen plead poverty or the financial burden of unmarried children some better-off Catholics think the price worth paying. In 1604 Talbot is granted a *"License ...... to be absent from church on paying £20 a month"*, turning his fine into a kind of subscription. And from a subsequent receipt for £160, it looks as if he pays up regularly.

This laissez-faire attitude changes for the worse after the Gunpowder Plot of 1605 when, to a shocked government at least, every Catholic becomes a potential Guy Fawkes.[54] James I's Statute the following year requires the churchwardens and constables of each parish to give the local magistrates an annual list naming all "popish" recusants; adults, children and even family servants. Churchwardens can claim a reward of 40s for every such recusant who is subsequently fined, the money coming from the recusant's estate. The idea, of course, is to drive all Catholics from the locality. As such it is an early form of ethnic cleansing and just as morally palatable. Although the Worcestershire Presentment of 1640 does not list a single recusant in the parish, its successor in 1642 suddenly finds thirty, including four from one family, the Willamsons. Several family groups are also named, including Ralph and Ann Taylor, along with their servant, William Matts; and the widow Margery Waters, with her children, Clement and Catherine.

But there is more here than first meets the eye. Three-quarters of named

---

[54] Old hurts ran deep. As late as the mid-19th Century, Bromsgrove schoolboys collecting firewood for Guy Fawkes Night would not call at farms owned by Roman Catholics, as a matter of honour.

FAIRLY MOUNTED ON A HILL

Worcestershire recusants are women, as is over half the Bromsgrove group of 1642. Is this just a cruel predilection for picking on the easiest target, or might it actually be coded evidence of a rather more pragmatic attitude by those in authority locally? It all hinges on the State's ability to extract money. As women - particularly married women - cannot hold property they simply have no estate to fine. Perhaps the lack of names in 1640 is actually an attempt by someone to protect the local Catholics. The sudden emergence of thirty names only two years later might then be a calculated compromise to limit the damage by naming those who had least to lose. The churchwardens at St John's can be seen to be doing their job, the Quarter Sessions magistrates have a satisfying list and the local recusants are kept out of real trouble. Although the presentment does include three "Gents", the Talbots are conspicuous by their absence. As we shall see, both presentments take place while the vicar of the time is very much preoccupied with his own problems, and it is very possible that a little aristocratic pressure is being applied to the churchwardens and constable responsible for collecting names.

Dissenters and Sectaries

While the argument over the nature of State religion rages within the respectable classes something rather more radical is happening beneath their feet. The old Roman Catholic ritual provided a set language of belief as well as a common pattern of religious conduct for every man and woman. Invited now to think about their own beliefs it is very unlikely that everyone will think the same. The progressive introduction of printed English Bibles through the 16th century makes Scripture available in an unexpurgated form to the increasingly literate yeoman classes, rather than filtered through the prejudices of lay and ecclesiastical rulers. The Word of God turns out to be far less supportive of any form of temporal Authority than has been preached from the pulpit. It is promptly seized upon as a weapon with which to challenge not only the Episcopal structure of the

CHAPTER 5: A DIVIDED HOUSE

Established Church but the very monarchy itself.

The Geneva Bible of 1560, with its strongly Calvinist footnotes, is a major catalyst in this process. Almost every book of the Old Testament provides ready-made examples of the fate of unjust rulers and idolatrous peoples, and the Bible's English editors-in-exile are not shy of drawing the appropriate, if guarded, parallels. The Geneva Bible fuels a growing band of amateur preachers, often from the poorer end of town, with an encyclopaedic if selective knowledge of the Old Testament and a talent for ranting. These ultra-Puritans, collectively known as Separatists, preach a Christianity separated from any formal church or civil government, a millenarian universe in which a literalist interpretation of the Bible is the sole source of all authority and justice. Familists – members of the splendidly named Family of Love – believe that Scripture can only be understood by inner personal revelation. Anabaptists reject infant baptism, tithes and all the other trappings of State Church control, and firmly promote the concept of a divinely chosen Elect.[55]

Unsurprisingly, this is anathema to the bishops. They see the English Bible as a dangerous tool that should only be handled by university-trained clergy and kept well away from what Bishop Jewel in 1562 calls *"the ungodly, unlearned riff-raff"*. And women are even more dangerous than men. As early as 1543 Henry VIII passes an Act forbidding anyone below the rank of gentlewoman from reading or even discussing the Bible. Despite the universal puritan rejection of Catholicism, successive Anglican Bishops of Worcester regard the more radical puritans as an equal threat to civil order and apply the recusancy laws to them with the same vigour. Bishop Sandys (1559-71) lambastes dissenting puritans as

---

[55] While the later Baptist movement owed some of its antecedents to the English Anabaptists, the two groups are not the same. The original Anabaptists were a radical 16th century German sect that eschewed any lay or church authority on earth and adopted a sometimes-violent policy of civil disobedience. In England the term was more loosely applied and eventually became a pejorative catch-all for any religious dissenter, rather as we would use "extremist" today.

FAIRLY MOUNTED ON A HILL

"pretended favourers and false brethren who, under the colours of reformation, seek the ruin and subversion of learning and religion". Although relatively few dissenters of any colour appear on Worcestershire recusancy lists, the Calvinist John Whitgift, Bishop of Worcester from 1577 to 1584, has an intense hatred of them, a position in which he is considerably helped by his right to appoint the county's Justices of the Peace.

By the 1580s, separatists are beginning to form a serious threat to Anglican order and the first "Act against Seditious Sectaries" is passed in 1593 to suppress them. It does no good. The Word of God is now directly available to a class of people unused to having such power in their hands, and by the early 17th century, England is Bible-mad. To many ordinary labouring men and women the Bible carries longed-for messages of social reform, common ownership of land, political representation, natural justice, even sexual liberation and equality: indeed *"the private life and doings of every man"*, as the 1603 Introduction to the Geneva Bible proclaims. Every chapter is pored over, sung about, quoted in Parliament and pasted onto cottage walls. Every phrase is subjected to dissection and interpretation in countless books, pamphlets and treatises, each proving the unique insight of its often-untutored author into the mind of God.

Allied to this theological impetus there is also a human factor. The financial inflation of the early 17th century pushes prices steadily upwards, enriching the entrepreneurial merchant classes but impoverishing agricultural workers on wages officially fixed below subsistence level: 6d a day, the average labouring wage in the 1620s, buys one loaf of bread. Adding to their woes the increasing enclosure of land for sheep pasture is driving those already on the margins of settled society off their smallholdings and squatter cottages. Dissent is therefore strongest amongst the poor, those who have most to gain from a movement that proclaims the equality of all men before God, regardless of rank or station.

CHAPTER 5: A DIVIDED HOUSE

Through the first decades of the 17th Century these early dissenters meet as semi-secret congregations, sometimes seeded by Separatists returning from banishment in the Low Countries. But after the breakdown of State censorship in 1641 a whole host of extreme sects emerges into the open, combining an apocalyptic religious outlook with radical political aims. Seekers, Ranters, Quakers, Adamites (a deeply odd nudist sect), Muggletonians and Fifth Monarch Men all in one way or another look for the imminent Second Coming and the establishment of Christ's reign on earth, of which they each consider themselves an essential catalyst.

With such a stew of denominations, sects and sub-sects a certain disrespect for any form of organised religious observance begins to show itself in various outbreaks of civil disobedience and blasphemous behaviour around the country, including a curious incident that comes before the Worcester magistrates in 1623. Two Bromsgrove men, Walter Dennys, a butcher, and Edward Banyster, a labourer, induce Jane Bigg and Stephen Knight, one of the churchwardens, to go through a blasphemous mock-eucharist using a pin and a piece of wood in place of the bread and wine. Knight and Bigg promptly flee to the local magistrate and inform on their tormentors. Warrants are issued against Dennys and Banyster but no one can agree on what was actually said and the case is never proven.

What dark purpose lies behind this otherwise inexplicable behaviour? At first glance it almost sounds like witchcraft – pins and mock-masses do have an uncomfortable feeling about them after all. But evidence for witchcraft in Worcestershire is sparse and this is not sorcery. Nor is it simply youthful trouble-making. No, these men are probably Familists and their little prank is a taunting jibe at the straight-laced churchwarden and his despised, ritual-bound, clergy-infested church. The previous year Knight had reported Dennys to the bishop *"for selling flesh in times of Divine service"*, so this is some sort of revenge. However, only a true radical would dare keep his butcher's shop open on a Sunday morning.

Twenty-five years later such irreverent behaviour will characterize the Ranters, *"blasphemously counterfeiting the sacraments of the Lords Supper"*, in the words of a contemporary critic. Ranters' provocative behaviour - drinking, swearing, smoking, public blaspheming and sexual promiscuity – all demonstrate their Godly immunity from sin, in their own eyes at least. But Ranters are unknown in the 1620s and our two miscreants sound like part of the group from whom they will grow. The next two decades will not be easy ones.[56]

The Established Church

Stuck in the middle of this storm, the Church of England struggles to maintain equilibrium under the relatively tolerant James I. His attempt to establish a definitive version of Scripture acceptable to all Protestants produces the great King James Bible of 1611 - the Authorised Version – still in use today. This is based on the excellent Geneva version, but with those provocative footnotes carefully removed.

However, the consensus begins to break down under James's son. Charles I leans increasingly towards High Church, not to say popish, church practice, a stance popularly attributed to his Catholic French wife, Henrietta Maria. Charles reinforces his absolutist view of monarchy by appointing William Laud as Archbishop of Canterbury in 1633 with a specific remit to drive out Calvinism and Presbyterianism and to re-establish the Anglican Church as an agent both of the monarchy and the Church Universal. Lists of puritan vicars are compiled and the culprits deprived of their parishes; a more elaborate Eucharistic service is introduced behind railed altars and candles, confession and clergy celibacy are re-instated. This drives a wedge between Anglicans and Puritans, who are infuriated by what they see as the reintroduction of Roman Catholic practices when the

---

[56] Dennys and Banyster's actual words do sound very Ranterish, mimicking the Prayer Book to the letter. One can't help wondering how Knight and Bigg got themselves into the situation in the first place.

CHAPTER 5: A DIVIDED HOUSE

faith itself is still outlawed and punishable. From the liberal, secular outlook of the 21st century, these distinctions may now seem like so many minor differences of degree. But in the England of the 17th century, religion and politics were seen as one. The way in which God was worshipped was a direct reflection of the way in which the country was governed and dissenting clergy were therefore a direct challenge to Royal authority.

Where did Bromsgrove's church stand in this bitterly divisive climate? Things certainly got off to a bad start with the sudden death of Richard Harforde's successor, Peter Weaver, late in 1558 after barely eighteen months in the vicarage. Faced with a desperate need to raise funds from a diocese stripped of many of its assets at the Reformation the dean and chapter had stooped to leasing out the presentation of vicars - and the tithes that went with them - to local landowners.[57] So it was with Bromsgrove, where the dean had granted the presentation of the next vicar to Roger Folyott of Worcester and Robert Arden of Westbury (Gloucs) back in 1550.

Whatever the original relationship between these two men, it had seriously deteriorated by December 1558, when the time came to choose Weaver's successor. Inevitably, they chose one each. Folyott picked the university-educated Richard Hall, while Arden named John Persey, precentor of Hereford Cathedral. The dean and chapter favoured Hall but Persey apparently pulled rank and won the contest. He barely had time to settle in before the dean craftily pulled the rug from under him. First, he revoked Arden's portion of the lease and reassigned it the following February to William Warmestry, the diocesan registrar, and Ralph Wyatt, a Worcester clothier. He could then safely deprive Persey of the living and trust his now-compliant lessees to present Richard Hall again. Incumbents have

---

[57] The year after Weaver's death Bishop Sandys of Worcester apologised to Lord Burghley for his meagre New Year's gift, telling him, *"such ys the barrenness of this contie that it bringeth nothing forth fit to remember you by"*.

99

the freehold of the vicarage and it took a year to extricate Persey, but Hall was successfully presented on 7th March 1560 and took up residence soon after.

There is no certain evidence why Persey was so unacceptable, but Peter Weaver's death coincided with that of the Catholic Queen Mary after six troubled years of Counter-Reformation. It is therefore possible that this little tussle over Bromsgrove reflects the battle for souls in the nation at large; between a Catholic-inclined Arden and an Anglican Folyott, each with his own man for the job. Such unseemly wrangles were happening up and down the land as this new Church of England tried to find its feet.

Hall himself lasted barely a year before dying at the beginning of 1561. His successor from 1st February, Robert Avys MA, died in 1581 and was replaced by Thomas Hearle on 5th September that year.[58] In the absence of any parish registers for this period these early post-Reformation vicars leave little record other than their names. No doubt they were perfectly orthodox men, just doing their job under new management, although Gervase Carington, prebendary canon[59] of Worcester Cathedral and Hearle's successor from April 1590 to 1611, sounds an easy-going sort. Happy to baptise or bury almost anyone who asked for it, stranger, gypsy or pauper, he sometimes enlivened the first surviving register with parishioners' nicknames, such as *"Thomas Badger, commonly called Badger with the Reade heade"* and *"Humphrey Hall, alias Said-I-well"*. He also found time to take on at least two other incumbencies at the same time, as vicar of nearby Stoke Prior from 1597 to 1599 and as rector of the rather more distant Weston-upon-Trent (Staffs) from 1594. Collecting parishes was actually something of a habit with Mr Carington. Starting in 1568 as vicar of Powick, just south of Worcester, he then

---

[58] This succession is taken from the diocesan registery at WRO and does not agree with the list in Shepherd or the vicars' board in the church. Shepherd omits Persey, Hall and Avys but records a Robert Notingham, not mentioned in the register, between 1561 and 1581.

[59] A salaried Canon of the Cathedral and therefore a favoured candidate for preferment.

CHAPTER 5: A DIVIDED HOUSE

acquired the benefices of Longdon (Gloucs) in 1571, Hazleton (Gloucs) in 1574, Beckford (Gloucs) in 1576, Marston Sicca (Gloucs) in 1579, Cropthorne (Worcs), in 1581 and Brinklow (Warks) in 1583 – all before coming to Bromsgrove. Pluralism – the holding of several benefices at the same time – was a frowned on but common practice, especially when there were assistant curates on hand to mind the home parish. While we might condemn the greed that drove some to pluralism others resorted to it through sheer necessity. We have already seen how vicars' incomes – the so-called "living wage" – were steadily depleted through the loss of chantry benefactions and the sub-letting of glebe lands, and what remained had to support the families of now-married clergy. Worcestershire was particularly impoverished, with many churches badly neglected and priests reduced to penury. Carington's personal circumstances are not known but we might at least give him the benefit of the doubt.

Gervase Carington died in one of his other parishes on the 17th August 1611.[60] His multiple benefices so confused later historians that they entirely failed to spot his successor (if successor he was), the hitherto unnoticed John Aldworth. A Gloucestershire man, Aldworth gained his Master's degree in 1601 and took up his only recorded benefice at Bromsgrove in 1606.[61] But he left no trace of his name in the parish registers and his death early in 1613 at the young age of 37 is only known from the inventory of his possessions taken on 26th February. There is no known will, nor any record of his burial. Now, here is a little mystery - a clergyman who has simply vanished from the record. There is one clue. The next recorded vicar, John Archbold, was presented on 9th September 1611, barely a month after Carington's death, but was not formally instituted in the vicarage until 4th May 1613, two months after Aldworth's death. Did Archbold, like Richard Hall before

---

[60] At least, he left no local will or record of his burial. His wife, Elizabeth, was buried at St John's in July 1594.

[61] According to Alumni Oxonienses only. The bishops' register records his exit but mysteriously not his arrival.

101

him, have to wait until the previous resident was out of the way? The bishop's register notes that Archbold was first presented *"by lapse or otherwise"*, a strong hint that the absentee Carington had let the parish go to seed and that one of his assistant curates had taken up residence in the vicarage as a locum.[62]

The impression is reinforced by the fact that John Archbold, a royal chaplain and prebendary at Worcester, was presented by King James I himself.[63] This was a present the dean and chapter could not refuse, especially as Archbold's wife was the niece of Edward Conway, Secretary of State and friend of the dean of Worcester. John Archbold gives every impression of being a fixer sent in to get a failing parish back on its feet. The Stuart ideal of an Anglican clergyman, the Eton and Cambridge-educated Archbold already had his bachelor's degree in divinity when he became vicar and gained his doctorate two years later. As the beneficiary of royal favour he could be counted on to toe the moderate Anglican line and to resist any pressures from the presbyterian faction in his congregation. Bishop Thornborough went so far as to call him *"a special ornament in this church"*, no doubt with an ear to the puritan hatred of ornaments. Archbold too had a turn at Stoke Prior between 1620 and 1622, and his reliance on a succession of assistant curates to sign the registers at St John's suggests that he too was well used to spreading his workload. As the father of ten children he needed every penny he could get.

But trouble was again looming in the turbulent years after Charles I's accession,

---

[62] The lack of a burial record in the parish register is harder to explain, especially as Aldworth's inventory was made in Bromsgrove. He may have died unexpectedly while journeying away from the parish and his body could not be returned for burial. Sudden death would also explain the absence of a will. When Archbold was finally installed in 1613 the bishop's register records his predecessor's fate as "deceased or otherwise", hinting that even the diocese did not know what had become of the unfortunate man.

[63] James' extravagant conception of royal patronage meant that many early 17th century institutions merely formalised royal presentations.

CHAPTER 5: A DIVIDED HOUSE

when the fragile consensus within the Established church under James I began to crumble before his increasingly partisan son. Faced with a clash of loyalties many people in Bromsgrove looked to their vicar for leadership, and two remarkable individuals provided it. Resolute men of strong personal conviction they successively held St John's together for the next thirty-five turbulent years and guided it along the narrow path of moderation between royal absolutism and radical dissent. Modern sensibilities may find them perhaps rather severe - intolerant even. But they were both honest, thoughtful men, trying to keep their rapidly revolving world the right way up; and their experiences tell us not only something of St John's itself but illuminate the wider world in which they worked and prayed.

John Hall

While awaiting appointment as dean of Bristol – yet another potential income – John Archbold died unexpectedly in early December 1623, leaving his large family suddenly destitute. His wife tried to persuade her uncle to install a relative who would support her family, but the dean felt that this would court scandal and although sympathetic to her plight, could not agree to the suggestion.[64] He chose instead a bright young man who was about to make an indelible mark on Bromsgrove and its church.

John Hall, the 25 year-old son of a Worcester clothier, was installed as vicar of St John's on 6th June 1624, his first and only parish.[65] He quickly found a partner in Ann Fownes - from one of the big local families, the Fownes's of Dodford Priory -

---

[64] Even Bishop Thornborough felt unable to intervene. Archbold had been a royal presentation and the bishop was unwilling to pre-empt any similar recommendation for his successor, although none was ultimately forthcoming. He did at least have the decency to arrange charitable assistance for Mrs Archbold and her children.

[65] Calamy records that Hall first served at Kings Norton. If so, it was as assistant curate, not vicar. As we have seen with Aldworth, the distinction was sometimes lost on observers.

and married her in February 1626, barely twenty months after arriving. The young couple applied the same no-nonsense approach in starting a family, and children arrived with a certain degree of regularity: Elizabeth in January 1627, Hannah in July 1628; twins Sarah and Rebecca in October 1630; John - the only boy - in January 1633, and the baby of the family, Phebe, in October 1635.

Amidst all this fecundity Hall apparently carried out his pastoral duties well enough, with perhaps just a hint of youthful academic hubris in the Latin epithets he sometimes added to entries in the church register. His degree from Pembroke College Oxford should have been a guarantee of conformity and his first ten years do seem to have passed without undue incident. There is certainly little to indicate any personal inner conflict. In those confused times John Hall, like many other moderate puritan clergy, followed his conscience as far as it would allow without actually breaking away from the broad Anglican communion. But when it came to matters of authority Hall showed his true colours.

In a rural parish the local gentry could browbeat their agricultural tenants into submission, suppressing open dissent through fear of eviction. Bromsgrove, however, was an expanding town of traders, small-time business people and craftsmen, with their own modest properties and a regular income. Clothiers, tailors, butchers, chandlers, apothecaries and ironmongers, they owed little duty to a feudal superior. They saw bishops and the church courts over which they presided as agents of royal authority, unwarranted intruders in the local governance of a church in which lay people were playing an increasing role. This new "middle" class looked instead to the magistrate for civil order, and to the vicar himself for spiritual discipline. These two figures became the linchpins of authority in many such towns, an alliance described by Elizabeth I as "the Word and the Sword". Their roles complemented each other; regulating behaviour, directing consciences and punishing malefactors – and building in the process a

CHAPTER 5: A DIVIDED HOUSE

work ethic that would underpin the future economic growth of Britain. John Hall's clothier father was one of this new breed of industrious men, and the disciplined and self-governing structure of Presbyterianism was their natural home.[66]

John Hall came from this stock, and when a problem arose in the church he reached naturally for the magistrate. In 1628 Hall sought the indictment of his own curate at Kings Norton in the Worcester Quarter Sessions. Tobias Giles had charged young John Field a mere twelve pence for a licence to marry his sweetheart, Mary Badger, when the going rate was upwards of 3s 6d. After Giles applied the same kind-hearted but strictly illegal discount to a second young couple Hall hauled him before the magistrate and had him fined. Satisfied that the letter of the law had been applied he apparently forgave the lapse, for Giles remained at Kings Norton until 1639.[67] Hall also involved himself in purely civil cases when necessary. In 1633 he supported his churchwardens in a complaint to the same court that they had assiduously maintained the road between Bromsgrove and Kings Norton at their own expense, even though it should rightly have been a joint obligation with the Kings Norton folk.

However, as the country edged towards civil strife and sides began to be taken, John Hall's Presbyterian leanings began to get him into trouble. In 1635 Hall simply disappeared from the record. He no longer signed the register, leaving his assistant curate to cover all the services, baptise the newborn and bury the dead. Hall left absolutely no clue as to his whereabouts, leading earlier writers to

---

[66] Richard Baxter, of whom more anon, described them as *"the tradesmen, and freeholders, and middle sort of men; especially in those corporations and counties which depend on clothing and such manufactures"* - as Bromsgrove did.

[67] Hall's clergyman brother, Edmund, was similarly inclined. His 1653 book, *"A Scriptural Discourse on the Apostate and the Antichrist"* complains about the extortionate fines levied by church courts on couples that married without a licence. The cost of such licences effectively made marrying in church the preserve of the well-to-do. But church court or civil, poor couples still had to pay up.

FAIRLY MOUNTED ON A HILL

speculate that he was another pluralist. But as Bromsgrove is his only recorded parish it is rather more likely that Hall found himself on Archbishop Laud's list of puritan ministers and was suspended from office, forbidden from officiating at services or preaching. Suspension was worse than *"scolding"*, the lightest of Laud's penalties, but more lenient than *"depriving"*, which would have put Hall and his large family onto the street.

Just as the timing of Hall's disappearance coincides with Laud's purge, his reappearance follows Laud's fall in November 1640, when the Long Parliament impeached the archbishop for treason and, ten weeks later, sent him to the Tower. On 7th July the following year Hall resurfaced in the record, when he signed a certificate for William Reynolds, a conforming recusant Catholic who *"has according to the order of the Church of England received the Sacrament and does constantly come to his parish Church to hear Divine Service"*. Come what may the rule of law had to be kept and John Hall had no quarrel with civil justice.

While Hall was out of action his curates kept the presbyterian flag flying. Richard Flavell belonged to a large local family of Puritans and became Hall's assistant curate some time around 1628. An anonymous contemporary remembered him as *"a faithful and eminent minister and a person of such extraordinary piety that those who conversed with him said they never heard one vain word drop from his mouth"*. He married another Ann the same year as Hall and his equally vigorous approach to family life hints at a close friendship between the two young clergymen.[68] And while Richard provided a strong right hand, Hall already had his successor in mind. Thomas Flavell, Richard's younger brother, first appeared in St John's as a churchwarden, serving for two years in 1630 and 1631. Then after a gap of four years - just long enough to train for the clergy - he reappeared as curate in 1635,

---

[68] Richard passed his puritan convictions onto his eldest son. John Flavell was born in Bromsgrove in 1630 and later achieved fame as "Flavell the Divine", a Presbyterian minister in Devon and a writer of note. None of the Flavells had Oxford or Cambridge degrees but this was not unknown.

CHAPTER 5: A DIVIDED HOUSE

the year that Hall disappears. Did John Hall see trouble ahead? Did he spot potential in the Flavells and encourage their training as locums in case he was removed? It certainly looks that way.

But in 1640 the registers stop altogether. 1641 too is a blank and 1642 records only one birth, one marriage and nine funerals - unlikely in a town with over 1500 inhabitants. The world was turning again. Charles I's repeated failure to comply with parliament's Grand Remonstrance of grievances - and the furore that followed - led to his dissolving parliament and setting up the royal standard at Nottingham on 22nd August 1642. After an early skirmish at Powick Bridge, just south of Worcester, the battle of Edgehill in north Oxfordshire followed on 22nd October, barely a day's ride from Bromsgrove. A number of puritan clergy left their parishes around this time, some to flee what they saw as the approaching Armageddon and others to join the parliamentary forces as military chaplains.

What did John Hall do? The church register for 1642 is not quite blank. For, on a single sheet at the back of the book is a faded and plaintive note that reads:

"The Warres began in England in the yere 1642 which was the occasion this register was neglected for the minister was faine to fly and diverse ministers were placed in his roome until he could return, which was not until May 1647"

John Hall took flight, and he was not alone. Two vicars had already left their Worcester city parishes in January of that year, followed by the vicars of Witton and Severn Stoke. More importantly for St John's, the great Richard Baxter, one of the key commentators on the Civil War years and a persistent critic of Oliver Cromwell's more absolutist tendencies, left his position as lecturer at St Mary's, Kidderminster in October 1642 to seek refuge in the parliamentary garrison town of Coventry before serving as an army chaplain.[69] But if Hall took his cue from Baxter's precipitate action, he had a different destination in mind.

FAIRLY MOUNTED ON A HILL

There are two sides to every story of course, and not everyone was sympathetic to the finer feelings of a Puritan vicar. Late in 1642 someone complained to the authorities about Hall's absence from Bromsgrove and this time the complaint went to the top. On 26th February 1643 King Charles wrote to Bishop John Prideaux about a number of *"schismaticall and seditious preachers"* in the diocese, including John Hall. Hall, he said, *"hathe been a greate promoter and stirrer up of this unnatural rebellion against us (in which he is himself now active), he hath forsaken his Cure of Soules within the said parish"*. Suspension had obviously not taught Hall his lesson. Charles therefore invoked the ultimate sanction and ordered; *"Turn out J.Hall Vicar of Bromsgrove, a rebel, and admit Anthony Fawkner to supply his place"*. But by then it was too late. The country was at war with itself, Charles was in no position to enforce his command and whatever his merits may have been, there is no evidence that Fawkner ever actually arrived at St John's.[70]

But read the words of the accusation again. Hall is no mere passive victim of circumstances but one of the agitators for reform. To do this he had to be in London. As Hall tells us in his will:

"Before the warrs began, what through the evill of those times and by reason of oppression, it was great mercie to mee that I had liberty to dwell in peace and to Sustayne my Familly. When the Warrs began God caused me to Flye and hide mee and my Family in a strong Citty from the drawne Swords and afterwards restored mee to my habitation and the Congregation with whom I had lived from my youth"

---

[69] Lecturers were official preachers, ordained but non-parochial clergy paid by local parishioners or town corporations to deliver weekday and Sunday afternoon sermons in parishes where the incumbent had no preaching skill. Reflecting the religious leanings of their patrons, the merchant and yeoman classes, lecturers formed the backbone of moderate puritanism in the county and could have large popular followings. Some lecturers were also vicars or, like Baxter, effectively acted as such. The majority of Worcestershire clergy supported the Parliamentary cause in one way or another.

[70] Fawkner was a royalist army chaplain under Lord Capel. Charles I ordered a very similar substitution at Oldbury the same year.

CHAPTER 5: A DIVIDED HOUSE

Hall may also have had another rather more domestic reason choosing London as a bolthole. Royalist Worcester – his parents' home – was obviously unsafe and his wife's family at nearby Dodford, although themselves puritan, were equally exposed.[71] London by contrast was not only strongly parliamentarian; it had also been the home of his maternal grandfather, John Bonner, a London merchant who had sheltered puritan clergy during the last years of Elizabeth I's reign and left a legacy to provide them with financial aid. Bonner had been something of an inspiration to his children and it is entirely possible that the Halls simply headed for the relatives who could best shelter them. Hall did not remain idle. He found a position at St Botolph's, Billingsgate, an old City church crammed amongst the warehouses on Botolph's Wharf.[72] With its sequestered vicar gone to join the king at Oxford, Hall spent the next few years preaching to a willing audience and sent his son John to the Merchant Taylors School, as the family's clothing business entitled him to.[73] He also took an active part in the wider spiritual life of the capital by helping to set up the Fourth London Classis in 1646, one of several convocations of presbyterian ministers in the capital.

Without the protection of its vicar, St John's weathered the next five years as best it could, although the bare trickle of entries in the register hint at a church functioning at the most basic level. 1644 has just three entries, all baptisms; one baptism in 1645, one in 1646. And four of the five are children of a single family, the Westwoods of Chadwich.[74] These sparse records are written in several different hands, in Latin or English, on whatever scraps of paper were available to the anonymous "diverse ministers". There were no deaths; no marriages - or

---

[71] John Fownes of Dodford was one of the Parliamentary Committee for Worcestershire in 1646.

[72] Nathaniel Salvay of Severn Stoke also headed to the capital. He took over the rectorship of St Martin's Vintry on Thames Street, another dockside church, replacing its royal chaplain incumbent. Both churches were destroyed in the Great Fire of 1666.

[73] Master at the time was William Dugard, a Bromsgrove man and something of a royalist. His father, Henry Dugard, had been Master of Bromsgrove School from 1606-11.

at least, none recorded. Life must have gone on but there were now far more pressing needs than logging the minutiae.

For the town was vulnerable, whatever the convictions of its citizens. Although Worcestershire was ostensibly a royalist county, Bromsgrove and its neighbours were perilously close to the border with parliamentary Warwickshire and got the worst of both worlds. As the war developed, each side raised money for its armies from local taxation, using an ordinance of February 1643 signed by Parliament and – under duress – the King. The Parliamentary Committee for Worcestershire, based in Evesham, assessed the county at £550, while the royalist garrison at Worcester demanded its own hefty levy of £3000 to maintain the royalist forces. Bromsgrove, caught in the middle, had to pay both but showed the true spirit of John Hall by defaulting on the royalist payment.[75] This would not have gone down well at Worcester. If the reaction of Colonel Sir Henry Bard, governor of the royalist garrison at Chipping Campden, is anything to go by, such refusals did not go unpunished. Threatening the south of the county for a similar misdemeanour, he wrote as only a military man could:

"Know you that unless you bring unto me [at a particular time in Worcester] the monthly contribution for six months you are to expect an unsanctified troop of horse among you, from whom if you hide yourselves they shall fire your houses without mercy, hang up your bodies wherever they find them, and scare your ghosts".

Battle-hardened officers like Bard had no time for compromise and such official

---

[74] John Westwood became churchwarden in 1653, as one might expect of such a law-abiding Anglican. He paid for his loyalty to the Crown after the final royalist defeat in 1651, when he and the equally loyal William Sheldon were compounded (fined) for £112 6s and £96 respectively against the threat of losing their estates.

[75] Not everyone in Bromsgrove supported the parliamentary cause. In an undated petition to the House of Lords from 1642 or 1643 John Biddle of Bromsgrove complained about the seditious – that is, anti-monarchist - language used by Ralph Bowars, the flag-bearer of a company of soldiers billeted in the town.

CHAPTER 5: A DIVIDED HOUSE

extortions were frighteningly common as the war dragged on and Royalist supplies began to run low. As we will soon see, Bromsgrove's church may carry its own silent evidence of just such a threat.

John Hall began to sign the registers again on his return in 1647, after Charles I's surrender to the Scots. But the paucity of entries in the following two years shows the continuing disruption to local life that the Civil War and its brief but bloody revival created. Births and deaths remain fairly constant but Hall recorded only five marriages in 1650 and nine the following year. Compare this with 21 marriages in 1603, a typical pre-war year. Was this just the forgetfulness of a preoccupied clergyman or was marriage furthest from people's minds in this troubled time? The post-war disorder was exacerbated by the failure of the 1648 harvest, depressing wages, inflating food prices and driving many poor families to the brink of famine while gentry and clergy continued to enjoy the fruits of parish tithes. Radical elements in the parliamentary army mutinied over pay arrears and lack of representation the following April, and for a while it looked as if England would descend into a chaos worse than the war itself. Although Cromwell eventually succeeding in imposing order, now was not a good time to be a minister of the Church.

John Hall certainly had his hands full, but he did not stand alone. As well as Richard Baxter, now restored to Kidderminster,[76] Hall had the support of his two younger brothers, Thomas and Edmund, both of whom became clergymen and shared his Presbyterian outlook. John appointed Thomas successively as curate at Wythall from 1632, at Moseley from 1635 and – replacing Tobias Giles - at Kings Norton from 1640, thus keeping both ends of Bromsgrove parish in one family as well as of one mind. Having trained him up John then stood aside, allowing

---

[76] While Baxter does not refer directly to John Hall in his writings, the fact that one of Baxter's correspondents could ask him to leave a reply at *"Mr Hall's house minister of Bromsgrove"* for a messenger to pick up, suggests that Hall was a trusted colleague. (Nathaniel Stephens to Baxter, 25th April 1653).

FAIRLY MOUNTED ON A HILL

Thomas to become vicar of Kings Norton in his own right, a position he kept until forced to leave in 1662. Edmund had broken off his studies at Pembroke College, Oxford, to take a commission in the parliamentary army on the outbreak of the Civil War. A moderate Covenanter in both church and state, he left the army in 1647 when the radical factions within it began to turn against its Presbyterian officers, and returned to his studies. Edmund became a Fellow of Pembroke College in 1650 when he took on John's son, the younger John Hall, as a pupil, although his anti-Commonwealth pamphlets landed him a short spell in prison soon afterwards.[77]

Even after the King's trial and execution in 1649 John Hall remained an irritant to the largely royalist county gentry. Although the Church Settlement of 1646 legitimised Presbyterian clergy the disruption of the Civil War years had encouraged a certain degree of carpet-bagging. A parliamentary survey in 1649 found that the rectory manor, and therefore all the tithes, had been rented out to the Cockes (later Cookes) of Bentley since November 1599 for a miserly £26 a year, although worth £151 16s 8d.[78] Hall, like his predecessors, was subsisting on his own resources and while the vicarage was worth £60, it did not put food on the table. The Parliamentary Trustees of the fund set up to dispose of dean and chapter lands therefore granted him a further £30, a tacit acknowledgement of his worth.

The law-abiding John Hall had one final score to settle. During Hall's absence from the parish in 1644 one of the local gentry, Roger Lowe of Perry Hall, had

---

[77] Edmund eventually became Rector of Abington St Nicholas in 1676 and of Great Rissington in 1680. Outliving both his brothers, he died in 1687.

[78] A lease of 17th Nov 1640 between the dean and chapter and Henry Barnes, a gentleman of Oxford University, transfers this lease to Barnes for 21 years on Cockes's death, reserving only the right to appoint vicars. It was called in by the dean and chapter and reassigned to Charles Cockes of Cleeve (Gloucs) on 30th June 1641, after it had apparently passed to the Barnesleys of Barnesley Hall, Bromsgrove, by marriage in the intervening period.

CHAPTER 5: A DIVIDED HOUSE

given £400 to the royalist cause and ordered the church bells to be rung in support of the King. Bellringing was still officially sanctioned for major events and holidays but it was most definitely not for drumming up this sort of partisan support and Hall got to hear of it. As Lowe had died before Hall's return, his son was reported to the Parliamentary Commissioners instead and had to pay a hefty fine to regain his right to Perry Hall.[79]

His position secured by this final Parliamentary victory, John Hall remained vicar until his death two years later. His last years were blessed with some worldly success. Hall acquired some land at Callow Hill, near Feckenham, saw his eldest girl married off to a local Presbyterian clergyman, took on a keen young assistant and built up a modest wealth, a prosperity he readily attributed to Divine providence. He was able to leave his three unmarried daughters a generous £100 each, while passing his library and property to his son. Hall died on 19th August 1653.[80] He was buried below the chancel of St John's in a tomb now hidden and his widow continued to live in Bromsgrove until her own death in January 1658.

John Hall's 24-year incumbency is a testament to both his own stalwart character and his undoubted local popularity. But who was his successor? The records of this troubled decade are anything but clear and we will have to join a number of broken threads if we want to piece together the man – or men – who next moved into the vicarage below the hill.

---

[79] This is probably the same Roger Lowe who was fined for refusing a knighthood (and the financial obligations that went with it) from Charles I in 1630. The law-abiding John Westwood was another. A large number of minor gentry had been unfairly summoned to accept knighthoods after Charles's accession, on the spurious basis of their lands being worth £40 or more. Stiff fines were exacted on the defaulters, many of whom had not been given proper instructions on what was required of them and were in any case ineligible for knighthood. These *"useless and unreasonable"* penalties were finally revoked by parliament in August 1640.

[80] Nash incorrectly records the date on Hall's now-lost gravestone as 1652. Hall's will was made on 3rd June 1653.

FAIRLY MOUNTED ON A HILL

John Spilsbury

As patrons, the Dean and Chapter of Worcester had always presented new vicars to the parish. But England was now a republic and Presbyterians themselves had been pushed aside by the Independents, who were nearer Oliver Cromwell's own religious outlook. Deans and Chapters had been abolished in 1649 and a congregation of Independents now occupied Worcester Cathedral under Simon Moore, Hall's old curate at Moseley. Without any higher ecclesiastical authority to consult, many vicars were simply elected by the parish itself and they naturally tended to reflect the sectarian leanings of the most influential parishioners. The next claimant to the title in Bromsgrove is a 30-year-old Warwickshire man called Joseph Ainge; but John Hall has left a cuckoo in the nest.

John Spilsbury was born in Bewdley on 25th May 1628, one of seven children to William and Anne Spilsbury. He was first appointed in 1644 as an unlicensed curate at Chetton, a remote little settlement at the end of a long lane some twelve miles northwest of Bewdley. When the royalist vicar, George Benson, was ejected during the War in 1646, the task of caring for this rather humble parish fell to the eighteen year-old Spilsbury. Here in 1648, he signed the Testimony of Shropshire Ministers in support of the Solemn League and Covenant *"against the Errors, Heresies, and Blasphemies of these times, and the Toleration of them"*. Like many other clergy, Spilsbury initially saw Presbyterianism as the only alternative to Anglican orthodoxy while remaining within a national church. Even the narrow "toleration" advocated by Independents was anathema[81] and although Spilsbury was later to change his mind, this ultimately doomed attempt to change the course of state religion was sufficiently close to his own early convictions to merit

---

[81] The London Presbyterian clergy had protested to the Westminster Assembly on 18th December 1645 that *"we cannot dissemble how we detest and abhor this much endeavoured toleration"*. The Presbyterian minister and polemicist Thomas Edwards denounced toleration as *"the grand design of the devil...the most ready, compendious and sure way to destroy all religion"*. In this febrile atmosphere, compromise was unlikely.

CHAPTER 5: A DIVIDED HOUSE

his signature. The meagre salary from Chetton may also have helped to fund his university studies. Spilsbury entered Magdalen College, Oxford the same year but, with Bishops gone, he eventually had to travel to Derbyshire for ordination by the Wirksworth Classis.[82]

Despite his apparent presbyterian credentials, young John Spilsbury's more radical tendencies were already evident in his friendships with several members of the early Baptist congregation in Bewdley itself. This group had been founded in 1649 by John Tombes, curate at Bewdley's half-timbered Anglican chapel. Tombes was one of the leading dissenting figures of the Commonwealth period, and to understand John Spilsbury's subsequent trajectory we must first learn a little more about this complex and disputatious character. Born in 1603, John Tombes went to Oxford at the young age of 15 and rose through Anglican ordination to become "Catechetical Lecturer" at Magdalen Hall. Like many radicalised clergy in Charles I's time he acquired an early interest in Calvinist theology, and his sermons against infant baptism eventually cost him his house and job in 1627. Convinced that he could reform the Anglican church from within, Tombes accepted the position as vicar of Leominster, Herefordshire, in 1630. When war broke out he moved to the relative safety of All Saint's, Bristol in 1643, only to flee the city the same year after its capture by the royalists. Like John Hall, Tombes ended up in London, where he took two successive incumbencies but lost each in turn after preaching against infant baptism.

After Charles I's capture in 1646, Tombes accepted a request from the congregation at Bewdley to become its curate and returned north. As Bewdley was then a chapel-of-ease to Ribbesford all baptisms had to be carried out in the mother-church, and Tombes could neatly avoid a confrontation over his antipaedobaptist[83] views

---

[82] But not until 17th December 1656. Several other Worcestershire clergy had a connection with this Classis, including Thomas Hall and Humphrey Waldron, rector of Broom, who was ordained there the previous March.

while maintaining an otherwise orthodox Anglican ministry. Bewdley itself was something of an antipaedobaptist hotbed, fuelled no doubt by its regular river trade in clothing with the strongly Calvinist Low Countries. Its church, like many at this period, was split on the subject of baptism and a splinter group eventually left to form their own dissenting congregation in 1649. Sympathetic but unwilling to make the split himself, Tombes acted as their part-time pastor and thus maintained a vital bridge between the two sides of his now-fractured congregation. And this is where John Spilsbury found him - or perhaps Tombes actually found Spilsbury. Here we have a little mystery to solve, for there are other John Spilsburys around. They have very tempting links with our own man and they may just explain his own Baptist sympathies.

The Bewdley and Ribbesford parish registers confirm that a "John Spilsbery" was baptised on 25th December 1589, one of four known children to Robert Spilsbery. Our John Spilsbury's father, William, is not among them but there is only one family of Spilsbery/Spilsburys (the family spelled its name both ways) in Bewdley at this time and the appalling handwriting of Bewdley's vicar may conceal William's name. Down in London, another John Spilsbery, a firebrand preacher in contact with Low Countries Anabaptists, published several strongly worded tracts against infant baptism and established the city's first Particular Baptist congregation in Wapping sometime around 1633.[84] Are they the same person? The dates and continental connection are certainly suggestive. If so, it is plausible that the London John Spilsbery is our John Spilsbury's uncle and the reason for young John Spilsbury's Baptist sympathies then becomes clearer. If John Tombes's own antipaedobaptist preaching put him in contact with John Spilsbery during his time in London, perhaps Spilsbery was Tombes's pointer back to Bewdley, along

---

[83] Literally, "against infant baptism"; a contemporary phrase used by adherents and critics alike.

[84] Particular Baptists were a strict Calvinist branch of the Baptist movement who entirely rejected infant baptism, restricted salvation to a predestined elect and acknowledged almost no other denomination, including General Baptists. In Britain, the two branches reunited in 1891.

CHAPTER 5: A DIVIDED HOUSE

with a recommendation to look out for his young nephew.

Although our John Spilsbury never formally joined the Bewdley Baptists he certainly sympathised with their strength of conviction - and perhaps the trip into town also provided some relief from the deeply rural life at Chetton. He retained a strong link with Baptist colleagues throughout his life, and with one man in particular. John Eckells was still in his early teens when Spilsbury met him and encouraged the young man in his growing faith.[85] Eckells became known as the *"boy preacher"* in Bewdley's infant Baptist congregation and took over as its pastor when Tombes left to become Master of St Catherine's Hospital, Ledbury, in 1650. A year later, the sixteen year-old Eckells came to Bromsgrove to learn the trade of clothier and expanded his evangelical work to support a new group of dissenters in Bromsgrove's congregation. Spilsbury went with him - and thus he met John Hall. Hall must have been impressed with Spilsbury's earnest beliefs for he gave the young man pulpit space at St John's, where Spilsbury preached his first sermon on the 27th August 1652. He soon formed a firm friendship with Hall's son John[86] and an admiration for John's sister, Hannah that was eventually to grow into something deeper. John Spilsbury was therefore already established at St John's when Hall died in 1653. He may well have acted as locum during in the interregnum, and when Joseph Ainge was appointed in either 1653 or early 1654, Spilsbury soon left the moderate newcomer in no doubt where he stood.[87]

---

[85] Many years later, Eckells recalled that Spilsbury *"thought it not too much below him to converse familiarly with children themselves about their souls concernments. Of which I am an instance. Almost 50 years ago he stooped to me."*

[86] Having four sisters of his own, plus a fifth who died in infancy, Spilsbury may well have found common cause with the only son in his patron's family. Spilsbury's only brother, James (b.1639), also became a clergyman.

[87] Spilsbury's formal position is unclear but he may have been acting as lecturer rather than curate. He was certainly acting as locum at Bewdley. In January 1654 he stood in by popular request for Henry Oasland, Tombes's successor as curate, while Oasland was out of town one Sunday preaching a double lecture with Richard Baxter. This did not go down at all well with John Boraston, the strongly royalist rector, who questioned Spilsbury closely about what the congregation had prayed for. Bewdley people were obviously trouble.

FAIRLY MOUNTED ON A HILL

Like Bewdley, Bromsgrove was now a divided congregation, albeit one that still occupied a single building. Ainge had been promoted by a number of prominent parishioners with landed connections, including Edward Sheldon, one of the churchwardens and a member of a wealthy local royalist family. Their Anglican outlook was not shared by many ordinary folk in the congregation and barely months after Ainge's unauthorised installation the murmurings of discontent flared into open argument. During a bad-tempered exchange in church on the 20th August 1654 Sheldon openly accused Spilsbury of having *"a low [i.e. an unrefined] voyce"*. One of the dissenters in the congregation, Humphrey Potter, leapt to Spilsbury's defence and shouted back: *"If he had a low voyce, he had a true voyce"*. *"Soe have I"*, interjected Ainge in an attempt to calm the proceedings but Potter snapped back, perhaps unwisely, *"Noe, you have tould lies in the pulpit"*. Churchwarden Sheldon was having none of this and together with a colleague, Nicholas Hill, he had Potter immediately hauled before the Quarter Sessions at Worcester on a charge of misbehaviour in church. The loss of the Calendar Rolls for this period annoyingly deprives us of the court's decision, but it is interesting to see that the magistrate himself was not entirely convinced of Ainge's credentials. Rude parishioners he could deal with but the rights and wrongs of clergy appointments were above his head.

Spilsbury, however, knew what to do. Under Oliver Cromwell's personal direction a new Church Settlement had been imposed on the country in 1654, to rescue England's rapidly collapsing national Church from the confusion that had enveloped many parishes like Bromsgrove over the previous five years. The work of leading Independents it firmly rejected Presbyterianism and put all church governance solidly under the control of civil government. The key Ordinance of the new Settlement was enacted on 20th March that year, setting up a central appointing body of lay commissioners known as Triers, for the *"trial [i.e. interviewing] of public preachers and lecturers"*. By taking clergy appointments

CHAPTER 5: A DIVIDED HOUSE

out of local hands the Triers could weed out inadequate clergy and build up a consistent standard of pastoral care and preaching across the country, a task they accomplished with some success.

Emboldened by his supporters, Spilsbury left little Chetton in the hands of William Baggeley, its lay rector, and applied for the incumbency of Bromsgrove. Barely a month after the Quarter Sessions he was presented to the Committee for the Approbation and Presentation of Ministers for consideration as minister at St John's. His obvious talent impressed the committee, for they promptly sequestered and ejected the unfortunate Ainge. John Spilsbury was formally admitted as vicar on 28th September, to the delight of most of the congregation. Joseph Ainge appealed to the Committee for the Maintenance of Ministers but his appeal fell on deaf ears and we hear no more of him at St John's, although his failing was no more than trying to be an Anglican in an age driven to extremes.[88] The same committee approved a petition on 10th July that year to augment Spilsbury's income by £50, on the grounds that Bromsgrove was *"a great market town and the means small"*.[89] Someone had seen John Spilsbury's worth, and that someone was probably his old friend John Tombes. With nonconformists now running the country, Tombes was appointed a Trier in 1654 and he may well have been a friendly face across the interview table when Spilsbury needed it most.[90]

Christian Concord

His position secured, John Spilsbury could now build on his earlier foundations. Kings Norton was still in the safe hands of Thomas Hall. While Grafton was beyond his control, Moseley remained a dependent church and Spilsbury now

---

[88] Joseph Ainge continued to live in Bromsgrove, where his son Samuel was born on 7th June 1656.

[89] William Tylt, one of the two parish Constables had attended an enquiry into church livings in September 1650 at Droitwich with two other representatives, Daniel Higgs and Edward Hill.

[90] Tombes regained the incumbency of his old parish at Leominster the same year and stayed until his ejection in 1662.

appointed Joseph Cooper, a likeminded soul, as minister. Spilsbury could also count on the support of the moderate and tolerant Richard Baxter.

[Picture 10] Richard Baxter

Like Tombes, Baxter is a pivotal figure in John Spilsbury's life, but in an entirely different way. Tombes dealt with his divided loyalties by keeping a foot in both camps; Richard Baxter found his solution by building a united front. In the vacuum left by the abolition of Episcopal authority, Baxter set up his "Assembly of Associated Ministers of Worcestershire" in 1652. This self-regulating association published guidance on preaching, catechising and personal instruction, issued

CHAPTER 5: A DIVIDED HOUSE

joint statements on matters of national governance and provided a lively discussion forum for local clergy of various religious viewpoints, Anglican and Nonconformist. Meeting monthly in the five market towns of Worcester, Upton, Evesham, Kidderminster and Bromsgrove, the association reviewed recent cases of Christian indiscipline, carried out routine church business and formally debated an agreed topic of religious import after a communal dinner. Although its presbyterian respect for religious self-governance was at variance with the state control advocated by the Cromwellian Settlement, this gentle model of mutual support was much admired and widely imitated elsewhere over the next few years, including Shropshire, Cumberland, Westmorland, Wiltshire and Ireland.[91]

[Picture 11] Baxter's church: St Mary, Kidderminster in the early 19th Century, above the Staffs and Worcester Canal

---

[91] Although ordained an Anglican and doctrinally a Presbyterian, Baxter refused to label himself other than as a *"Meer Christian"*, a telling description later adopted by C.S.Lewis to describe his own faith.

121

FAIRLY MOUNTED ON A HILL

Baxter set out the Association's inclusive tenets in "Christian Concord", first written in 1653,[92] and reinforced his life-long message of unity in several explanatory memoranda to prevent, he said, *"the causeless dissent and separation of any sincere Christian from our churches, or any sincere Minister from our Associations"*. Chief of these was the agreement of 1656 *"for Catechizing or Personally Instructing All in their several Parishes that will consent thereto"*. Recognising that *"the people perish for lack of knowledge"* the agreement set out in the clearest and most sensitive manner the need for high quality instruction in the basics of Christian belief, and explained how that instruction could be made available to everyone of whatever level of knowledge without condescension or confusion, *"the plainest necessary truths in the plainest words"*, in Baxter's telling phrase. If people were unwilling or unable to come to church, instruction could be arranged at home in a group, or individually if that avoided social embarrassment. Young women would however not be taught in private *"lest malicious wicked rumours should make it an occasion of scandal and reproach."* Baxter knew that the old were in many cases more ignorant than the young but were less willing to acknowledge their weakness. In these cases, he said, *"we shall as carefully as we can avoid the exposing of the weaknesses of parents and masters in the hearing of their children, or servants, in any way that may tend to the diminishing of their authority or respect"*. This masterful little booklet was to be read out in churches on an agreed Sunday, after which it was distributed to every family that would accept a copy, for reading at home. With its inviting - rather than threatening - language and its liberal, gently inclusive tone, the Worcestershire Agreement held local churches together at a time when radical sectarianism was tearing other areas apart, and it saw St John's and many other churches safely through what Baxter called *"the Darkness of this land"*.

---

[92] Its full title was *"Christian Concord: or the Agreement of the Associated Pastors and Churches of Worcestershire, with Rich. Baxter's Explication and Defence of it and his Exhortation to Unity"*. It was updated in 1654 and again in 1656.

CHAPTER 5: A DIVIDED HOUSE

The Worcestershire Association ultimately had seventy-two clergy members and John Spilsbury's ministry truly reflected its precepts. Richard Baxter, who knew Spilsbury well, acknowledged him as a man of *"Extraordinary Worth, for Moderation, Peaceableness, Ability, and Ministerial Diligence, and an upright Life"*. Edmund Calamy, the near-contemporary Puritan historian, confirmed Spilsbury's gentle and accommodating nature, his *"happy way of explaining Difficulties and reconciling seeming differences in Scripture to the great satisfaction of those who heard or consulted him......He was thought to be a man of great wisdom and therefore much advis'd with in most cases."* In Calamy's eyes, Spilsbury was the Worcestershire Agreement personified. *"Whoever heard a rash word come out of his lips?"*, he recalled, *"His moderation of Persons of differing sentiments from him was great"*. Even the bald entries in the parish register occasionally betray Spilsbury's compassionate nature. He records the burial of *"my dear friend"* John Pearks from Stoke Prior in October 1660, and, with obvious sadness, *"a poore boy whose name I could not learne"*, one cold day in February 1658.

Although Spilsbury counted both as friends, Tombes and Baxter themselves had fallen out some years previously over Tombes's unyielding objection to infant baptism. Baxter had actually recommended Tombes for the curacy at Bewdley in 1646, believing him - baptism apart - *"orthodox in all things else (or I then thought he was)"*. But Tombes's increasingly strong antipaedobaptist preaching at Bewdley began to irritate the paedobaptist Baxter and after a heated exchange of correspondence through the autumn of 1649 he challenged Tombes to a debate in Bewdley church on the 1st January 1650. In front of a expectant congregation of around 1500 the two men preached against each other from 9am to 5pm without a break before retiring exhausted, each confident that he had won the case. They

---

[93] The university-educated Tombes initially wanted a written exchange of views, to which he could bring his scholarly pen. His dislike of the *"disorderly throngings"* of a live debate was not shared by the populist Baxter, whose *"ready wit and speech"* he reluctantly acknowledged. Thomas Hall was not so reticent about going into print against Tombes and easily matched him, both in biblical exegesis and well-aimed sarcasm.

continued to trade letters in the succeeding years but never really healed the rift.[93]

John Spilsbury therefore bridged the theological ground between Tombes and Baxter, and throughout the Commonwealth period he kept a carefully neutral position, unwilling to commit himself overtly to either camp or to alienate either friend. Although he still maintained a close friendship with some of the Bewdley Baptists, Spilsbury never formally joined their congregation. And while Baxter counted him a member of the Worcestershire Association and spoke warmly of him, Spilsbury never actually signed the Agreement.[94] It was a dangerous game to play, for either side might see him as a waverer and therefore not to be trusted. His Baptist sympathies were a particular worry to Henry Hickman, an old colleague from his student days in Oxford. Writing to Baxter about other matters on the 22nd May 1657, Hickman offered his *"kind respects to Mr Spilsbury, concerning whom I should be loath to learne that he doth not close with his brethren of the ministry but attempt that other strict way for which so little can be said from Scripture or church practise."* [95]

But perhaps there is more to this than indecision or double-dealing. It is always tempting to see the religious divisions of the period as mutually exclusive doctrines with immutable boundaries. Their leading proponents certainly worked hard to stress the differences, with each faction the self-proclaimed sole true inheritor of Christ's reign on earth and the others Babylon incarnate. But the divisions were anything but clear-cut to many ordinary people, who could easily find themselves pulled this way and that by the latest public debate, pamphlet or pulpit ranter. Faced with bewildered and contentious congregations, many puritan clergy did what Tombes and Spilsbury did: they maintained their parochial

---

[94] Spilsbury's name does not appear on either the 1653 or 1654 manuscript copies of the Worcestershire Agreement, nor the two printed editions of 1656. The only mention of his membership is on the list included in Baxter's autobiography of 1696.

[95] In 1652 the ultra-presbyterian Thomas Hall condemned Baptists as *"that troublesome, impure and disordered sect"*.

CHAPTER 5: A DIVIDED HOUSE

responsibilities while not entirely rejecting the dissenters in their congregations over essentially minor differences. It would count against them in the long run, but as the world turned, so did the clergy. John Hall, trained an Anglican, had followed his convictions and become a Presbyterian; and now John Spilsbury, trained a Presbyterian, followed his own more liberal convictions and went one step further. Presbyterianism was on the wane, its stern intolerance divisive and unpopular; Spilsbury could see that well enough from the bickering in his own congregation and the travails of his Baptist friends. He owed his own appointment to the new provisions of Cromwell's Church Settlement, and he would never have regarded himself as anything other than an Independent minister at St John's.[96]

While John Hall had had to withstand the orthodox tendency in his church, the threat to John Spilsbury and his colleagues more often came from the opposite direction. Some people now felt that, from being too radical, these moderate puritan clergy were not really radical enough. Quakers were a particular threat to any moderate clergyman. Developing out of the Seeker movement in northern England early Quakers were anything but pacifist and often resorted to direct and sometimes violent action to make their point. In Worcestershire even their non-violent activities had a certain edge to them, including running naked through the streets proclaiming the Word of God, and attempting to raise the dead.[97]

Baxter's Worcestershire Association was therefore anathema to them, a pandering to moderation when armed revolution was the only answer to the nation's spiritual ills. Richard Baxter thought Quakers were a "Fanatick Strain" and his anti-Quaker Worcestershire Petition of 1652 in favour of an ordained and salaried ministry was signed (he said) by over six thousand people. The ill-feeling was entirely mutual.

---

[96] Baxter refers to him as *"accounted an Independent"* while at St John's.

[97] At least this was the presbyterian accusation, and William Simson was indeed whipped in 1659 for *"passing naked through the streets at Evesham in a Prophetick manner as a Sign to the People"*. But going naked for a sign (as it was known) usually involved stripping to one's underwear, and *"raising the dead"* referred to reawakening the inner spirit of God in the individual rather than reanimating a corpse!

FAIRLY MOUNTED ON A HILL

The Quaker Benjamin Nicholson dismissed Baxter as *"one of England's blind guides"* in 1653 and a Quaker pamphlet three years later condemned by name the forty-two clergy who had signed the Agreement that year.

A favourite Quaker tactic was to infiltrate parish church services and wait quietly for the sermon, then jump up and harangue the preacher until the churchwardens threw them out. The local judiciary hated Quakers, and it hated Jane Heeks of Chadwich in particular. Jane had first incurred their wrath on 7th September 1656, when she interrupted Thomas Hall at Kings Norton in the middle of his sermon *"by questioninge his Doctrine"*, which earned her a spell in Worcester Gaol. Two years later, *"concerned to bear her Testimony to the Truth to the People assembled at their Place of publick Worship in Bromesgrove"*, she tried the same tactic on the rather more liberal John Spilsbury. He put up with her interruptions for a while although each outburst still landed her in the town stocks outside the Market Hall, once for an overnight spell. But even Spilsbury had his limits. Jane's fifth interruption was one too many and she was promptly hauled before the Worcester Quarter Sessions. Justice Milward obviously felt that the Truth did not need her testimony and he packed her off to Worcester Gaol again to cool her heels.[98]

A puritan minister had other enemies apart from Quakers, not least the local gossips. And there was no better sport than to accuse a pious clergyman of

---

[98] Jane was only following in the footsteps of Mary Tilsley, who had *"exhorted the people there, after the Priest had ended his sermon"* one day in 1656, for which she got sixteen hours in the Bromsgrove stocks. Jane was sentenced under the new Lords Day Act of 1656, brought in to stop this sort of behaviour. Before then, disturbances in church such as Humphrey Potter's outburst in 1654 had to be dealt with under legislation dating back to Mary Tudor's reign. Chadwich was actually something of a Quaker hotbed. Richard Farnsworth, one of George Fox's closest associates from Yorkshire, stayed at Chadwich Manor in February 1655 and held a public debate in the house with two members of the Worcestershire Association. Fox himself may have visited Chadwich the same year and a small but active Quaker community was soon established in the village, latterly with a meeting house of its own. These visits probably provoked the subsequent incidents at St John's. Thomas Milward, the magistrate, had been a captain in the parliamentary army and a member of the Worcestershire county committee.

CHAPTER 5: A DIVIDED HOUSE

naughtiness with one of the local girls. Richard Baxter had fallen foul of this calumny on one occasion and Mary Peake thought to try the same trick on Spilsbury in May 1655, whether on her own account or at the prompting of one of his opponents. In what sounds like a beer-sodden tirade, she claimed that one Mary Owen *"was a whore and that these and fortyscore more of you have been havinge that Rogue"*. *"What Rogue?"* retorted the no-doubt livid Owen. *"Spilsbury, that Rogue"* came the riposte, meaning of course our Godly but unmarried vicar. Any court in the land could see that this was a wild accusation and no doubt the Quarter Sessions gave the backbiting Peake short shrift.

Spilsbury At Large

When the Monarchy was eventually restored in 1660, the primacy of the Anglican Church was quickly re-established. Bishop Morley was installed in Worcester Cathedral that October and he would soon come looking for puritan blood, whatever its particular hue. John Spilsbury saw what was coming and rather than cause further division he left St John's voluntarily the same year, accompanied by at least some of his congregation.[99] After preaching from his own house for a time he founded the town's first Independent chapel in a barn behind the High Street belonging to Nicholas Blick, a sympathetic landowner and former churchwarden at St John's. Despite house arrest, banishment from the county for a while and several terms of imprisonment in Worcester Gaol for preaching without an official licence, Spilsbury continued to minister to his dissenting congregation, saying to a colleague on his release that *"I shall not henceforward fear a Prison as formerly; because I had so much of my Heavenly Father's Company as made it a Palace to me"*. Not everyone could say the same.

---

[99] His brother James took the Declaration of Uniformity in 1662 and remained as vicar of Bewdley. John Tombes was ejected as vicar of Leominster in 1662 but conformed as a lay communicant. His only argument (he said) was over infant baptism, a position he maintained for the rest of his life to anyone who would listen.

FAIRLY MOUNTED ON A HILL

There was at least one silver lining to this cloud. After one of the longer courtships on record, John Spilsbury finally found the time – or courage – to marry Hannah Hall on the 5th June 1661.[100] Like many late marriages theirs was a happy union of two like-minded souls. The 38-year old Hannah took a considerable risk in bearing the new couple's only child but mother and baby both survived and young John Spilsbury was duly baptised at St John's in July 1667. The Spilsburys lived latterly at "The Parsonage", 92 High Street, a house built for them at the same time as a new chapel for Spilsbury's Independent congregation.

But the years of struggle eventually took their toll. In July 1698 the 70-year old Spilsbury developed a cancer in his foot and was confined to bed, unable even to get up without assistance. Despite the constant procession of well-wishers he bore the corroding pain without complaint and cheerfully found the strength to counsel or pray for any that asked. But he had little time for anyone's sympathy. When John Eckells made the mistake of commiserating with him that *"I am sorry that you must thus go down groaning to the grave"*, Spilsbury told him tartly; *"good man, I do not groan – I am contented"*. But in darker moments he confessed his secret fears. Had all the struggle, the pain, anger and separation been worthwhile? *"I have been endeavouring to do some good and they say I have done a little"* he told Eckells shortly before he died, *"but I am nothing"*. Approaching death, Spilsbury imagined himself *"before the tribunal of God – whither I am going – and have supposed what I could plead for myself; and found there nothing but the mercy of God in Christ I can rest upon"*. He died on 10th June 1699 at the age of 71 and was laid to rest at St John's, in John and Ann Hall's vault below the chancel.

Invidious as comparisons are, John Spilsbury's will is a revealing counterpoint to his father-in-law's. John Hall died a relatively prosperous man and made elaborate

---

[100] But not at St John's, where the new Anglican incumbent was unlikely to be sympathetic. Instead, the couple journeyed across the county to Redmarley D'Abitot, whose vicar, William Kimberley, was husband to Hannah Hall's sister Elizabeth.

CHAPTER 5: A DIVIDED HOUSE

arrangements for disposing of his latter-day wealth through his children, while his "desolate" wife had to content herself with a short sermon on faith in hard times. John Spilsbury left nearly everything to his *"loveing and dearly beloved wife"*, money as well as household goods, along with the discretion to dispose of any income from his investments as she thought fit. The younger John inherited his father's library, but even this was subject to Hannah first choosing any books she would like to keep for herself. No sermon here; no last lecture to a grieving family. What John Spilsbury leaves is a heart full of love, as well as a rather modern sense of equality between the sexes. His son would inherit everything in good time but Hannah came first. She survived him by thirteen years, dying on 10th August 1712.

We know what Spilsbury's contemporaries thought of him but we also have his own words to judge him by. A *"plain and familiar"* preacher, according to Calamy, his sermons were *"filled with a variety of clear well digested Thoughts; very ingaging to his Auditory"* although his natural modesty prevented him from committing his sermons to print, despite the pleas of his many friends. While many radical writings of the period are harsh and uncompromising, there is no doubt about John Spilsbury's one surviving work - his own funeral sermon. This is the authentic voice of the man himself, written shortly before his death in the knowledge that he would never preach it. Instead, he entrusted the sad task to his oldest friend, John Eckells. Spilsbury's sermon is the voice of a gentle man, refined and chastened by his long journey of faith. *"Maintain humble thoughts of yourselves"* he says;

"Have a care of spiritual pride…let your dependence be on the grace of God in Christ for acceptance and salvation….Be content to wait on God's time and be content to stay until he calls. One moment's being in heaven will make you amends for all"

The cul-de-sacs of radical zeal, Calvinist exclusivity and millenarian imminence that afflicted so many Puritan preachers are all conspicuously absent, moderated by Spilsbury's gentle nature and a lifetime's ministry to the real people of Bromsgrove. *"Never was a Minister more concerned about a people"*, Eckells tells us. And the people of Bromsgrove obviously agreed, for *"the sorrowful countenances, bedewed cheeks and throngs of sighs"* that punctuated his funeral service were an eloquent expression of the regard the town had for its old minister.

There is a curious coda to this story. Despite a Puritan father and his lifelong friendship with John Spilsbury, the younger John Hall took the path back to conformity. Ordained a Presbyterian in 1655, Hall was re-ordained an Anglican in 1661 and accepted a position as Charles II's chaplain for a period. Secular and religious promotion soon followed and he became Bishop of Bristol in 1676. A refined and learned prelate who trod a careful line along the sectarian divide, Bishop Hall still kept his old links with Bromsgrove and bought Broom House about half a mile southeast of St John's. He also remembered his old friend and used to stay with the Spilsburys for several weeks on his annual visits to the town.

Hall's friendship extended to the whole family. Young John Spilsbury had followed his father's footsteps and became minister of the new Independent chapel in Kidderminster in 1693 in succession to Richard Baxter's friend Thomas Baldwin, although his uncle Hall had given him every encouragement to take up an Anglican parish. Having no children of his own Bishop Hall wanted his old home town to benefit from the wealth he had latterly enjoyed, and he entrusted young John with the task of making it happen. Bequeathing Broom House to young Spilsbury in his will, Hall instructed him to use £800 from its sale to buy land and use the annual income from it to help the poor. Spilsbury bought Urloxhey, a deforested estate in Elmbridge, three miles west of Bromsgrove, vested it with a group of trustees and set to work. Every September the trustees complied a list of needy townsfolk and put £20 aside to provide them with clothes, each suit costing no more than 13s for men or 7s for women. No-one received clothes two years

CHAPTER 5: A DIVIDED HOUSE

running and people already receiving other alms were excluded. The clothes were distributed between 1st November and 2nd February under Spilsbury's direction and any residual income was used to buy bibles for the townsfolk of the county.[101] Despite various vicissitudes Bishop Hall's Charity survived to the present day and his generosity still supplies the Bibles for St John's, amongst other aid. Bishop John Hall died on the 4th February 1710 and his alabaster monument, a rather elaborate tribute to a *"modest and holy"* man, hangs on the Chancel north wall in St John's. Its gilded wooden crosier and mitre proclaim his earthly status but the stark carved skull beneath sends out a more sombre message - even bishops are food for worms, it says. Episcopal purple notwithstanding, Bishop Hall had Presbyterian blood in his veins.[102]

We cannot leave this remarkable family without seeing how Thomas Hall fared at Kings Norton. A *"plain but fervent preacher"*, he had converted to the dissenting cause through the mission then active in Birmingham, at that time a hotbed of Presbyterianism. The Civil War was harder on Thomas than his brother, John. Although a friend of Baxter, Thomas's hard-line presbyterian convictions prevented him from joining the more moderate Worcestershire Association, which may have shielded him from the worst attacks.[103] Instead, his membership of the Kenilworth Classis from 1654 marked him out as a sitting target for royalists and Quakers alike. *"Many times plundered and five times imprisoned"*, as Calamy relates, Thomas outlived his elder brother but was ejected as vicar of Kings Norton in 1662 under the Act of Uniformity, for refusing to compromise his convictions. His last years were spent in great poverty in Kings Norton, supported and loved

---

[101] Hall wanted the Spilsbury family to maintain personal control over this process, to avoid it falling into neglectful hands. It remained with successive generations of Spilsburys until well into the 19th century.

[102] The mitre and crosier originally hung from a long-gone wooden canopy over the monument.

[103] Baxter, who regarded the term "presbyterian" as a broad synonym for puritanism generally, said that Thomas Hall was the only Presbyterian (in the strict Scottish sense) he knew.

FAIRLY MOUNTED ON A HILL

by his many friends. He died on 13th April 1665 at the relatively young age of 54, and was buried by his own wish in an unmarked grave at his old church. Now remembered as much for establishing Kings Norton grammar school as for his religious convictions, Thomas Hall's real love was writing, at which he excelled. He penned a number of theological works typical of the period including the snappily titled *"The Font Guarded with XX Arguments, containing a compendium of that great controversie of Infant Baptism"*, which he favoured. Infant baptism was one of the great religious divisions of the time but this work of 1652 now has another claim to fame, for it was the very first book actually published in Birmingham.

[Picture 12] Thomas Hall's church: St Nicholas, Kings Norton, in 1789

The 17th Century Church

While our puritan vicars were subject to the vagaries of political fortune, it would be wrong to think that church life entirely ground to a halt in these troubled years. Curates such as the Flavells continued to take the services in Hall's absence, and the churchwardens and other officers maintained the day-to-day running of

CHAPTER 5: A DIVIDED HOUSE

the parish, albeit on a basic level. The parish clerk had a particularly important role. An early description of his work at St John's, dated 6th December 1573, includes ringing the Angelus bell before the service, ringing the morning and evening curfew for 30 minutes between Michaelmas and Lady Day, reading the first lesson at Morning and Evening Prayer, keeping the bells in good order (even if they were no longer rung) and attending the clock that *"yt may goe right and true"*, perhaps the earliest known reference to the mechanical timekeeper that would eventually supplant the old curfew bell. The town crier, or bell-man, also had a number of church duties, including being in church every Sunday by the second peal of bells to carry out various assisting duties, keeping the church steps and paths clear, sweeping the church aisles and digging the graves at a penny a time. An employee of the churchwardens, he also accompanied the vicar and curate on Rogation Day, when the parish bounds were "beaten" to affirm their extent.[104]

A more contentious appointment was that of registrar. Sanctioned by the Barebones Parliament of 1653, registrars placed the responsibility for maintaining the parish registers in the hands of a lay officer, elected by the townsfolk. Most revolutionary of all, they took the solemnisation of marriage out of the hands of ordained clergy and created in effect the very first civil weddings. Banns could either be placed in church or the market hall if preferred, which a number of Bromsgrove couples did. The registrar then made out a certificate that the couple took to a magistrate, made a simple promise to live as man and wife *"in the presence of God"* and were declared to be so. William Suthwell, Master of Bromsgrove School, took on the role at St John's in 1653 and his scholarly handwriting fills the registers through the Commonwealth years to 1658, when John Spilsbury began to conduct weddings in church again.[105] Whatever Spilsbury may have felt, John

---

[104] So called because the boundaries were ritually beaten with willow wands by young boys. In some parishes, the beating was actually administered (lightly, one hopes) to the boys themselves, to make them remember the ancient boundaries in the days before reliable maps.

[105] After legislation passed in April 1657 permitted marriage by a church minister again.

FAIRLY MOUNTED ON A HILL

Hall evidently thought enough of the new registrar to let him witness his will.

While some of these roles and responsibilities survived the years, there are very few physical reminders of this troubled period in the fabric of St John's. Indeed, it was perhaps the single least productive period in the history of church building. However, one or two tangible clues have survived to support our human story. The present chantry chapel altar is an early 17th century oak refectory table with four turned baluster legs joined by stretchers. Most stone altars, with their five incised consecration crosses, had been removed by order in 1550 as part of the general stripping out of ornament that had taken place through the latter part of the 16th century. Their successors were usually wooden tables, whose domestic appearance was both a deliberate attempt to avoid popish imagery and a reminder of the original setting for the first ever communion – a meal. Being moveable these tables had a tendency to stray westwards, especially under puritan vicars. They sometimes ended up placed centrally in the chancel with their long axis east-to-west, allowing the congregation to gather round all four sides and thus emphasise the communal nature of the sacrament, which they received standing up or sitting down but never kneeling.

Archbishop Laud's attempt to establish Anglo-catholicism under Charles I included a decree that all such tables be returned to their medieval position hard under the west window and made sure they stayed there by ordering the back legs to be firmly fixed to the wall. Wooden rails were added to enclose the altar, not just for kneeling against but also to keep the dogs that frequently accompanied their masters to church off this supposedly sacred spot. But in 1643, the House of Commons overturned the now-imprisoned Laud's decree, the hated rails were ripped out by the cartload and altars became once again freestanding communion tables, on which churchwardens did their accounts, round which the vestry met and under which the local children played. Although there is no certain record of

CHAPTER 5: A DIVIDED HOUSE

St John's chantry chapel altar in the church before the 20th century, it is nicely contemporary with John Hall and may just be his - or Spilsbury's - communion table.

One other piece of evidence suggests that our communion table was placed well down the chancel. In the early 1640s, Thomas Habington found the chancel cluttered with monuments, some of which appear to have been moved out of the old chantry chapel. Elizabeth Talbot's tomb lay about halfway along the chancel north wall (about where the vestry door now sits) while her son's triple monument occupied the north-east corner and George Lyttleton's railed and arched memorial blocked part of both windows on the south side of the chancel. Talbot's daughters' plaques were fixed to the floor in front of their father's monument but these all played second fiddle to Humphrey Stafford's table tomb, which occupied pride of place in the middle of the floor, a location that would have pleased Alienora no end. Any altar at the east end would therefore have been all but invisible behind this mass of monuments. All were to move yet again in subsequent years but for the moment the chancel was entirely theirs, a family mausoleum.

Beside the old communion table now stands an old oak lectern of roughly contemporary date, again devoid of any ornamentation. Its single baluster leg is held at the foot by four arched braces and supports a plain bookstand in the form of a lockable box. This lectern used to carry a 1609 copy of "Jewel's Apology", written in 1562. John Jewel, Bishop of Salisbury, was one of the foremost Elizabethan churchmen and his "Apology [or justification] of the English Church" was a key early statement of orthodox Anglican doctrine in the teeth of Rome. In common with many church books it was secured to a hasp on the box by a stout iron chain to prevent pilfering. The fact that it remained in position until the mid 20th century shows its importance to a church beset by pressures on both sides.

135

FAIRLY MOUNTED ON A HILL

Jewel's "Apology" was one of a hundred near-contemporary volumes that once constituted the church library. Now in the safekeeping of the cathedral library at Worcester, these books typify the Anglican mindset that prevailed in a typical 17th century parish church. Church libraries were not only sourcebooks for the vicar's sermons and other theological doctrine but also practical resources for church and parish governance, policed by official censorship. So here are standard theological works such as "Against Celsus", a refutation of an early heresy by the 3rd Century Alexandrian scholar, Origen and printed in 1677; compulsory classics of Anglican writing such as Foxe's Book of English Martyrs in two volumes of 1631; factual works such as Andreas Osiander's "Church History" in four volumes of 1607 and 1608; Bible commentaries like St Clement's "Epistle to the Corinthians", an edition of 1669; and Cotton and Newman's "Concordance" of 1643; legal guides including Sir Thomas Ridley's "Civile and Ecclesiaticall Law" of 1634: and more individual religious treatises with charming titles like "The Soule's Conflict with its Selfe" of 1635, and "The Sanctuary of a Troubled Soul", no doubt a comfort to the hard-pressed John Hall. The oldest volume is a copy of Erasmus's Paraphrases, written in 1508 and another standard in church libraries. St John's copy was published in 1539, just three years after the great Dutch scholar's death. All these books are fairly orthodox, with little if any hint of the troubled years of their publication. State censorship, which had collapsed in 1640, was reintroduced in 1660 and anything too radical would have been quickly weeded out.

One other piece of furniture typifies the 17th century church - the parish Poor Box. A key role thrust upon Churchwardens at the Reformation was as Overseers of the Poor. The medieval church, and medieval society in general, accepted the poor as an inherent component of a fixed social order, helpless victims whose lowly state was sanctioned by an immutable God. Charitable giving to the poor both assisted the beneficiary and added to the donor's list of good works that would speed his path to heaven. In return, the prayers of the poor were considered

CHAPTER 5: A DIVIDED HOUSE

especially favoured by God and wills like that of James Lynalle in 1543 often contained payments *"for poore people to pray for me"*, in his case a generous 6s 8d.[106]

Calvinism changed all that. Its stern new worldview - that industrious labour was one of God's commands - recast the poor as malingerers in an increasingly materialistic world and ushered in the era of the protestant work ethic. The enforced closure of monastic houses between 1536 and 1540 left nowhere for anyone in distress to turn to and the roads of England now carried a throng of ex-soldiers, widows, orphans, unmarried mothers and the dispossessed of society. A Poor Law had been necessary as early as 1547 to deal with this flood, putting the onus of maintenance on each parish and setting up, in effect, a passport system to allow vagrants to travel between parishes. It was reinforced in 1575 and several times subsequently, each time increasing the punitive powers of its local administrators. State charity was both impersonal and uninfluenced by considerations of medieval piety. It was strictly utilitarian, grudging and conditional, designed to return the "sturdy" poor to work and to punish the remainder, *"the refuse and off-scouring of the world"*, in one particularly revealing description.[107] Churchwardens were made responsible for implementing the Poor Law at parish level. Under the authority of the magistrates rather than the vicar, they now became local agents of the civil state.

The painted 17th century Poor Alms box at St John's, next to one of the south arcade piers, was once a common church fitting but is now a rare tangible reminder of this early form of social control. By law all clergy were ordered to encourage their congregations after the sermon to contribute to the "Poor Mens

---

[106] Although Lynalle was seemingly unaware that private alms-giving had actually been made illegal in 1536.

[107] Originally from Lamentations 3:45, where it refers to Israel's suffering at the hands of her enemies. St Paul requoted it in 1 Corinthians 4:13 to describe the defamation of early Christians by detractors. Later users applied it, rather more cynically, just to the poor.

Box", and the sexton would stand at the door as the congregation left, calling out *"remember the poore"*, the legend now painted on the box itself. Post-Reformation wills also mark this shift in giving. Six years after James Lynalle, Richard Tybson gives 20d *"to the poore mens box"*.[108]

Giving to the poor was also a mark of personal status in the parish and larger donations were duly acknowledged in public. St John's retains an early benefactors' board dating from 1636, during John Hall's first absence. Its donors are an interesting cross-section of local society; from the aristocratic Staffords, whose "dole" paid an annual sum of 20s to the poor at Christmas and Easter, through gentry like William Sheldon, William Baylis and Nicholas Lylly, to tradesmen such as one *"Palmer, a butcher from Alcester"* and the upholsterer, Henry Brookes, both of whom gave 10s. The four churchwardens also add their names, keen to be seen to be doing their job.

And what sort of building housed these now-scattered relics? Despite the many subsequent changes in furnishings and decoration, the strict guidelines laid down for Anglican churches in the 17th century allow us to hazard an informed guess at the general appearance of Hall and Spilsbury's church. The shape, size and general internal appearance is much as Hall's predecessors left it. Although the rood loft went in the 1540s, a law of 1561 had ordered the retention of chancel screens and many remained for some years, especially where (as here) they marked the boundary between patronal and congregational responsibilities. The spate of successive ordinances in the early 1640s demanding the removal of statues, organs and fonts also suggest that earlier attempts at iconoclasm were less than thorough. However, it is difficult to imagine either John Hall or John Spilsbury condoning such a divisive piece of joinery and the lack of any mention of a screen in later documents suggests that it finally came down around the 1640s. It would be nice to know what became of the medieval font, though. Spilsbury was not

---
[108] His only other monetary gift was 12d to the vicar, for forgotten tithes.

CHAPTER 5: A DIVIDED HOUSE

avowedly against infant baptism although it is difficult to imagine the original font surviving the war years. But such potent objects were sometimes buried rather than smashed and its remains may yet lie somewhere below the churchyard grass.[109]

The whitewashed walls were undeniably stark compared with their medieval counterparts but they were not bare. The predominance of the written word extended to decoration and after 1560 the walls either side of the chancel arch would have carried the Ten Commandments in stern black letters, an equally uncompromising message to that of the old Doom painting but now aimed at a literate congregation. Other walls carried other messages - the Lord's Prayer and the Creed were both mandatory – making the whole church a sort of communal prayer book at a time when individual books could only be afforded by the well off. The nave furnishings were as plain as the remaining table and lectern. A panelled wooden pulpit replaced its stone medieval predecessor, the still-existing wooden lectern carried the all-important church Bible, and simple oak pews filled most of the remaining floor space. Paid for by individual parishioners, these afforded just a little more comfort and shelter than draughty open benches for John Spilsbury's lengthy sermons. It was an unadorned church but not unhandsome, its airy medieval carapace still dominating the homely fittings within.

Of all the 17th century joinery at St John's only one piece actually carries a date. "1656" is carved into the crossbeam of the lych gate at the top of the church steps, in bold, slightly naïve numerals, protected these last three centuries by the tiled roof. The top of a steep flight of steps is an odd place to find a canopy for sheltering coffins and it is probable that this gate has actually been moved from one of the other entrances to the churchyard when wider access was needed at some time. The empty mortises and shortened brackets do hint at a structure cut about to

---

[109] The *"small plain font"* at the west end of the centre aisle noted by Lacy in 1778 was probably its Restoration successor. Such fonts were sometimes little more than shallow basins on slim pedestals.

suit a new location, not least the removal in 1861 of the central post that carried pedestrian gates, unpractical on a flight of steps. Perhaps it was a companion to the "lydiate"[110] recorded at the top of Crown Close in 1600, moved to this spot when the churchyard wall was rebuilt in 1815?

Puritans are often perceived as iconoclasts and many churches did indeed suffer severely from image wreckers. The lack of notable damage to St John's is therefore interesting in itself. The Stafford, Talbot and Lyttleton monuments were barely touched although gentry tombs were defaced elsewhere, as much a protest against local landowners as for religious reasons. It is also uncertain how much of the stained glass at St John's was actually destroyed at this time. At least two lights in the 15th century east window glass survived until the late 18th century, including an image of St Wulstan and several bishops' heraldic shields. The carvings of the three saints on the tower also escaped damage, although well within range of a musket ball. In the south porch, the old holy water stoup had its bowl smashed to prevent filling but was otherwise unharmed, and perhaps yet more survived than is now evident. It seems that some local people thought enough of their already-old church building to keep it intact through all the vicissitudes of the Civil War, and we shall see that the depredations of fashion and philistinism did far more to harm the fabric of St John's than ever Oliver Cromwell could.

---

[110] Literally a sliding gate, and usually denoting an opening wide enough for carts.

CHAPTER 5: A DIVIDED HOUSE

[Picture 13] The lych gate c1900. The old houses in St John Street below were cleared in the 1960

FAIRLY MOUNTED ON A HILL

St John's may carry yet one more memento of this troubled period. On the outside north wall of the tower, a series of small, circular depressions marks the stonework just above eye level. Stand beneath them and you will see that they form a crude arc around and above you, just as a volley of musket balls fired at close quarters might. Although there is no firm proof, are these the silent record of a Civil War execution? If so, who was it? One prime suspect must be Sir William Waller, whose parliamentary force plundered Bromsgrove on the 13th June 1644, just twelve months after Royalist troops had similarly stripped the town. Waller was an uncompromising, punitive man, and his army's rampage through Worcestershire that month was described as "without control". Executions of deserters and uncooperative civilians by military firing squad are certainly recorded elsewhere and it is tempting to wonder what small tragedy may have played out in the shadow of the tower one dark day in the mid-1640s.[III]

Common Prayer?

The complexities of the Civil Wars and the Commonwealth that followed them are subjects in themselves and this story can only touch the edges. The Anglican Church that emerged after the restoration of Charles II in 1660 was rather different to its Cromwellian incarnation, purged of extremes and hardened by the divisiveness of the previous twenty years. Charles was pragmatic enough to acknowledge that English Christianity could not realistically be brought back under one roof and he initially promised *"liberty of conscience"* to all Christians. This was a little too liberal for parliament, which persuaded him into enacting a number of restrictive measures collectively known as the Clarendon Code. The first measure, the Corporation Act of 1661, required local government officers to set a good example by regularly taking Anglican Communion and swearing an

---

[III] The lack of any surviving burial records between 1642 and 1646 now makes this impossible to prove. The execution of three Leveller soldiers in the churchyard at Burford, Oxfordshire in 1649 comes to mind. Although not a garrison town Bromsgrove did have a gunpowder magazine for the local militia. If this was stored in the church, as it often was, any execution may well be related.

CHAPTER 5: A DIVIDED HOUSE

oath of allegiance. The Act of Uniformity, passed on 19th May the following year, demanded that all clergy make a public declaration before St Bartholomew's Day, the 24th August, acknowledging the authority of the bishops, promising not to take up arms against the King (a pointed reference to all those former parliamentary chaplains like Baxter) and, most importantly, giving their *"unfeigned assent and consent to all and everything contained and prescribed in and by the book entitled The Book of Common Prayer"*.

The reissuing of this small volume in 1662 encapsulated everything that the restored Church of England now stood for. Its compilers had no illusions about the task they faced. In 1646 the old Prayer Book had been replaced by the "Directory of Public Worship of God", a Presbyterian rubric that gave individual clergy considerable leeway in the content of services, removed infant baptism but retained the Anglican Eucharistic and marriage services. Even after 1660, Presbyterian clergy held out for the retention of these key features. The newly reinstated bishops thought otherwise and the two sides battled it out at the Savoy Conference in April 1661, twelve bishops against twelve puritan ministers led by Richard Baxter. Although it claimed to *"keep the middle way between the two extremes"* the 1662 Prayer Book made almost no concessions to puritan sensibilities. Instead, it positively rubbed their noses in the power of state-sponsored religion. Out went presbyterian references to pastors, ministers and congregations; in came priests, deacons and church. All dissent was summarily dismissed as the action of *"factious, perverse and peevish spirits"*, as opposed to the *"sober, peaceable and truly conscientious sons of the Church of England"* who toed the Anglican line, of course.[112] To be fair, the presbyterian demands would have placed far too much authority into the hands of individual ministers, reducing congregations to silent witnesses whose only contribution to services would have been the occasional amen. Despite some unfortunately triumphalist insertions much of Cranmer's

---

[112] In the words of Bishop Sanderson's uncompromising preface to the new Prayer Book.

old Prayer Book survived into its last great incarnation, and it formed the basis for Anglican worship for the next three centuries.

Ostracised by government and church, nonconformism nonetheless continued to grow and the more responsible dissenting groups coalesced into the Baptist, Congregational and Presbyterian (both now combined as United Reformed) churches we know today, each with their own formal structures. These dissenting congregations also offered a safe haven to the two thousand Anglican clergy who refused to subscribe to the Uniformity Act and therefore found themselves homeless in August 1662. Some of these removals were forcible. Joseph Cooper, Spilsbury's curate at Moseley, found out just how uncompromising the new regime could be *"when a troop of horse came and carried him out of the pulpit on the Lord's Day"*, consigning him to Worcester Gaol for six months. The same process worked in reverse as well. Amongst the many Anglican vicars who now emerged from enforced sabbatical to fill the new demand for orthodox clergy, Joseph Ainge at last found his spiritual home as vicar of Handsworth from 1661. He obviously liked it there, for he stayed 30 years.

More sanctions were imposed in the following years. The Conventicle Act of 1664 banned gatherings of more than five non-related nonconformists for religious worship, forcing Independent ministers like John Spilsbury to preach from their own houses. John Hall's old curate, Richard Flavell, was less fortunate. Arrested in 1665 while preaching at a house in Covent Garden, he was imprisoned in London's notorious Newgate Gaol, where he and his wife succumbed to the Great Plague that ravaged the city that year. The same year's Five Mile Act tried to ban even home preaching by forbidding any former Anglican minister from preaching as a dissenter within five miles of his former town, forcing Thomas Hall to move temporarily from Kings Norton and imprisoning Richard Baxter. Nonconformists remained second-class citizens throughout the reign of Charles II (whose

CHAPTER 5: A DIVIDED HOUSE

sympathies increasingly tended to Anglo-Catholicism) and they continued to be harassed and fined for their dissent. The Bromsgrove churchwardens reported twenty-one people to the magistrates for *"not coming to church to hear Divine Service"* in 1669, and several of John Spilsbury's Independent congregation were *"levey'd"* £4 on the 25th October 1671 for not attending St John's.

The worst penalties were removed in March 1672, when Spilsbury was finally licensed as a Congregational preacher and his home as a Congregational meeting house.[113] The unquestionably Protestant William III's Toleration Act of 1689 finally allowed freedom of worship to all registered dissenting protestant congregations[114], including the three hundred nonconformists counted in Bromsgrove for the Compton survey of 1676; out of a total population of 2325 adults, this was the largest number by far in the whole county. Nicholas Blick's old barn had only provided the barest of comforts for Spilsbury's first dissenting congregation and his own house was a rather cramped alternative. Now able to worship openly Spilsbury's people needed proper accommodation. On Blick's death in 1691 his widow Alice sold 22 yards of land to the younger John Spilsbury, who funded the building of a purpose-built chapel for his father at his own expense in 1693.[115] This in turn was replaced in 1832, again on the same site, by the present building, initially a Congregational chapel, then a United Reformed Church. Together, these buildings provided a continuous venue for nonconformist worship in Bromsgrove for over three hundred years until the final closure of the church in 2013. These resolute folk were an indication of the continuing popularity

---

[113] This also gave him the freedom to buy land with several others in Kidderminster in 1673, to set up that town's first Congregational chapel.

[114] But not alas Catholics, who were specifically excluded from the Act. Exemption from penalties only began in 1778 and full religious emancipation had to wait until 1829.

[115] Blick left *"my very worthy and good friend John Spilsbury the elder"* £5 in his will *"as a thankfull acknowledgement of the many favours and kindnesses I have had and received from him"*. The younger John Spilsbury was named as one of the four overseers of the will, with powers to settle any inheritance disputes.

of the nonconformist message amongst the working population.

John Spilsbury was also – albeit indirectly – responsible for the town's Baptist community. Several members of Spilsbury's congregation including John Eckells and Humphrey Potter – he of the 1654 court case – had left St John's with their vicar in search of religious freedom. After a few years preaching illicitly from Potter's home in Holy Lane (now Church Street) Eckells founded Bromsgrove's first Baptist chapel in 1666 in a yard behind the house. Like Spilsbury himself Eckells was imprisoned for his faith but released on bail of £1000, paid for by a sympathetic Worcestershire MP. Without the comfort of tithes and parish endowments nonconformist ministers had to survive on the generosity of their congregations, many of them from the poorer end of town. Clergy, even nonconformist clergy, were regarded as minor gentry and were taxed accordingly. In 1690 John Spilsbury's poll tax bill of 12s was the third highest in town, the same as the vicar of St John's. But Eckells' bill was even higher, a crippling £1 9s.[116] With seven children to feed and a naturally generous disposition Eckells spent his latter years in great poverty and died at Coventry in 1711, aged 76.[117]

Baptists remained a defiant challenge to the Anglican hegemony. Although 17th century English Baptists bore little resemblance to the old German Anabaptists the distinction was conveniently lost on most Anglicans. "Anabaptist" was a useful stick with which to beat them and Anabaptists they became. Bromsgrove's Baptists certainly succeeded in annoying the increasingly self-important

---

[116] The usual charge was 1s per head. Catholics and Quakers were charged double.

[117] After more than 30 years as Bromsgrove's Baptist pastor Eckells was dismissed in August 1696 over a curious incident that offended a faction in his congregation. It seems that a young woman he knew had misbehaved in some way (possibly an illicit pregnancy, from the reticence of the record) and Eckells discreetly sent her away to avoid a public scandal rather than bring her before the church elders. Disciplined by the elders for his high-handedness the unrepentant Eckells appealed successively to the Upton-upon-Severn and London Baptist congregations, both of which largely exonerated him. As the Bromsgrove congregation was still unwilling to forgive him he left his old church by agreement in July 1700 and established a separate Baptist congregation with a number of supporters.

CHAPTER 5: A DIVIDED HOUSE

churchmen at St John's over the next hundred years. On January 9th 1670 the Revd Thomas Willmott complained bitterly to the Quarter Sessions about some bad behaviour during a funeral he had been conducting outside the south porch of St John's for Jane Eckols, the wife of a John Eckols.[118] While the vicar struggled through the noble prose of the Book of Common Prayer, he was by *"a tumult of Anabaptists affronted and disturbed"* who *"no sooner came to the grave but irreverently threw the Corps thereinto"*. Without removing their hats in respect the crowd peremptorily kicked the earth back into the grave with their feet. Pushing the hapless Willmott aside, one Henry Waldron finished the job off with a spade stolen from the sexton's house. Baptists didn't have much time for ritual when it came to funerals, or any other services for that matter.

A century later, things had still not improved. John Lacy noted in 1778 that Bromsgrove accommodated *"a meeting house for the Anabaptists, who are very numerous and whose present minister is but too successful in gaining converts from the lower and illiterate class of people to his Diabolical and wicked principles"*. It was no good blaming the Devil. The real problem was that these supposed miscreants were rather successfully evangelising the growing working class population of the town away from the Established church, and were therefore posing a threat to posteriors on seats – and coins in the Poor Box - at St John's.

At the other end of the doctrinal spectrum the radical sects gradually faded away as the years passed, although their underlying message of social reform re-emerged shorn of its apocalyptic imagery in the radical politics of the early nineteenth century. Only the Quakers outlived this period in any numbers, organised into a coherent body under their charismatic leader George Fox. Ostracised by the newly re-empowered Anglican Church, they turned

---

[118] Almost certainly the same man as John Spilsbury's friend. Eckells was 52 when he married Elizabeth Butler in September 1687 and Jane, although unrecorded in the parish registers, may have been his first wife.

FAIRLY MOUNTED ON A HILL

progressively from radical action towards the quiet discipline and industry for which they were later known and ceased to bother the Establishment. Quiet or not, Quakers kept to their principles and refused to acknowledge any aspect of Established religion. The noisy Jane Heeks was among forty-seven local Quakers committed to Worcester gaol on 8th January 1660 for refusing to take an oath of obedience before the magistrate. Quakers were equally independent over rights of burial. This could lead to awkward situations like that of 6th September 1661 when Anthony Cole, another Chadwich Quaker, was buried twice in one day, once by the Quakers in their own meeting house yard off what later became Hanover Street and then - after a quick and no doubt bad tempered exhumation - at St John's.[119]

It took more than royal writ to overcome the many years of lingering resentment that had built up between families in this divided town. Not everybody liked the Halls or the Spilsburys, and when an opportunity came along there was always someone prepared to keep the fires of personal animosity fanned. Another Quaker, Elizabeth Bache, saw her chance in March 1679, when she wrote and distributed a *"scandalous song"* involving Elizabeth Hall's husband, William Kimberley, and a mysterious baby.[120] Kimberley accosted Bache and demanded to know all the words. The duplicitous minx told him that she had a copy in her house but needed him to read it to her, as she was illiterate. As Kimberley tried to make out the words in the gloom of her parlour Bache launched into the song, adding four lines of her own at the end for good measure. When news of the song

---

[119] Jane Heeks's appearances before the Magistrates stop in January that year but she was presented by the churchwardens in 1676 for not coming to church. She was buried in the Quaker meeting house yard on 9th May 1700. The "widow Heeks" who was buried at Bromsgrove's small Quaker Meeting House on 25th March 1660 may therefore be her mother, whose death just before the restoration of the monarchy and established church at least spared her the unseemly treatment meted out to Anthony Cole eighteen months later.

[120] Kimberley was vicar at Redmarley until his ejection in 1662, after which he took up teaching at an unnamed school, "in which some thought he excelled most" (Calamy). His son became Dean of Bristol, another beneficiary of Bishop Hall, his uncle.

CHAPTER 5: A DIVIDED HOUSE

got to the authorities Bache denied anything to do with it and told Kimberley that she would say she had learnt it from a copy lying in the street. Elizabeth Bache was a known troublemaker from a family of troublemakers, but it is tempting to wonder just what that song was about.[121]

Whatever their religious outlook in these difficult years the people of Bromsgrove expressed their beliefs through declaration, through protest, through a prison sentence if necessary. But sometimes just a name was enough to declare their point of view. From all the anonymous Annes, Marys and Elizabeths on offer, John Cookes chose the simply charming Sweet-my-footsteps to be his bride on 17th July 1677. Only a child of the puritan revolution could ever bear such a name, and her proud parents must have thought that the mid 1650s truly were just a step away from the Second Coming.

And what of the Bible, the ultimate source of this revolution? The proliferation of sects in the 1640s and 50s had shown that however potent a spiritual guide it was the Bible was no basis for a universally agreeable model of civil government. This troublesome book was therefore brought back under episcopal control, with a set lectionary of readings to ensure that its meaning could not be taken out of context by unsanctioned and untutored preachers. It retained its place at the centre of Christian belief of course, but faded from the political stage. Instead of rabble rousing, the Bible's message was now used to enforce the status quo of a rigidly stratified English society, rich and poor.

A Parade of Vicars

Where did the Revd Dr John Woolley MA, Trinity College, Oxford, stand in this

---

[121] A predecessor, Margaret Bache of Chaddesley Corbett, had been excommunicated at the diocesan visitation in Bromsgrove on 29th April 1603 for *"misbehaving her tongue towards her mother-in-law"*. By then, excommunication was a largely symbolic act, usually added to other physical punishments as a sop to the church courts. She was subsequently presented to the county sessions court in 1614 as a *"common skould and a sower of strife and disorder amongste her neyghboures"*.

149

newly re-established Church? John Spilsbury's 43 year old successor was *"inducted and legitimately admitted to the possession of the Parish Church and Vicarage"* on 1st September 1660. Already Prebendary Canon of Stafford, his ostentatious Latin announcement in the register shows that the spiritual pendulum had now swung decisively from dissenting Puritanism back into diocesan-controlled Conformity and that this man was no Spilsbury. Officially sanctioned or not, Woolley had little chance to prove himself as he died unexpectedly eighteen months later in March 1662.

The dean and chapter took no chances with his successor and appointed one of their own. Dr Thomas Warmstry was installed as vicar on 20th September 1662 and came with something of a pedigree. A moderate Puritan before the war, he had initially attempted to reconcile the opposing factions in the church before throwing his hand in with the royalist cause and joining the king at Oxford in 1642. Ejected from his parliamentarian Warwickshire parish of Whitchurch in 1643 Warmstry gained a position as a chaplain with the royalist army and thus found himself in Worcester during the siege of 1646. During a truce on 17th June he met Richard Baxter, then a chaplain on the parliamentary side, and had an odd but good natured discussion on the battlefield about the holiness or otherwise of church buildings, from which the two apparently parted amicably. After the city fell to the Parliamentarians Warmstry became a fugitive and helped fleeing royalists in London before acquiring a remote parish in Shropshire during the Commonwealth. Here he met Baxter again in 1653 to discuss the Worcestershire Agreement, and he agreed to promote it in Shropshire - or so he told Baxter. Baxter was therefore incensed when Warmstry changed his position after secretly consulting his less compromising London colleagues. He still supported the concept of the Agreement (he now said) but not Baxter's interpretation of it. Baxter saw this disingenuous little statement as a betrayal of trust and he never forgave Warmstry for it.

CHAPTER 5: A DIVIDED HOUSE

Thomas Warmstry acquired something of a reputation through the 1650s as a evangelical zealot, *"converting Infidels, Industrious in Redeeming the Loose and Establishing the Wavering"*, as a royalist apologist recalled. Infidels seem to have been of special concern to Warmstry as he devoted one of his books to them in 1658, excitingly titled *"The Baptized Turk, or a Narrative of the happy Conversion of Signior Rigep Dandulo"*.[122] After all this enthusiastic zeal, the odd puritan minister was not going to be much contest and at the Restoration he was quickly installed, first as Canon of Gloucester, then Dean of Worcester, with a writ to sort out the nonconformists.[123] Before coming to Bromsgrove, Warmstry had already been sent to bring St Mary's, Kidderminster back under diocesan authority with a hectoring three-hour sermon of *"vehement, tedious invectives"* after Richard Baxter's ejection that year, *"to cure them of the Admiration of my Person"*, as Baxter remarked bitterly. His remit at St John's was no doubt the same, although his various diocesan responsibilities kept him out of the parish for long periods. The churchwardens even plucked up sufficient courage to complain in their 1663 presentment to the bishop *"that our Vicar has been absent from us twentie weeks"*. But Warmstry was first and last the bishop's man, and no doubt his curate William Broughton just had to soldier on in Bromsgrove without him.

Thomas Warmstry stayed barely three years at St John's before dying in 1665 at the relatively young age of fifty-five. However, this was quite enough time to knock any lingering puritan inclinations out of the local congregation and we hear no more talk of nonconformity at St John's from now onwards. Warmstry's replacement in

---

[122] Turks were a contemporary fascination, provoked by the first English translation of the Koran in 1649. Warmstry's sympathies might be gleaned from another of his titles: *"A Hand kirchife for Loyall Mourners, or a Cordiall for Drooping Spirits, Groaning for the Bloody Murther and Heavy Loss of our Gracious King"*, published the same year. In April 1661, Warmstry showed his versatility by converting Issac Grosner, a Jew from Smyrna and christening him Paul.

[123] He was also appointed Master of Kings School, Worcester.

[124] The number of vicars who died in office at this period hints at the shortage of younger conformist clergy in the years after the Restoration.

151

FAIRLY MOUNTED ON A HILL

October 1666, the Edinburgh educated George Glen, came from Derbyshire but barely lasted eighteen months.[124] The vicarage then remained empty for the next year and a half while the dean and chapter pondered who to inflict next. They pondered rather too long, and the right of appointment reverted to King Charles. Perhaps John Spilsbury - still around and still very popular – was a distraction.

Thomas Willmott

Whatever the reason the next incumbent was rather more resilient – and youthful - than his predecessors. Thomas Willmott, a 22 year old local man from a respectable Hartlebury family, was installed on 22nd November 1669 and decided to stay…and stay…and stay. In fact, he stayed thirty years until January 1699, when his son and namesake took over for a further forty-two, a remarkable family performance. To ensure a smooth succession the elder Willmott actually tried his son out at Kings Norton beforehand, first as curate, then vicar for a couple of years. We have already met the newly installed Willmott struggling against a pack of recalcitrant Baptists, and he may have had his own reasons for doing so. Just two years previously, as the rather inexperienced vicar of Wolverley, he had stood surety for the good behaviour of a number of parishioners who had been rounded up by the local militia after going to hear a Fifth Monarchy Man preach at Oldbury chapel. Such a liberal outlook was not going to go down well with the very royalist Bishop Skinner and Willmott's subsequent behaviour at Bromsgrove hints strongly that someone had a quiet word with him about which side he was on.[125]

The passing of the draconian Second Conventicle Act in 1670 must also have quickly dissipated any lingering liberalism. For whatever his previous inclinations

---

[125] The preacher Steele, alias Fraser, bolted when a small company of militia under William Perrott approached. Perrott locked the large congregation into the chapel and awaited the arrival of reinforcements but they forced their way out, easily overpowered the four soldiers and ran off into the countryside. Perrott could only grab a few stragglers, Wilmott's straying parishioners among them. The case came up before the final Quarter Session Assizes of the year at Worcester.

CHAPTER 5: A DIVIDED HOUSE

Willmott now became a true ecclesiastical product of the Restoration, firmly orthodox in his beliefs, subservient to civil authority, intolerant of every other denomination. So when Robert Hill, a Bellbroughton miller and Quaker, used the opportunity of a friend's burial one day in November 1677 to speak *"a few words to the People by way of Exhortation to Repentance and Amendment of life"* at the graveside, Willmott saw a *"seditious Conventicle"* in the making. Satisfied that the group were acting *"in other manner than according to the Liturgy or practice of the Church of England"* he lost no time in passing their names to Justice Leonard Simpson. The Conventicle Act imposed a five-shilling fine on first offenders, and a swingeing £20 fine on the preacher. Hill simply did not have that kind of money and most of his household goods and chattels were seized in lieu.[126]

Just two years later the full weight of Thomas Willmott's heavy hand fell on John Boweter, one of several Chadwich Quakers reported as "Sectaries" in the churchwardens' presentment of 1674. Boweter had made the hazardous crossing to America in 1677 and visited fifty-five Quaker communities across New England before returning to old England the following year. Willmott was waiting for him, and armed with a writ for the non-payment of his Small Tithe of 6s he had Boweter thrown into Worcester Gaol in 1679. It was the first of several such incarcerations. Willmott came after him again in 1681 with another writ for the same default, for which Boweter was committed to Worcester for five months and then to the appalling Fleet prison in London. In his absence Willmott had a heifer worth £1 10s seized in compensation. Not one to take such punishment lying down Boweter wrote an *"Epistle"* to his colleagues from jail, setting out his side of the story and thoroughly castigating Willmott as *"this Merciless Man"*, the epitome of false prophets. Further letters to his friends in Chadwich and elsewhere confirm that the unfortunate Boweter was still (or again) in jail in 1683, 1684 and 1687. A

---

[126] The five named persons - John Crowe, William Astmore, Thomas Haden, John Chandler and the slanderous Elizabeth Bache - were the minimum number to qualify as a conventicle under the Act. The baker Matthew Cartwright, also present, joined Willmott and his manservant as an informant.

debt was a debt to Thomas Willmott, and the Small Tithe paid his salary.

Catholics fared no better. Sarah Christopher, a local girl, fell for John Staples of nearby Beoley and the young couple decided to get married. Being Catholics they had a choice – conform against their conscience and marry in St John's, or marry illegally in their own faith. They chose the latter, found a priest in the Catholic mission at Edgbaston who was willing to perform the ceremony and settled down quietly in Bromsgrove as a married couple. Early in 1687 someone discovered their secret and told the vicar. Thomas Willmott promptly demanded to see a marriage certificate. They refused – because they had none - and he reported them to the bishop, requesting that the unfortunate pair *"may be proceeded against according to Law"*. Turning a blind eye was not in Mr Willmott's nature.

Rather than face constant discrimination some Catholics chose to suppress their own faith and tried to live a normal life – church papists, they were disparagingly called. The carpenter John Wallis appeared a model of respectable conformity, so much so that he was elected churchwarden at St John's in the early 1670s. As if proof were needed of his orthodoxy Wallis and a colleague, John Asmore, actually reported the two remaining wardens *"for not receiving the sacrament"* in an undated presentment from this time. But something was simmering inside. It cannot have been easy working with a new vicar whose rigid adherence to the law brooked no other point of view than his own. Perhaps Willmott demanded one demonstration of conformity too much. Whatever the reason, in 1674 Wallis was himself reported as one of the *"chief of the Papists"*, now ostracised by the very church he had once helped to govern.[127]

But Thomas Willmott did not believe in letting anyone off the hook lightly, and he eventually forced Wallis back under legal duress. Willmott signed a Sacramental

---

[127] The form of Wallis's report is odd; a paragraph added to the bottom of the main presentment in his own rather untidy hand, as if someone – Willmott perhaps? - had forced him to write it.

CHAPTER 5: A DIVIDED HOUSE

Certificate of attendance on the 24th April 1679, declaring that Wallis had now been regularly attending St John's for several weeks and *"during the whole time of Divine Service and Sermon reverently behaved himself there and that upon Easter Day last past...he reverently consumed the holy Sacrament of the blessed body and blood of our Saviour Jesus Christ according to the customs of the Church of England."* Wallis bore the hurt for a while, but four years later he let the town know how he really felt about the people who had humiliated him. *"Ye Protestants were noe better than Dogges"* he blurted out one day, *"for they were of noe religion"*. This cost him a punitive 40s fine and a summons to appear before Justice Jolliffe and affirm his good behaviour towards King and country. He never recanted again. As late as 1706 the now-blind Wallis and his family were still being reported as *"Papists or reported Papists"* by Wilmot junior.[128]

John Wallis would not have appreciated it but he was in good company. Alongside the fourteen prominent Catholics in the 1674 presentment, Thomas Willmott's now-craven churchwardens named thirteen important Presbyterians and Independents, including our old friends Thomas Flavell and Nicholas Blick, nine chief "Annabaptists" including John Eckells, twelve Quakers[129] and, most surprisingly, two "reputed Jewes", one – Anne - the wife of the Baptist ironmonger Walter Bradley. After centuries of persecution and banishment the door had been opened for Jews to return to England by Oliver Cromwell in 1655.[130] Many

---

[128] The younger Wilmot spelled his surname differently to that of his father, probably to distinguish himself in correspondence.

[129] John Blick, presumably a Quaker relative of Nicholas, was reported for not paying his contribution to the parish clerk's wages for twenty years and discouraging others to do so. Martin Blick followed suit in 1696. By ancient custom the clerk's wages were paid by contributions from householders, 4d per house and 2d per cottage in 1573. A miscellaneous collection of gentry, Quakers and Baptists including Walter Bradley and John Crowe collectively owed £4 13s in 1685. At least they had ethical reasons for doing so: the second-highest defaulter – owing 12s - was the vicar himself.

[130] After Cromwell's Whitehall Conference debated the issue rather inconclusively in December that year. Cromwell was equally interested in religious liberty and merchant banking. Readmission started properly in the 1660s.

radicals acknowledged them as a people called by God; they saw Biblical Israel as a metaphor for a millenarian England and promoted toleration. But Cromwell was dead now and Willmott could safely indulge in a little anti-Semitism.

Catholic, Quaker or Anglican, everyone was supposedly equal in death. But even death was not exempt from politics or taxes. The Burial in Woollen Act of 1666 was intended to bolster the flagging English wool trade by requiring all bodies to be wrapped in wool, rather than *"any shirt, shift, sheet or shroud"*, as the act rather alliteratively stipulated. The parties then had to swear an affidavit in front of the local magistrate that wool had been the only material used, on pain of a £5 fine. Many people thought that £5 was worth paying to avoid this cumbersome and unnecessary law, and it was widely flouted. Not by Thomas Willmott, though. When the Act was strengthened in 1678, he proudly recorded the funeral of Ann Pinock, widow, *"the first buried in woollen"*. By contrast one can imagine the note of disapproval in his memorandum of 1696 that *"John Hunniott was interred on the 8th June in linnen in the Quaker graveyard."* To Willmott at least Quakers were always going to be trouble, living or dead.[131]

The Winds of Change

In all his dealings Thomas Willmott only did what the law required of him, albeit rather strictly. But the world was turning again and the role of the Anglican Church as the nation's moral policeman was changing with it. Through the 1660s and '70s the churchwardens faithfully reported all the *"multitudes of Sectaries of different persuasions"* in their annual presentments, as if these people were lapsed Anglicans rather than the conscientious Nonconformists that many actually were. By 1684 though, the redundancy of this process was becoming apparent. The churchwardens that year noted: *"the greatest part of dissenters are already*

---

[131] Hunniot was one of the Quakers reported in the 1674 presentment and owed 2s for the clerk's wages in 1685. His wife Mary was buried in the same way on 26th January 1704.

CHAPTER 5: A DIVIDED HOUSE

excommunicated and have continued for many years", and even more despairingly in 1693, *"wee have diverse persons under Excommunication who have been presented formerly & wee know not what care is taken in it"*. After the passing of the 1689 Toleration Act the churchwardens adopted a new stock phrase. *"Wee confess we have a good many dissenters from the Church of England"*, they admitted in 1690, *"who (we suppose) are tolerated by Law"*. "Tolerated by law" became the common element in presentments over the next twenty-five years, until even this became meaningless and the churchwardens turned to the rather easier target of sexual misdemeanour.

But Thomas Willmott clung to his vision till the last. Six years before the Toleration Act he noted optimistically that *"notwithstanding the toleration our congregation dayly increaseth & Wee hope in a little Tyme the Sectaries (w'ch in our large parish are numerous) will joyne themselves to the Church of England (as many dayly do)"*. John Spilsbury would have told a different story, had anyone asked him. But the Bishop only saw Willmott's version and no doubt comforted himself with the thought of a strong vicar in a tricky town. Thomas Willmott saw himself in the same role; *"exactly conformable"*, as successive churchwardens dutifully noted. In 1693 they expanded this into what can only be read as a good conduct reference for more than twenty years of service. *"Our vicar"*, they report, *"is an orthodox Divine & perfectly of the Church of England; hee is constantly resident on his Vicaridg: hee constantly reads prayers & preacheth twice every Lords Day; Hee constantly catechises the youth of the parish in the Church Catechism in service time on every Lords Day & is every way regular"*. Conformity and regularity were the Anglican touchstones now, and it would be hard to find a better description of a late 17th century vicar.[132]

---

[132] The presentment is in Willmott's hand, like many of this period, and one wonders how much say the churchwardens had in it.

157

FAIRLY MOUNTED ON A HILL

The Vicarage

Away from his draughty workplace Thomas Willmott lived in modest but noticeable comfort, for the old vicarage had expanded steadily through the 17th century to accommodate both the status of the vicars and the size of their families. The early 16th century replacement for the original vicarage was a wide hall-house with 2-storeyed gabled cross wings, typical of many late medieval gentry homes. It sat on level ground at the foot of the church hill and faced south onto St John's Street behind a courtyard. One of the church paths, Parson's Hill, ran across the back of the house from a narrow entry off the High Street and separated the vicarage from its garden in Crown Close. With its various outbuildings it must have been a house of some pretension.

But at the beginning of the century the vicarage – then lived in by the elusive John Aldworth - sounds more like the farmhouse it undoubtedly was, with a brewing furnace, cheese press, salting vats, a corn and hay barn, and storerooms piled with malt, bacon and hops, and a decent dung-heap in the yard. With his equine transport in its stable, a cow and calf grazing in Crown Close and pigs rooting amongst the stubble in the glebe fields, Aldworth was perhaps the last generation of farming vicar, a pattern of life that harks back to the very beginnings of St John's Church.

By the time Willmott and his new bride Johusha moved in during 1669, the house had expanded to include great and little parlours in one cross wing, the hall itself (apparently still open to the rafters), a kitchen and buttery in the other wing and a lower buttery in a lean-to. There was one main bedroom over the parlour and a further four bed chambers, including a maid's room. While this hardly sounds adequate for John Hall's six children or George Glen's nine it was still common practice for families to sleep several to a room – or even a bed - with younger children tucked into truckle beds that slid under the main bed when not in use.

CHAPTER 5: A DIVIDED HOUSE

With little or no bedroom heating, body warmth was a necessity, even for a vicar. Fireplaces were generally restricted to the living rooms on the ground floor, at least to start with. John Woolley's vicarage had four fireplaces in 1662 and George Glen's had five in 1668, but the following year Thomas Willmott unaccountably paid his Hearth Tax for eight. As he only owned four domestic fire grates the canny tax-assessors must have counted every single hearth of the new and inexperienced incumbent, including the brewing vat and wash-tub stoke hole.

The rooms themselves may have been on the cold side but the house now reflected the clergy's steadily rising status in this prosperous market town, with pictures on the walls, silver in the dresser and decent hangings on the feather bed testers. Although the building itself was only in *"tolerable repair"* in 1687 Willmott apparently celebrated the Glorious Revolution of the following year with major home improvements, and the wardens' presentment of 1693 excitedly reported that the vicar's *"mansion house"* – no less - was now *"in excillent good repair"*.[133] By the end of the 17th century the old vicarage was a gentleman's home, echoing to Johusha's attempts on the harpsichord and her husband's pot shots at passing woodpigeons with his favourite fowling piece.

A Kind of Peace

Thomas Willmott died in early August 1699 – just six weeks after John Spilsbury - bringing this turbulent century at last to a close. Over the next hundred and fifty years the great parish church of St John the Baptist would settle, like the Church of England itself, into a deep Hanoverian torpor - self-satisfied, intolerant and quietly crumbling. The war years and the Commonwealth that followed had been deeply traumatic. Families had been torn apart, forced to take oaths to a conflicting succession of temporal and ecclesiastical rulers, hide a secret shame,

---

[133] At least until all but the main house was *"consumed by a Dreadfull fire"* in 1714, according to the churchwardens' presentment of 9th July that year.

turn traitor for a lost cause. Most ordinary people now just wanted to forget - to put these years behind them and to observe the conventions of worship without challenge or contention. The poet William Fairbrother summed up this mood eloquently in a verse written for Charles II on his accession, and perhaps he spoke for the battered people of Bromsgrove as well:

And thus we all may wear the Mourning weed
Few are the men who not your pardon need
It's wisest then for me to point out none
Lest others numb'ring, number me as one

I have rather taken the side of our puritan vicars, impressed with their strength of conviction. But there were just as many sincere and pious royalists, or Catholics, or Quakers, all of who could tell you a similar story of oppression or loss - and it is quite possible to read this story from their side if you have a mind to. Even our diocesan fixer Thomas Warmstry was no villain; rather, a pragmatic clergyman who stuck to the faith he had been ordained into and lived to enjoy its eventual triumph. And who could condemn a man that at the peak of the Civil War wrote a book defending Christmas carols. *"If they be...of holy and sober composure"* he pleaded, they *"may be profitable if they are sung with grace in the heart"*. John Hall, by contrast, would have been right behind Parliament when it banned the celebration of Christmas and Easter on the 8th June 1645. He and Warmstry stood at opposite corners of the same Church and it is to our 18th century church, with its two thousand parishioners, that we must now turn.

CHAPTER 6: THE SLEEPING CHURCH

1700 to 1850

Churchwardens

It is time we met properly some characters who have so far lurked in the background but whose increasingly influential position underpins the next stage of our story. The office now known as churchwarden was first recognised by the Council of London in 1129, and from the beginning the role reflected the dual authority of the medieval church, ecclesiastical and lay. While the priest had the cure of souls, churchwardens attended to the practical running of the church and its parish. They administered church funds, maintained the building fabric, bought church requisites, ensured the safety of the church silver, collected rents and tithes on church property, farmed the glebe land and sold its produce, and they prosecuted non-attenders, blasphemers and other breakers of church laws. Dealing in the hard currency of cash, tithes and civil justice, churchwardens were influential men in the locality and were usually appointed from the town's leading citizens. Their office not only survived the Reformation intact but acquired onerous new civil duties when they acquired the responsibility for poor relief in 1547, together with a ragbag of other tasks including the maintenance of local highways, the punishment of vagabonds and the destruction of vermin. Churchwardens were the detailed recorders of the parish's affairs and we shall look at St John's in the 18th and early 19th centuries through their beady eyes.

Churchwardens were elected annually at the Easter Vestry meeting on Easter Monday. As they authorised most parish expenditure their names were recorded both on paper and in the fabric of the building itself, either as authorities or witnesses. Although five names are given alongside John Hall's legal presentment in 1633, St John's traditionally had four wardens. The incumbent proposed two - the vicar's wardens - while the parishioners put up the two people's wardens to maintain the balance of power in this still-large parish. Their occupations show the influence of those who appointed them. In 1784, for example, Richard Wilkes and John Boulton Burton are both noted as "Gent" – landowners who did not have to work for a living – while John Higgs and his successor in 1785, William Freeman, are both working farmers. The contrast is even more pronounced in 1777, when John Dowdeswell and William Greaves are again "Gents", while William Thomas and William Shenstone are blacksmith and miller respectively. One wonders how well they got on.

Perhaps the dinners helped. However hard the work, churchwardens made sure that they were adequately compensated with food and drink. The churchwardens spread their patronage as widely as possible and the local hostelries seem to have done particularly well out of St John's: *"Cross Inn Bromsgrove, Beer and eating – 5s"* in 1790; *"Dolphin Bromsgrove, as per bill – £3 9s"* the same year; *"King's Head Inn, Churchwardens Dinners, ale and lunch - £2 15s"*; and the positively Bacchanalian *"12 dinners, ale and tobacco, servants, at the Black Cross"*, both in 1799. All rather smack of a comfortable and expansive view of the job. Somebody else obviously thought so too, as a rather terse entry in the 1706 account book orders *"no ale until the business is done"*.

Right and Wrong

As the various Nonconformist congregations progressively became part of mainstream society through the 18th century Anglican disapproval, unenforceable by any law, began to sound merely peevish. Thomas Wilmot junior tried to keep the flame of intolerance alive in 1706 with a neatly scripted list of papists, twenty

CHAPTER 6: THE SLEEPING CHURCH

men and twenty-seven women including servants and guests. But the wardens last bothered to report religious dissent of any sort in their 1714 presentment and turned their attention from Sabbath observance to affairs of the heart.

It was relatively easy to identify a Catholic or Quaker, and indeed many would readily profess their faith. Illicit sexual unions were rather more difficult to prove and the churchwardens had to rely on the old and unreliable process of *"common fame"* - that is, hearsay. Elizabeth Smith, Ann Shayland, Ann and Mary Crowe – but not their menfolk - were presented under common fame for adultery in 1676, but the wardens of 1714 managed to pair up the miscreants rather more successfully. Edward Heath and Sarah Mallet, Joseph Worman and Elizabeth Wall were obviously lovers, although *"Thomas Hill and his daughter"* were presumably guilty of separate demeanours, albeit *"to the great Scandal and Offence to Many in our Town and Parish"*. But hearsay is hardly a reliable source of evidence for human relationships and one wonders just how many petty jealousies found their way into the record as unquestioned fact.

Slightly easier to prove was the visible misdemeanour of bearing an illegitimate child. The wardens presented Rachel Shurnford *"upon fame for having a bastard child"* in 1693, and Ann Howle for having a second illegitimate child the same year.[134] No less than three widows, the Mrs Baxter, Athersitch and Carpenter, all presented children in 1705, although the wardens were fairly sure that Benjamin Goode was the latter's paramour. Women sometimes tried to protect their lovers. Elizabeth Baggott refused to name her baby's father in 1709 although the prime suspect, Robert Moore, promptly *"ran away"*, leaving Elizabeth to fend off the pointing fingers by herself. Sometimes running was the only option for either party. The following year the wardens had to confess that *"a strange woman supposed to come from Cofton was delivered of a child in our town but made her*

---

[134] Mary, born 13th October. Ann's first child, Hanna, was born on 21st November 1690. She married John Cartwright in 1716.

escape before we could have her examined". One can only guess at her feelings.

This interest in sexual behaviour was only partly driven by moral considerations. Of far more interest to the churchwardens was the financial aspect. Illegitimate children were an added expense to feed, clothe and house under the Poor Law, on top of the heavy cost of maintaining the adult poor of the parish.[135] Tracing the fathers was the best option but failing that, the wardens tried to find someone else to shoulder the cost. Their interest in interrogating the girl from Cofton was primarily to see whether they could confirm where she lived and thereby pass on the responsibility for maintenance to her home parish.[136] As the 18th century wore on the religious justification for presenting illegitimate children gave way to the requirements of civil law. Rebecca Badger, reported in 1728 for *"having a Bastard Child born on her body, the father thereof we know not"*, was the last to appear in a church presentment at St John's. From the early 18th century onwards the unplanned offspring of Bromsgrove were entered into the sad pages of the parish bastardy records, still kept by the churchwardens but now in their municipal capacity as Overseers of the Poor.

A Bouquet of Roses

While the Churchwardens dealt with management of parish affairs the sexton cared for the church on a day-to-day basis. The title is an old one, a corruption of sacristan, although modern sacristans deal mainly with the communion vessels and altar furnishings. Sextons' duties could vary according to ability or the degree of responsibility they were prepared to accept, and a good sexton was a vital Jack-of-all-trades who knew his church inside out. In Bromsgrove at least, the 18th century sextons' duties absorbed those carried out in the 17th century by the bell-

---

[135] In 1696 the churchwardens reckoned this cost to be £323 8s 0d "as neare as wee can guess".

[136] This could be taken rather literally. In May 1753 it was agreed that a poor child found lying inconveniently across the parish boundary between Bromsgrove and Stoke Prior should be maintained at the expense of both parishes.

CHAPTER 6: THE SLEEPING CHURCH

man and parish clerk, and if there is one name that runs like a thread through the story of St John's at this time it is that of "Sexton Rose".

The Roses were a remarkable family and rather made the job of sexton their own. William Rose started it all, succeeding John Hill on the 2nd August 1772 on an annual salary of £2 5s, paid at Michaelmas. He earned a further £1 a year for patrolling the church during services and maintaining order, a necessary job when congregations regularly exceeded a thousand and not everyone had come willingly. Thomas took over on his father's death in 1789, while Thomas' brother, Joseph, became churchwarden in 1794. Thomas died in 1824 and was succeeded by one of his sons, also Joseph, while his other son, William, became parish clerk in 1819. On William's death in 1850, Joseph also took on his late brother's role, serving as both sexton and parish clerk until his own death in 1868. Joseph's son, John, then took over as sexton until his untimely death in 1879, of which more anon. Undaunted, the parish promptly voted in John's nephew, Joseph William, who served a further 61 years until his retirement in 1940 at the age of eighty. This brought the total record of family service to an astounding 168 years, over five generations.[137]

Thomas was undoubtedly the entrepreneur of the family. As this was a job that had elastic sides he cannily ensured that the terms and conditions were clearly stated before taking up the post. In addition to *"looking after the body of the church"* (that is, keeping the place tidy), he had to make ensure that the communion wine was always *"ready and sufficient"*; ring the curfew bell at 5am and 8pm; keep the bell ropes were in good order; dig the graves, and ring the funeral bell. This last was properly part of the parish clerk's job but Thomas agreed to take it on when the clerk, John Southall, unexpectedly dropped dead while opening up the church

---

[137] The family's relationship with the Established church had not always been so cordial. Two earlier Roses, Walter and John, both butchers in Bromsgrove, took part in the dispute over infant baptism at Beoley on 13th August 1651 that occasioned Thomas Hall's Birmingham pamphlet of 1652. Their antipaedobaptist stance implies that they were probably Baptists.

FAIRLY MOUNTED ON A HILL

on the morning of 30th May 1804. Thomas soon made himself an indispensable part of the church and was keen to expand his role. By agreement with the churchwardens, he now also kept the monuments and vestry clean; opened the door to all visitors; rang the ting-tang[138] bell before services; attended all vestry meetings to report on the state of the church, and generally assisted the churchwardens as needed. Like his father, Thomas would also *"walk the church on Sundays, according to custom"*. All these additional duties earned him an enhanced salary of £2. 2s 6d per six months and provided him with a lantern.

Joseph, born in 1794, continued what was now becoming a family tradition, albeit one fully supported by the congregation. He added to his father's tasks that of chorister, possessing a fine bass voice that must have boomed out from the old west gallery. He also kept up the alarming practice of *"walking the church"*, tiptoeing about the pews in his slippers and rapping the heads of dozing parishioners with the long white rod that was his badge of office. We shall see the Roses in action as we look at the church itself.

Repairs and Alterations

The church fabric seems to have come through the depredations of the Civil War and its aftermath relatively unscathed – well, most of it anyway. A diocesan visitation on 22nd August 1674 to assess Civil War damage found that *"the church is in good repayer but the chancel is not soe and theyr surplis is nought."*[139] The lack of surplices is hardly surprising, given that neither Hall nor Spilsbury would have dreamed of wearing Anglican vestments and their Restoration successors were

---

[138] An untuned bell rung separately to announce services. It replaced the old Angelus bell after the Reformation.

[139] By contrast, Chadwich was *"out of repayer and there is noe minister"*. In the 1740s the villagers petitioned the bishop of Worcester to be allowed to restore the chapel at their own expense and for the owner of the manor, Christ Church College, Oxford, to provide a minister. Christ Church apparently baulked at the expense of funding a curate in this small and unremunerative settlement, as the chapel was in ruins by the late 18th century and has now disappeared completely.

CHAPTER 6: THE SLEEPING CHURCH

largely transient. By contrast, the chancel owes its poor condition to the Cockes. Ever since the Dean and Chapter had leased out the rectory in 1599, the obligation to keep the chancel in repair had rested with this family or its sub-lessees. The lease had been renewed for £44 per annum just two years before the diocesan visitation with an explicit reminder, but Charles Cockes, now of Norton, Suffolk, seemingly felt that an obligation in distant Worcestershire could safely be avoided. He was right. Builders were *"employed about the church"* the following month but the churchwardens had to admit that *"the chancel which belongeth to Mr Chetle, an undertenant to Mr Cox [Cockes] to repair is out of repair"*. The chancel was still *"very much out of repair"* in April 1676, and although some work was undertaken that autumn it was probably the minimum necessary. The condition of the chancel was again causing concern in June 1728, this time the southeastern buttress. It was still precarious nine years later, but now joined by the decayed plaster ceiling. No doubt funds were eventually found to patch the place up but the chancel is still the least altered part of the church today.

Although the shape and size of the church remained as its medieval builders had left it, the now-elderly building needed regular maintenance and alteration work to keep it fit for its growing congregation. Such work now begins to occupy a sizeable portion of the churchwardens' accounts, allowing us a unique insight into the lost 18th century interior of St John's.

We must start with the roof. The flat roofs of the late medieval church were leaded, a covering that can last over a hundred years in good conditions. This was kept in repair by what would now be called planned preventative maintenance, although Thomas Boulton would just have called it good commercial sense. In July 1684, the churchwardens agreed to pay him 50s a year *"to keep the leades on the church in good repair During is life and to cast two sheets every yeare, to be the same weight as the old"*. The main nave was releaded in July 1758, the north aisle roof was re-boarded and leaded in 1769, more work followed in 1794 and repairs to other water-damaged roof timbers were carried out in 1779. Practical utilitarian men that they were, churchwardens saw little merit in propping up ancient history if it let the water in, and Alienora Stafford's magnificent chantry roof succumbed to their tender mercies in 1814, to be replaced by a plain flat plaster ceiling that continued the line of the north aisle. Not wishing to pass up the opportunity for yet another slap-up feast, the churchwardens had a sheet of lead destined for the new aisle roof fashioned into a drip tray for an ox roast at the Market Hall on 10th June that year, to celebrate the ending of the Napoleonic Wars.[140]

Internally, the medieval timber trusses were considered decidedly old-fashioned by the mid 18th century, a relic of a more barbarous age unbefitting the aspirations of a provincial Georgian town. Some churches succumbed entirely at this time to rebuilding in a fashionable classical style but St John's, thankfully, made do with a policy of concealment. In 1756 a new flat plaster ceiling was drawn under the old nave trusses, which had their carved spandrel brackets sawn off to allow a classical plaster cornice to be run round the perimeter. The old walls received little attention other than the occasional patching of decayed areas in the soft red sandstone. New stone was carted down from the quarry on Rock Hill for some unspecified repair in 1796, incurring a turnpike charge as the mason's cart passed through the toll gate on the Worcester Road. Internally, the plasterwork was whitewashed, in 1783 for example, both to offset the constantly seeping damp and to reflect as much light as possible into the cavernous interior.

Window glass was replaced regularly and the quantities used suggest that whole windows were being reglazed at a time. The outgoing churchwarden's account for 1744 includes the large sum of £8 4s for keeping the glazing in repair and *"ye other new windows"*, which he was still owed. Now, 18th century church glaziers do not

---
[140] A small brass plaque commemorating the event was found by workmen on the roof in 1919.

CHAPTER 6: THE SLEEPING CHURCH

get a good press. They often offered impecunious parishes enticing deals to re-glaze battered old stained glass windows with plain crown glass or poorer quality green glass, and then sold on the old medieval coloured glass for a tidy profit to landowners rebuilding their country houses in the newly fashionable "Gothick" style. Those awkward ogees and cusps were knocked off the tracery at the same time, making the job of re-glazing much simpler. While there is no explicit evidence of dirty dealing at St John's, it is at least suspicious that the remaining medieval glass in the east window - still in place when Treadway Nash saw it some time in the 1770s - mysteriously disappeared shortly after major unspecified re-glazing work in 1796. By the early nineteenth century the church windows were a mixture of plain quarries and *"some very good painted glass"*, rather different in appearance from medieval stained glass and much more to Georgian taste.

One part of the church did undergo physical alteration. At some point the 14th century chantry chapel against the north wall of the chancel became a vestry, when its monuments were cleared out and, as far as we know, destroyed. This probably happened during the early 18th century, as the churchwardens proudly recorded *"the first Parrish meeting ... to be keep'd at the Vestry"* on 5th March 1739. Access into the main body of the church was still by way of the archway into the Stafford Chantry, although this was rather crudely infilled at some point and a low doorway formed in the blocking. Whatever internal arrangements the chapel originally had were removed so thoroughly that there is no hint of their existence. The new, living, occupants valued comfort over piety and promptly installed a fireplace in one corner, its flue rising through the roof in an incongruous brick stack. In 1830 the architect Francis James further despoiled this already battered corner of the church by removing the entire roof and raising the walls two feet to allow a new flat plastered ceiling to be installed clear of the east window. Mr Woodhouse, the builder, rebuilt the gables with steeply inclined Gothick crenellations to match the genuine battlements on the nave and covered the new roof of Memel pine with best Broseley red tiles from Shropshire. The chimney stack was rendered to match, while the internal walls were painted out in a "neat stone" colour with a white ceiling. The dean and chapter paid the £72 bill, seemingly unaware that their monastic predecessors had cleverly sloughed off the obligation to maintain the chancel back in 1380 – or at least none of the churchwardens thought to remind them.

Inside

Although St John's is a church of stone and lead and glass, its 18th century interior was largely wooden, and the heavily used furnishings needed even more attention than the fabric. A building designed for medieval Catholic masses now had to accommodate the preponderantly non-Eucharistic services of the 1662 Book of Common Prayer such as Morning and Evening Prayer, while Holy Communion became a relatively minor service, compulsory only three times a year. This profound change of emphasis affected the whole layout of the church, concentrating activity in the nave and leaving the chancel largely unused. In common with most churches up and down the land, St John's became a "Prayer Book church".

The heart of most 18th century church services was the sermon, and this found architectural expression in the pulpit. From their usual medieval position on the nave north wall, pulpits moved to centre stage and grew both in stature and ornament. In January 1744 whatever John Spilsbury had preached from was replaced with that epitome of Prayer Book furniture, the three-decker pulpit. This oak-panelled monster consisted of a high square preaching desk reached by a flight of stairs at the rear and towering over two further desks, the middle layer a reading desk for the curate and the lowest for the sexton, all for a cost of £41 13s raised by public subscription. Anyone who has listened to a sermon in St John's will know that it is a big church to fill with a single voice. To ensure that no-one

CHAPTER 6: THE SLEEPING CHURCH

missed a word the pulpit actually sat a quarter of the way down the middle aisle of the nave, with the box pews gathered round it. Many faced sideways, looking across the church, while others faced west, away from the rarely used altar. Further amplification was provided by a large flat sounding board over the pulpit, supported from four oak columns and topped by a gold fringe and a glided dove bearing an olive branch in its mouth.[141] To complete the ensemble, the enormous church bible rested rather more comfortably than the vicar at that commanding height on a green baize cushion.

It was customary in most churches for those that could afford it to pay for their own seats, a practice that dated back to the very beginning of fixed pews. There was a simple system for doing so: the more you could pay the better the seat you got - bigger, cosier or in a more prominent position. When the 17th century pews were replaced by new box pews at the parish's expense in August 1720 the churchwardens ensured that their paying customers' new seats should be *"as near as posable to the Old Ones"*, to avoid disrupting the status quo. Renting sometimes became proprietorial over time, and family pews were frequently handed on to the next generation as an assumed right. In 1667, for example, the former churchwarden Edward Sheldon bequeathed to his two sons the *"seats or sittings which I now have and usually doo sitt in in the p'ish Church"*. Like the pulpit, the better-off box pews had green baize linings and cushions, as well as locks on the doors against interlopers. The churchwardens had their own pew, a large, square and no doubt comfortable box under the left hand side of the chancel arch, its four corners proudly displaying the wands of office. Those parishioners that could not pay were left with the remaining free benches immediately under the pulpit - draughty, uncomfortable and an obvious advertisement for their occupants' poverty. These social distinctions sometimes had to be enforced by decree. Notice was given at the Sunday services in March 1703 that *"no person*

---

[141] The fringe was unaccountably stolen in 1776.

shall sitt in the Bayliffs and Aldermens Seates but such substantall House Dwellers that the Churchwardins shall order and that no servants shall sitt in the Aldermens Wives Seates".

Over the next fifty years all this woodwork took something of a battering from its heavy-handed users, and the archdeacon's visitation in 1779 found all sorts of defects. Some pew benches needed replacement, and new doors and hinges feature prominently, as do the locks – these seats were private property, after all. Heavy-handed clergy were also in evidence, as repairs were needed to the pulpit steps, reading desk and handrail. Other joinery figures from time to time as well. The churchwarden's wands, prodders of the slumbering as well as badges of authority, were repainted and gilded in 1795. No doubt they looked splendid. The important woodwork out of the way, it was the turn of the ornate iron communion rails the next year, in a dignified Georgian colour scheme of white, chocolate and stone.

Galleries

18th Century Bromsgrove was a rapidly growing industrialised town, and its working population were not necessarily enamoured of a Church that preached the morality of a fixed social order. But with so many pews appropriated or allotted there was precious little room for attracting newcomers, of whatever persuasion. Even the regulars had trouble finding a space and tempers began to fray. By 1714 the churchwardens felt that action was needed. Their presentment to the bishop that year suggested that *"Wee think there would be a considerable addition to our Congregation if a Convenient Loft were erected in our Church which would likewise probably prevent such disorders and disputes as have of late too often happen'd for want of Convenient Seats"*. Perhaps the Bishop persuaded them otherwise, as nothing happened for a few years and the re-pewing of 1720 was probably a stop-gap to squeeze in more seats at ground level.

CHAPTER 6: THE SLEEPING CHURCH

But the pressure remained, and the churchwardens bowed to the inevitable in 1756 by building a west gallery for the choir and the parish reed and string band. This provided all the music in the days before St John's acquired an organ and its removal from the ground floor would have freed up a number of pews.[142] With an almost complete lack of grace the new gallery cut across the bottom half of the great west window and extended out beyond the tower arch as far as the first aisle column and across the south aisle to the south wall. A truly remarkable act of vandalism created a new external doorway through the south aisle wall, allowing the musicians direct access to the gallery from outside via a steep timber stair. Books, instruments and other necessities were provided through an annuity of 20s from Simon Crane in 1787.

At the beginning of the 19th century the urban aspirations of the better-off townsfolk demanded something more fashionable than a country wind band. On 15th June 1809 a new organ, built by Elliot of Tottenham Court Road London for £750, rose under the tower arch, its bulk almost totally obscuring the west window. With no resident organist to hand, the churchwardens had to bring in Mr Bishop Simms from St Philip's Church, Birmingham to give the organ its first outing on 9th July. It was obviously a success as the collection raised an enormous £63.[143] The mixed choir occupied the upper four rows of gallery seats in front of the organ, although the organist himself was screened from view by a red velvet

---

[142] It was common for congregations to turn and face the west gallery when singing. A correspondent to the Bromsgrove Messenger of 9th May 1908 claimed to have in his possession a primitive old bassoon from the church band, known as a "horse's leg". The musicians doubled as the town band and played outdoors at major gatherings.

[143] The oddly named Bishop Simms had seven brothers, four of whom were also proficient organists. A contemporary music dictionary noted of them: *"From their originality of style, genuine taste and neatness of execution they have not only established a high reputation in their respective situations but have called forth warm expressions of approbation from strangers."* Bishop's brother James was subsequently appointed as permanent organist at St John's on an annual salary of £30, paid out of the town weighing machine fund and supplemented by the occasional benefit concert. A prolific and accomplished composer of church music in his own right James Simms stayed 44 years and was succeeded by J.B. Tirbutt in 1854.

curtain on brass rings. To complete the ensemble a clock was fixed to the panelled gallery front, its large clear face and fretted brass hands easily visible to the vicar as he entered the second hour of his sermon. From all the galleries this alone survives, relocated and silent in the vestry.

But a west gallery alone could not provide enough space. A north gallery was built between May and September 1766, slung across the north aisle on great timber beams from the external wall onto the 13th century arcade, whose column capitals were cut away to take the beam-ends. Reached from a balustraded staircase in the chantry chapel this further intrusion doubled the capacity of the aisle while halving the natural daylight. Ever pragmatic, the churchwardens simply had the old aisle window heads and tracery knocked out and the openings extended upwards to the roof in ugly iron frames. To compound the felony, an entirely new hole – it must not be dignified with the term "window" – was punched through the wall over the north door and glazed in another iron frame. It is said that one of the churchwardens that year was an ironmonger and did well out of the work.

Last to come was a relatively narrow south gallery, completed on 9th September 1769. This sat well back from the slender south arcade on iron columns and was entered from a staircase rising through the medieval arch in the chancel south wall. Despite its size the gallery only contained thirty-one box pews, each a rather generous square. The space was clearly capable of taking more people and it was therefore completely rebuilt in 1824. While the other galleries were probably designed and built by local carpenters, the new south gallery was a Proper Work of Architecture. Pride or contacts pushed the churchwardens in the direction of Thomas Rickman, later to achieve fame for his chaste "Gothick" churches in Regency London as well as part of St John's College, Cambridge. At this stage in his career however, Rickman had just been established four years as an architect in Birmingham after working successively as a chemist, doctor, grocer, corn

CHAPTER 6: THE SLEEPING CHURCH

merchant and insurance agent. He charged a hefty £37 4s for designing the new gallery, as well as altering the other two to increase their capacity, although all the survey work was actually carried out by his no doubt poorly paid clerk. Reasonable or not, the churchwardens were no fools: they paid him late, with a discount for cash.

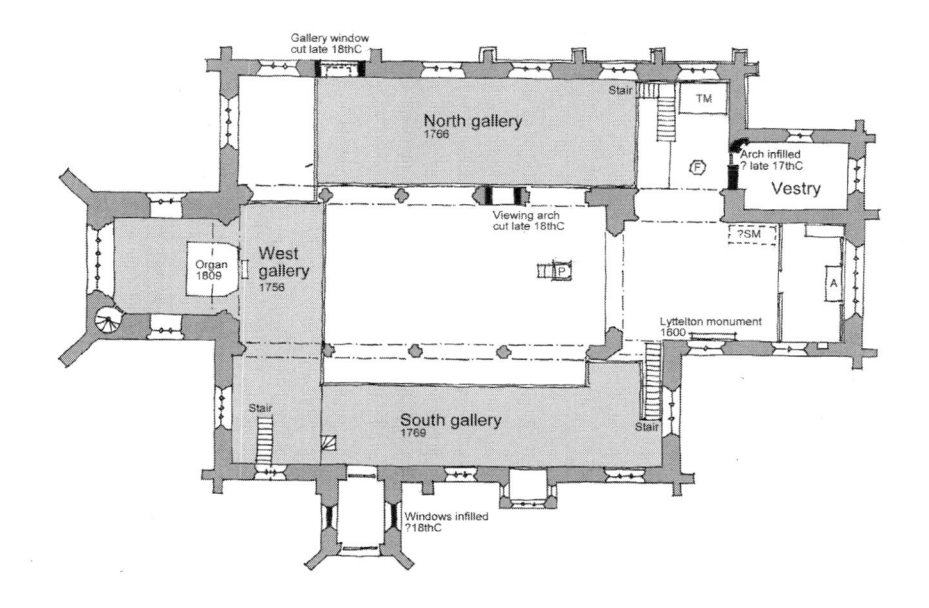

[Plan e] St John's c1800. Shaded areas indicate the three galleries, each with its' own staircase. The west gallery is dominated by the organ. The south gallery was rebuilt wider in 1824. The west end of the north aisle, the darkest and coldest corner in the church, was never infilled with a gallery. The 3-decker pulpit stands in the centre of the nave.

£481 7s 5d bought an oak panelled and deal floored gallery with forty-two pews, this time spanning the entire south aisle onto the back of the slender stone arcade. The builders, Messrs Hepworth and Davis of Birmingham, also re-floored and refaced the north gallery as well as overhauling other joinery round the church, including the pulpit stairs (again). Safety rails were put across the tall south aisle windows, the cills of which were dropped to admit more light to the now-gloomy ground floor. The organ was protected in a timber casing for the duration of the work, although the repairs found necessary when it was uncovered suggest that this was less than effective. The existing pew owners were allowed to confirm their entitlement to a new pew in the same vicinity as their old seat at a vestry meeting on 25th February and therefore brought no additional income to the project. To pay for the work itself, lots were drawn to allocate the best additional seats in each gallery and a further 17½ pews were sold at auction in the town hall, raising a total of £382 10s. By the time the inevitable cash discount was taken off the builder's account the churchwardens could congratulate themselves on their commercial acumen. Evidently Rickman thought it a good project too, as he submitted the plan to the Society of Arts' annual show.

Thomas Rickman made another contribution to St John's, and to every other church in the country in fact - he gave us the language to describe the place. Rickman was the first to analyse historic buildings by their architectural styles. His 1817 book, *"An attempt to Discriminate the Styles of English Architecture from the Conquest to the Reformation"*, established the historic periods by which medieval architecture is still described and gave Gothic architecture an academic respectability alongside the dominant Classical styles then in vogue.

The Forgotten Chancel

In contrast to all the activity in the Nave, the chancel was still largely the repository of the dead. The chancel had always been the prime place for burial over the rest of the church and this was reflected in the fees charged - 2s for a chancel burial in 1789, compared with 1s elsewhere inside the church.

CHAPTER 6: THE SLEEPING CHURCH

[Picture 14] The earliest known detailed view of St John's, drawn by Peter Prattinton on the 30th August 1812. Its naïve accuracy clearly shows the mutilated north aisle windows, their stone mullions crudely extended upwards in iron. The new opening over the north door is also visible

As the main chancel area was still occupied by the Talbot and Stafford monuments, lesser mortals had to make do with the periphery. William Chance for example, a descendent of the Barnsleys of Barnsley Hall, was buried in 1622 under the lowest chancel step. His wife and her sister lay nearby, while a robbed brass to a Barnsley ancestor lay a few feet west in the nave centre aisle. In 1768 the vicar, John Waugh, had most of the chancel monuments moved back into the old chantry chapel to make way for a splendid new marble altar donated by Mrs Hannah Moore, widow of Edward Moore of Barnt Green, together with an ornate set of iron altar rails and an oak reredos painted with the Ten Commandments, Lord's Prayer and Apostles' Creed. These typical late Georgian fittings restored at least some eucharistic dignity to this crumbling portion of the church, although how much they were actually used for that purpose is debatable. Their owners long gone, the old monuments sat gathering dust below the north gallery stairs for the next fifty years. They were joined in March 1807 by the font, uprooted from its location on a stone block under the west gallery, in what was rapidly becoming a dumping ground for old stonework. Not everyone thought the changes an improvement. Francis Laird visited the church in 1814 in the course of writing a description of the county and was *"sorry to observe that during the repair of the chancel some years ago, some very improper changes of the monuments and brasses took place. It were well indeed if an Act of Parliament were to take place to prevent the barbarous beautifyings which are so often executed by the orders of as barbarous churchwardens."* There would be other similar accusations in the years to some.

Up The Tower

From a low, pointed doorway in the southwest corner of the tower base, a narrow stone staircase spirals steeply upwards into the church tower. Despite its external prominence this strange vertical world was a secret from all but a select few, for it was a place not of prayer but hard physical work. Within its solid stone shell the interior of the tower is largely timber. Three massive oak floors span clear across the width, carried on deep timber beams. Even the spire is partly supported by timber, for its 15th century builders simply left their internal scaffolding in place as the spire rose around them.

An unbroken climb of 50 steps leads to the first and most frequently inhabited stage, the ringing chamber. This was (and still is) home to the bellringers, a select company of men whose names and feats adorn the many ringing boards

CHAPTER 6: THE SLEEPING CHURCH

around the room. Among many notable performances the full peal of Bob Majors rung on 29th December 1788 by a junior band including Joseph Rose must have been a real feat of endurance, involving no less than 12,000 *"changes"* over an incredible 7 hours 35 minutes of solid ringing, in an unheated tower at dead of winter. Compare this with the average peal of around 5000 changes over three hours or so. Ringers were unsurprisingly a forceful, thirsty bunch, quite prepared to press for more pay if they felt the work deserved it, and the churchwardens forbad any ringing without their express consent. 5s a day for regular ringing in 1693 had risen to 6s 8d by 1718, and special days counted extra. In this virulently anti-Catholic age, the 5th November was a celebration against all things popish and the bells rang out accordingly, at an inflated cost of 6s 6d in 1693 and 10s in 1703. When the number of bells was increased to eight in the Spring of 1774, the ringers contracted with the churchwardens to ring the regular services at no cost, provided that they could keep the profits from wedding peals and other special occasions. Although initially for three years only, this is still the practice today.

St John's complement of eight – later ten - bells certainly demanded stamina. The four bells recorded in the 1552 inquisition had presumably hung idle for some years afterwards[144] but were brought back into use in the more liberal days of James I, when their deficiencies became apparent. Stephen Knight (the churchwarden implicated in the mock-eucharist incident) commissioned a local man, John Tidman, to recast the peal in 1622 and add new metal to increase the weight of the tenor bell – the deepest – to 19cwt. The other four bells were to be tuned to match, at a total cost of £61 13s 4d. Tidman botched the work – or so Knight alleged, and he took the bell-founder to court. To Knight's claim that the bells were under-weight and had already cracked in use, Tidman countered that the new bells had all been approved and the damage must have been caused by disorderly ringing. This is not an accusation brought lightly against any ringer

---

[144] William Colyar gave 2s in his will of 1558 to repair the bells and bell ropes, hinting at a period of disuse under Edward VI.

and it is frustrating that no record exists of the outcome, particularly as Tidman was pressing for a Bond payment of £120. However, the fact that the whole peal was again recast into six bells on 11th October 1695 (again unsatisfactorily) suggests that Tidman won his case. John Martin recast the Fourth bell in 1698 but such was the churchwardens' lack of trust in bell founders that they imposed a penalty of 8d for every pound weight of metal lost from the bell during recasting.

It was left to the rather more reliable Abraham Rudhall to recast the whole peal again at his Gloucester bell foundry in October 1701. These six now formed the basis of the present peal, although only the Fifth (C#) remains in its original form, complete with its motto of "God Prosper This Parish". Thomas Rudhall increased the total to eight by March 1774, adding a Third (E) and the present Tenor (E) at a charge of £117 16s, of which £33 15 4d was subscribed by the parishioners. The Ninth (F#) was recast in 1790 and the whole peal was re-hung and re-tuned by Thomas Paul in November 1815. The opportunity was taken to add two more bells from Thomas Mears of London, the Second (F#) and Seventh (A), bringing the total to the present ten. Three years later William Rose, bellringer and newly appointed parish clerk, celebrated the new peal by buying the old Lower Dolphin Inn in the High Street and renaming it the Bell.

At some point in the 18th century the ringing chamber floor was lowered, cutting across the top of both the east window and the tower arch and presumably ruining the proportions of both. This can only have been to allow the ringers a better internal view up the church nave, as the original (and now restored) floor level does rather isolate the ringers from the service. With around ten feet of extra weight added to the already long bell ropes ringing cannot have been any easier, and the new ropes bought in November 1772 may be a clue to the date of this particular act of officially sanctioned vandalism.

Between the two main floors lies a third, a low dark chamber criss-crossed with

CHAPTER 6: THE SLEEPING CHURCH

arched braces, each one squared up with an adze and firmly jointed with carpenter's pegged mortises to take the great weight of the bell frames above. This is the clock floor. Early clocks did not have faces or hands but were primarily mechanisms for sounding one or more of the bells on each hour.[145] As we have seen, St John's had a clock from at least 1573 although the evening curfew continued to be rung by hand into the 20th century. While the medieval working man had laboured from curfew to curfew with little measure of the intervening hours, his Georgian successor could judge far more accurately where he stood in his working day - when to open his shop, have his lunch or measure his hourly output of nails. Two bells were cast as "chimes" in the 1622 dispute,[146] Edward Carter, the parish clerk, was being paid 22s a year to look after the clock and chimes in 1684 and the clock itself was repaired in 1701, when the bells were being recast.

Although the original mechanism has long gone, it would have consisted of a large iron or wooden frame containing the escapement and chiming drum, powered by a cast iron weight suspended on long ropes that hung down through the tower floors in a timber shaft. Various people were paid varying amounts to keep the mechanism wound each day. John Spinstowe had £4 a year in 1703 but William Taylor, the clerk, only got 30s for the same job in 1730. It had risen again to £6 in 1742 and dropped to £3 in 1774, all depending on the bargaining skills of the recipient, one suspects. Thomas Rose acquired the job as part of his sexton's duties in 1772 and left an entertaining analysis of just what effort this apparently simple job entailed. *"To wind up the church clock and chimes"* he wrote, *"I have 5 locks to unlock and lock each morning, which makes 1825 times a year, I have 47 stairs to walk up which makes 17155 stairs in the year. I have 7 cwt to wind each morning, which makes 2555 cwt or 127 tons 15 cwt. The number of yards I have to wind the*

---

[145] As the French name for a bell – cloche – implies.

[146] Driven by a two-note mechanism, known for obvious reasons as a ting-tang. The double notes sounded the quarter hours, distinguishing them from the deeper hour chime.

FAIRLY MOUNTED ON A HILL

weights up every morning is 30 and the total is 10950 or 6 miles 390 yards....I have 625 different times to ring a bell in the year, and to walk up 28 stairs each time which makes 17500 yearly". And that was on top of winding the town hall clock as well.

The clock finally acquired a face in 1752 when Henry Payton made a *"Dyall Plate"*, a lozenge-shaped wooden board 9ft square with painted numerals. This was fixed to the south face of the tower so as to be visible from the market place, its mechanism running back through the belfry louvres. Although Payton made a new chiming mechanism at the same time, it was again replaced in 1772, as being out of time with the Town Hall clock.[147] This new municipal rival to ecclesiastical time must have spurred the churchwardens to action, for in March 1775, Edward Dracott, a local brush maker, made a musical chiming mechanism for £100, which played simple tunes on the church bells. It did not work very well and Dracott was still owed 17s 6d in 1779 against outstanding repairs. But the town's imagination had been caught and William Norton of Birmingham was commissioned in 1794 to see what could be done to improve the variety of tunes played. He came up with a real mixture - two psalms, the National Anthem, a military march and four popular tunes, all for £105. By September the following year Norton had also rebuilt the mechanism to chime the quarter hours and had fitted a new cast iron face 8ft 4ins diameter on the east side of the tower, the numerals picked out in *"real gold"*. The £62 was well spent, for this clock-face has now been telling Bromsgrove the time for over two hundred years, since 1859 from a raised position on the spire.[148]

---

[147] This is first noted in 1697, when a surplus of £5 0s 5d was used to fund the clock and hand set up at the town hall. Early clock faces usually had just an hour hand.

[148] Joseph Rose records that the clock dial was cased with inch thick mahogany boarding in 1831 and a minute hand and quarter hours added in 1848. As the two prints of St John's from the 1840s clearly show a cast iron skeleton dial on the east face, it seems that the old wooden lozenge dial was retained on the south face (hidden on the prints) and gradually brought up to the same standard as its newer neighbour.

CHAPTER 6: THE SLEEPING CHURCH

[Picture 15] Bromsgrove from Hilltop, c1790. The lozenge-shaped clock-face can just be made out on the south face of the church tower. This is also the earliest known accurate portrayal of St John's

The Day-To-Day Church

Alongside the big expenses of repairs and alterations, the church had to be supplied with necessities. Communion wine had to be bought, in bulk usually. Three bottles of Tent, an inexpensive Spanish red wine, lasted around four months, showing a fairly low consumption in line with the generally debased status of communion services. Communion bread – again sparse – and candles also figure in the accounts, along with lamp oil and coal by the cart-load. Materials wore out from time to time: the vicar needed a new quarto size Book of Common Prayer and a new silk hood for £2 in 1794. The reading desk mat was scuffed beyond repair in 1779 and the bottom finally fell out of the old coal scuttle in 1781. Paperwork was as unavoidable in the 18th century as the 21st: letters had to be written and posted, registers replaced when full, almanacs consulted, confirmation cards printed, and public notices bought. One wonders what the

FAIRLY MOUNTED ON A HILL

"Abstract against cursing and swearing" bought in 1795 said, and to whom it was directed.

All that coal was needed to feed the church's heating system, such as it was. In 1684, Edward Carter was being paid to *"warm the church"*, presumably with an early stove of some sort. New cast iron stoves were bought in 1844 at £21 10s each, plus the cost of tall iron chimneys that projected out from the walls at high level. How effective they were in that lofty nave is not recorded but our early Victorian congregation probably added an extra layer of clothing in winter just in case, as their modern counterparts still do.

The "evening" services actually began at 3pm, to make use of whatever daylight remained in the waning winter afternoons. When daylight failed, oil lamps and candle power took over, in the form of a great wrought iron *"shandeylear"* bought for £22 15s in March 1773 and hung from the centre of the nave ceiling on a chain. As it could not be lowered to the floor the newly appointed William Rose either lit it from a long taper or risked his neck on one of those impossibly tall ladders that still occupy the dark corners of some old churches.[149] In 1835, however, Bromsgrove acquired its own gasworks in a yard off Worcester Road. The churchwardens soon started a subscription to install the new craze of coal-gas lighting at a cost of £126 15s 6d, and the first gas-lit service was held on Sunday, 11th September 1836.

Church cleaning was a perennial chore. The *"alleys"* between the rows of box pews had to be swept, the windows cleaned, the plate polished and the surpluses and altar linen washed. Brooms, brushes and mops regularly wore out and had to be replaced. The interest of these otherwise mundane tasks is that they appear in

---

[149] When the chandelier was moved into the gallery under the tower on 29th June 1854 Jonathan Brazier, a 27 year-old bricklayer, chose the latter course. From a platform built over the box pews, Brazier climbed a tall ladder steadied by four workmen, unhooked the beast and lowered it to the floor. He went on to found Bromsgrove's biggest building company, J & A Brazier Ltd.

CHAPTER 6: THE SLEEPING CHURCH

the churchwardens' accounts at all. It is a sobering thought that everything now done willingly for free was once paid for, however meanly - the four women paid for cleaning the church through 1781 were paid just a penny a week each. This apparently mercenary attitude becomes more understandable when we realise that the whole concept of voluntary work was alien to a society where labour was cheap, families large and every penny earned kept poverty from the door. These pennies put bread on a working family's table and we should rather see them as one way in which the church provided for its more humble parishioners, without resorting to *"charity"*.

Then there's the beer – gallons and gallons of it. 39 pints alone were ordered between the 22nd and 31st of May 1798 and ale figures on almost every page of the churchwardens' accounts. But these men are no secret soaks. Beer was the staple drink of all ages and both sexes in a time when the water supply was at best murky and often lethal. Workmen ran on beer, usually small beer with a low alcohol content, and it was considered such a necessity that it was generally supplied free. *"Beer at the Bels and att ye Spire"* when the bells were being rehung in 1787 is typical, as is *"Ale for John Sinfield's men whitewashing"* in 1783 at £1 1s; *"Beer for Mr Green's men at work in the church"* in 1792 at 10s 5½d; *"beer for Mr Brook for his carpenters and masons"* in 1794; and eight quarts of ale in 1796 for just one builder and his labourer. While the thought of beer-sodden workmen manoeuvring heavy masonry on timber scaffolding would terrify a modern health and safety inspector, the sheer exertion of manual labour quickly burnt off any residual intoxication and it is a fair bet that these hard-working men thoroughly earned their watery pint. The *"two gallons of London Gin"* in 1783 is harder to explain. As the churchwardens were also overseers of the poor it may have been for the workhouse, where gin was the female tipple of preference, as well as a primitive medicine. If so, the peppermint water (for indigestion) and hartshorn (smelling salts) bought in 1787 may be destined for the same place.

One set of payments really does seem at variance with the rest. In July 1676, the churchwardens had *"agreed that one shilling p' head shall be paid for all foxes killed within the parish and nothing for aney other varmint"*. The practical advantages of keeping the fox population down were obvious, but by the mid 18th century the local hunt was happy to do so without being paid for the privilege and the churchwardens turned their attention to a rather different creature – hedgehogs, at 4d a time. Nineteen were paid for in 1775, and John Boulton Burton, churchwarden from June 1785 to April 1787, shelled out for a mind-boggling 211, including twelve in one day. Far from their modern Tiggywinkle image, 18th century hedgehogs (or urchins) were considered vermin, egg thieves and spreaders of disease in grazing animals. Every urchin caught helped to preserve the local livestock and the reward was a useful inducement for the local lads to be vigilant.

Such payments occur regularly in most rural churchwardens accounts of this period, although the practice actually dates back to the days of Henry VIII. An Act of 1532 required every parish to keep down the local population of crows, rooks and choughs by catching them in a net kept for the purpose. A reward was later offered for each bird's head or unbroken egg taken to the churchwarden, together with an extensive list of other so-called vermin, including such diverse creatures as rats, kingfishers, foxes and otters, each with a price on its head. With such an easy cash reward on offer, it is perhaps a wonder that any wildlife survived the 18th century, although the humble hedgehog bore the brunt at St John's.

The Churchyard

The present appearance of St John's churchyard is largely a product of the 18th century. Those small, square 17th century headstones with their lively but none-too-refined lettering now make way for increasingly large and elegant monuments, top-heavy with pedimented scrolls, cartouches, cherubs, skulls and swags, all recording the unqualified virtues of their slumbering occupants in handsome

CHAPTER 6: THE SLEEPING CHURCH

calligraphy. The sheer size of some stones is impressive, both in height and thickness, for the local sandstone is not particularly hard and anything thinner might crack. The east end of the church was considered the prime position for burial, inside or out, and some of the best surviving stones gather here in sweeping lines across the brow of the hill. As earlier generations had thought the same, this area was anything but vacant ground. The older monuments were therefore simply uprooted and used to revet the sides of the footpaths, allowing a new layer of burials to take place over the originals but leaving no clue as to where all these stones came from.[150]

By the early 19th century, even this expediency was at its limit. The churchyard was literally packed and more space was needed. With roads or steep slopes on most sides, the only possible area for expansion was Crown Close, for many years now the gardens of the Crown Inn. In May 1815, the church bought the Crown's old bowling green, which lay just outside the northern arc of churchyard trees and was fronted by what is now Church Lane. Even this was not virgin ground. A building of some sort occupied part of the site, for its stone basement was converted into two 16ft long vaults for the Dipples, one of the town's oldest families.

Even with a full yard, grave-digging outside was considerably easier than an internal location. In 1789 the new sexton, Thomas Rose charged a flat fee of 6d, plus a further 4d for *"biering"* the coffin to the graveside. "Parish" funerals for paupers and other outcasts were cheaper at 4d, the same price charged for burying stillborn children, of which there were all too many. The young George Fletcher, whose lively reminiscences tell us so much about mid-19th century Bromsgrove,

---

[150] This process gave rise to several spurious legends as older monuments were unearthed, devoid of any identifying inscription. The recumbent medieval figure now in the south aisle oriel bay once rested on top of the old north wall of the churchyard. By the 18th century, Bromsgrovians knew him as the man who had sold his soul to the devil, on condition that he would neither be buried inside or outside the churchyard. His neat way out of the bargain was to perch on top of the wall.

FAIRLY MOUNTED ON A HILL

saw Joseph Rose attend to such a burial some time in the late 1850s. *"One day"* he recalled,

"Mr Rose had finished digging a grave in the churchyard opposite the porch, and came back to the "dusthole" [151] *and from underneath some coal and old rugs he produced a small oblong white wooden box, about two feet in length. I followed him out and he went back to the grave just ready, and dug a small hole in the floor of it, where he placed this box and carefully covered it with earth. Naturally, my boyish curiosity was aroused, and I asked him what it was for. He fenced with the question for a minute, and then said it was a peculiar sort of earth or soil which was prepared to help the decay of the coffin over it."*

Rose was alluding to quicklime, which was used for this purpose; but Fletcher later found out the truth about these sad little parcels. Stillborn – and therefore unbaptised - children could not officially be given Christian burial. By secretly burying the child below an adult coffin the burial rights were read over both, and Rose's sensitive approach speaks well of the man's charity.

Deaths were announced to the parish by the sexton ringing the passing bell - three rounds of three strokes for a man and two rounds of two for a woman. And while the grieving families stood by the graveside in whatever weather happened along, the vicar had at least the comfort of a large umbrella, bought for this purpose for a hefty £3 in 1773 but needing repair six years later. In 1804 this was upgraded to a *"Clergyman's box"*, a sort of portable sentry-box that could be carried to any convenient spot in wet weather, although it is not certain whether its occupant was similarly transported or made a run for it across the wet grass - under his umbrella, presumably. Just occasionally, the process of burial had to be reversed. It was found necessary to exhume the corpse of one Lidford in 1797, and the fact that the men were paid in food and drink may be an indication of just how unpleasant the job turned out to be.

---

[151] His storeroom under the west gallery.

CHAPTER 6: THE SLEEPING CHURCH

[Picture 16] Joseph Rose greeting visitors, sometime in the 1840s (enlarged from 1840s general view)

As the last resting place of so many local people the churchyard had to be kept neat. The grass had to be cut, but only when long enough to do so with a scythe, at the expense of 10s 6d, plus 1s 6d for the scythe – did nobody have one? And nettles had to be pulled, by Mr Dovey, who also swept the church steps at 2d a week. Before the days of tarmac and concrete, paths wore rapidly under the hobnails and wooden pattens of the walking public, and they required regular replacement. John Pinfield repaired the steps themselves in 1779, and Parson's Hill, Crown Close and the other church paths were resurfaced with gravel in 1788, and again seven years later. Although Crown Close itself was wide enough for wheeled vehicles the churchyard paths themselves were too narrow for any but pedestrians, and carriages had to be left outside the gates. The only vehicle access to the west door was by the precipitously steep little lane off Kidderminster Road later known as Adam's Hill. Wedding carriages and funeral hearses alike risked this treacherous climb, and Sexton Rose kept a supply of dry sand and gravel in his little cubby-hole under the tower to provide at least some grip for iron-shod wheels and hooves in wet weather.[152]

Perhaps the most characteristic feature of the churchyard appeared in 1792, when the present ring of lime trees was planted. There is no indication that these replaced an older ring but the fact that they follow the line of the ancient burh bank seems to indicate the continuance of a very old practice. When the hot summer of 1795 threatened their future, the ever-helpful Thomas Rose kept the saplings going by watering them continuously for eight weeks.

The yard also had to be kept secure, from man and beast. The old churchyard wall eventually succumbed to age in 1815 and was replaced by the present stone wall. All entrances were protected by wooden gates, which were periodically replaced and repaired, for example at the top of Crown Close in 1794. These gates were locked after the 8pm curfew, as the padlock bought in 1779 attests. A year later, however, someone forgot to use it and Mr Wooley's horse wandered unhindered into the churchyard, no doubt enticed by the luxurious uncut grazing on offer. Whatever damage it caused was slight, but the churchwardens insisted on compensation and its no-doubt aggrieved owner duly handed over one shilling for the trouble caused.

Padlocks were no use against a rather more serious intrusion when, early on the morning of Monday the 23rd November 1829, three graves were robbed of their newly interred occupants and the corpses spirited away. Grave robbing had one blunt purpose – to supply the burgeoning medical profession with a steady supply of bodies on which to practice anatomical dissection. Officially, only the bodies of executed murderers could be used for dissection. But while some hospitals made

---

[152] It had been hoped that the path around the south side of the church could be widened to allow carriage access from Crown Close but this was never done. The present roadway across the churchyard was far narrower before the 1858 restoration and could not take carriage traffic, although there was a cart gate from Crown Close into the churchyard for maintenance.

CHAPTER 6: THE SLEEPING CHURCH

do with the bodies of paupers, vagrants or other unfortunates who had no family to claim them, the larger city infirmaries needed a rather more regular supply for their medical schools than poverty or the public hangman could offer.

So a new profession came into being. For a fee, the Resurrection Men would supply a reasonably fresh body to order, no questions asked nor any answers given. And when the city cemeteries became too well policed, what more natural development than to take a trip into the country and see what a quieter churchyard like St John's could offer. Grave robbing was a persistent feature of the early 19th century and its practitioners, if caught, sometimes turned out to be the surgeons themselves. Be that as it may, these three unfortunates probably ended up miles away in the dissection rooms of a Birmingham hospital, and the £20 reward was offered in vain. The only vestige of this practice is the iron railings still visible around some of the larger monuments, their pointed tops a strong disincentive to go a-digging.[153]

A Certain Lack of Respect

Grave robbing was just an extreme example of the more general disregard in which the Established church was held by many in the 18th century, and the citizens of Bromsgrove were no exception. Previous generations had attacked St John's on the basis of their deeply held religious or political convictions. Now, they just attacked it for what they could get. In December 1797 someone succeeded in breaking into the church and taking unspecified valuables. Sir John Fielding placed an advertisement in the 20th December edition of the Bow Street *"Public Hue and Cry"* broadsheet offering a reward – unsuccessfully, it seems. It would not hurt a well-off church to lose a candlestick or two to a poor nailer before Christmas.

---

[153] The Anatomy Act was passed in July 1832, specifically to stop this practice.

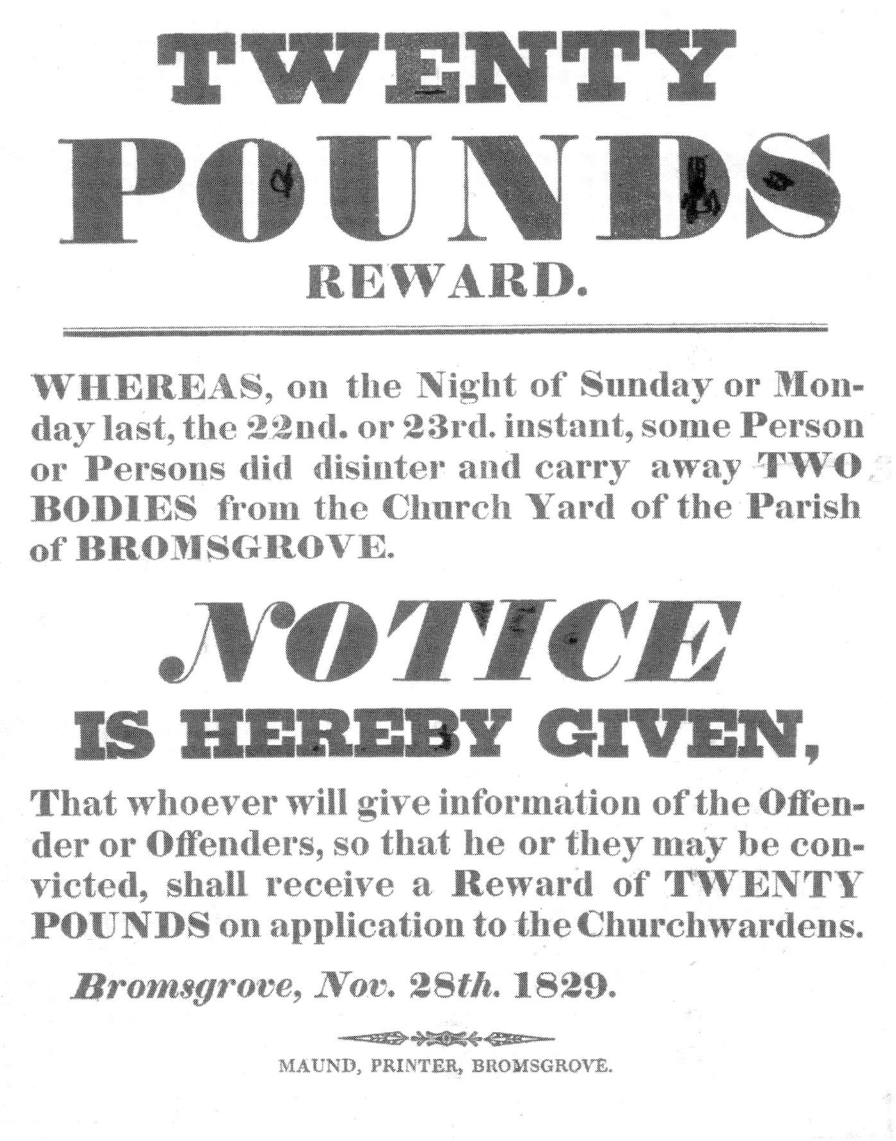

TWENTY POUNDS

REWARD.

WHEREAS, on the Night of Sunday or Monday last, the 22nd. or 23rd. instant, some Person or Persons did disinter and carry away TWO BODIES from the Church Yard of the Parish of BROMSGROVE.

NOTICE
IS HEREBY GIVEN,

That whoever will give information of the Offender or Offenders, so that he or they may be convicted, shall receive a Reward of TWENTY POUNDS on application to the Churchwardens.

Bromsgrove, Nov. 28th. 1829.

MAUND, PRINTER, BROMSGROVE.

[Picture 17] The reward notice posted after the grave-robbing incident. The number of bodies was incorrectly printed and has been altered in pencil to "3" on the original notice

CHAPTER 6: THE SLEEPING CHURCH

And after all, the miscreant was only following a precedent set by the lord of the manor himself. At the end of the 17th century its then-lessee Sir Scrope Howe had sold the manor of Bromsgrove to Thomas Hickman Windsor, newly Earl of Plymouth and owner of Hewell Grange in nearby Tardebigge. In 1728 Other Hickman Windsor, the distinctively named Third Earl, felt the need to reinforce his hold on manorial rights. Enlisting the help of Messrs Twitty and Bell, and Churchwarden Steedman, Windsor had the old parish records chest dragged out of its refuge in the tower. In his second capacity as servant to Lord Windsor, Steedman ordered William Davis, a whitesmith, to burst open the old chest's locks, allowing Windsor to remove a number of important documents, which he then destroyed. Although his primary objective was to change the ancient customs of the manor in his family's favour, Windsor also succeeded in obliterating irreplaceable historical records that would have shed a clearer light on Bromsgrove's early history, and he disturbed the reminder to such an extent that they were almost beyond saving when rediscovered many years later. Gentleman-farmer churchwardens were no match for an aristocracy bent on self-preservation.[154]

Disrespect works both ways of course. Protected by a succession of unswervingly Protestant Hanoverian monarchs, the Church of England felt no obligation to compromise with other denominations. The rather prim John Lacy was quite clear about where he stood when compiling notes for an unpublished history of Bromsgrove in 1778. The Independents and Presbyterians were by and large harmless, and therefore hardly worthy of note. The Quakers were suspect but of so few numbers that they were unlikely to do any harm. The Baptists, as we have already heard, were very active and therefore wicked. Catholics, still prohibited from public worship, were not even mentioned.

---

[154] The Windsors subsequently went to court several times to assert manorial rights: in 1729, over rights in Chadwich, in 1731 over copyhold estates in Tardebigge, and again in 1733.

FAIRLY MOUNTED ON A HILL

Although Bromsgrove's Catholics took care to keep themselves out of the limelight, no such discretion attended the rest of the population. Anti-Catholic feeling was still regularly stirred up any time the Establishment wanted a convenient scapegoat, fuelled by the residual attempts of Stuart Pretenders to claim the throne in 1715 and 1745. Consider the town's Court Leet. At every annual dinner from the mid 18th to the mid 19th century the town crier stood up and sang a song entitled "The Church and State, and No Surrender", which included these two verses:

The Bible was no longer read
But tales of sinners sainted
The Gods adored were gods of bread
And signposts carved and painted
When priests and monks with caps and cowls
Arrived here without number
With racks and daggers blessed by popes
And loads of holy lumber

Our trade abroad, our wealth at home
And all things worth desiring
Were sacrificed to France and Rome
While Britons lay expiring
The monarch, a priest-ridden ass
Did whate'er the priests suggested
And trotted day by day to mass
The slave of slaves detested

There is more in the same intolerant vein. The song's anti-Jacobite sentiments date it to the 1710s, the monarch so disparagingly referred to being the late and unlamented James II. That it survived to be sung at official dinners up to 1855 is an insight into the mindset prevalent amongst many in the Established church at

CHAPTER 6: THE SLEEPING CHURCH

the time.

Lacy had no love of straying Protestants. A Mr Bayliss had left money to buy land, the £8 annual income from which was to fund a hundred loaves for the poor at Christmas and Easter. But, relates Lacy with some horror, "by shameful doings amongst the feoffees [trustees], most of them Presbyterians, the land is now worth no more than £6 a year." All was not lost, however. The land was later bought back with a new set of trustees, all of them solid Anglicans; and bread production no doubt returned to its former generous level.[155]

The Established church carried a natural authority when it came to law and order but it could not stop the ordinary folk of the town gravitating towards the growing number of Nonconformist meeting houses that were springing up around the town, soon to be joined by the strong new shoots of John Wesley's Methodism. Anglican clergy were by and large docile but had still to be reminded that their continued employment depended on their orthodoxy. Edward Moore of Barnt Green no doubt had this in mind when he signed an indenture on 20th March 1745 granting an annuity of £5 to the then-vicar, William Phillips, so long as he continued to say daily prayers according to the Anglican rite. Failing this the money was to be given away in cloth to the poor. The co-signatories to the agreement included no less than five local clergymen. Had Phillips expressed rather too much interest in the looming Jacobite threat that year, and was this perhaps an attempt to deflect his sympathies?

Faced with pressures from several directions the Anglican ascendancy had to be preserved at all costs, and to do that the congregation had to be caught young.

---

[155] We should not be too hard on Lacy. His equally horrified reaction to the *"disagreeable and cruel sports"* of cock-fighting and bear-baiting at the annual Sidemoor Wake, held in the fields just north of the churchyard every July, is fully justified, as is his anger at the inability of the churchwardens and constable to stop the *"cruel, inhuman, cowardly and shameful Pastime"* of stoning birds on Shrove Tuesday. Church festivals had rather come down in the world by the late 18th century.

FAIRLY MOUNTED ON A HILL

Off to School

Despite their title Sunday schools were not the purely religious institutions they later became, and they provided a rudimentary general education as well as instruction in the basics of Christianity. Sunday was the only day of rest for most of the working population, adults and children, and all other activities had to take place then, including education. William Brook started the first known Sunday school in 1780, in a long-gone house in St John Street opposite the foot of the church steps, where the first class of two boys and seven girls were taught on Sundays and one weekday evening free of charge. When growing popularity made these domestic premises too small the girls' class moved to the nearby Quaker meeting house in Hanover Street, while the boys used the rather dilapidated town hall round the corner. This passed the point of decrepitude in 1823 and in the absence of any church hall only the old cotton factory in Watt Close had the clear floor area to house the still expanding school. Girls and boys were brought together here until the old building was commandeered as a fever hospital in 1832 to cope with a severe outbreak of cholera amongst the nail-makers' cottages that bordered the heavily polluted Spadesbourne.

The old enmity between Anglicans and Nonconformists, once the excuse for bloodshed, found a new battleground in education. By 1805 Bromsgrove had acquired a British School allied with the Congregational Chapel, whose pupils were taught a view of religion that owed nothing to the State. In this time of accelerating social change a nonconformist education could so easily lead a young man into the mire of radical politics and disrespect for his superiors. Action was needed and the Church of England duly fought back with the National School Society, set up in 1811. Although this genuinely aimed to provide local schools on a modest fee-paying basis there was a strong and deliberate bias in the teaching – all were welcome but the flavour was strictly Anglican.

CHAPTER 6: THE SLEEPING CHURCH

Sunday scholars were naturally expected to attend church as well as school, but their position was a lowly one at best. Unruly and inattentive (and who could blame them), they were confined to the dark space under the sloping west gallery on a grandstand of tiered benches built in 1824, the underside of which formed Sexton Rose's snug *"dusthole"*. Here the children could cause the least disturbance to an almost invisible and inaudible service.[156] Their one recorded moment of real excitement in this dim spot came on a thundery day in June 1852, when a lightning strike on the tower during a service hit the metalwork of the clock, travelled down the weight casing and blew out the panelling below the gallery with a fearsome flash. Faced with an enormous cloud of dust, piles of splintered wood and hundreds of screaming children, the congregation panicked and ran terrified from the church, many of the children getting to the bottom of Crown Close before they were stopped. It was a miracle that no-one was seriously hurt, although many of the victims were still suffering from delayed shock two or three years afterwards. The tower had been struck twice before in recent years, in 1843 and 1846 but the threat to life this time was enough to prompt some action. A thanksgiving service for the safe delivery of the children was held the same night and a lightning conductor fitted a few weeks later.

Even before the cholera outbreak the cotton factory was recognised as an unsuitable venue for a school. An opportunity to build something new eventually presented itself when the churchwardens decided to rebuild the tumbledown town hall, over which they had jurisdiction. Why not combine the two functions in a single building? A committee was formed on 17th November 1830 with the vicar as chairman, but the idea quickly proved impracticable. The site was just too constricted and the idea was dropped within the month. Instead, the parish bought another parcel of the Crown Inn's extensive pleasure gardens just outside the churchyard in Crown Close. Mr Woodhouse turned in a design *"as*

---

[156] John Noake remarked that the sight reminded him of *"a pen of yearlings at an annual show"* (1848).

FAIRLY MOUNTED ON A HILL

plain as possible", Samuel Hartle of Birmingham and his men set to work with spade and trowel in June 1833 and a fine new National School costing £1,244 6s 6d opened its doors on Christmas Day the same year. The link with St John's was cemented when the Sunday School was formally joined to it on 31st January 1834. The number of children at both the Sunday and Day Schools grew rapidly, so much so that it threatened to overwhelm the parish's resources. A long series of fundraising Sermon Sundays was held between the mid 1840s and 50s to raise the necessary running costs, which rose from £240 a year in 1845 to £414 in 1857.

[Picture 18] Church and school in the late 19th century. Note the open aspect of Crown Close and the gate into the earth forecourt of the school. The new vicarage was built in 1848

Although the Great and the Good had brought the National School into being, the driving force behind the actual teaching was John Netherton Harward, an energetic curate. Harward's obvious worth was recognised on his departure in 1838 when the congregation presented him with a massive silver service, together with a handsome portable communion set from the Sunday School itself. But why was everything left to the curate? [157]

CHAPTER 6: THE SLEEPING CHURCH

The Case of the Vanishing Vicars

We have seen the churchwardens at work and heard how the sexton, the bellringers, the workmen, the cleaning ladies and even the nettle puller all made their own contribution to the life of St John's. But there is surely one person missing. Where is the vicar? Where are the Georgian equivalents of John Spilsbury, steering their congregation through the complexities of 18th century life? The answer is that they are somewhere else. John Waugh, vicar from June 1754 to December 1777, was the last 18th century vicar who actually lived in the vicarage, and for a period of nearly seventy years St John's had no resident incumbent. This may sound remarkable but it was sadly the norm for many provincial parishes at this time. From January 1778 to July 1846 a succession of underpaid curates conducted the services, baptised the newborn and buried the dead, while their absentee employers enjoyed the fruits of preferment in various grander or more lucrative benefices. The Honourable - and saintly - St Andrew St John, for instance, preferred being dean of Worcester Cathedral during his two year incumbency from 1786, while his successor, Thomas Fountaine, managed to carry out two other jobs during his 27 years, as Prebendary of Worcester and Chaplain-in-Ordinary to the ailing King George III.

But perhaps the most prominent practitioner was George Murray. The Murrays were hereditary Dukes of Atholl, and while the eldest son inherited the title second sons were destined either for the army or the church, preferably somewhere comfortable and not too demanding. Our George Murray was the eldest son of Lord George Murray, Bishop of St David's and the Third Duke's second son, and he was obviously pointed in the same direction as his father. While nominally vicar of St John's between 1827 and 1846 on a generous stipend of £1,100 a year he

---

[157] Harward moved to Seal (Kent), where his daughter was born the following year. He became domestic chaplain to the Bishop of Rochester in 1840 – for reasons that will soon become clear – and vicar of East Grinstead in 1848, where he spearheaded the building of another National School in 1860. His two sons had distinguished military careers.

was also Bishop of Rochester, Dean of Worcester and Rector of Bishopsbourne, a parish in Kent.[158]

Murray actually came to St John's under something of a cloud. Appointed Bishop of Sodor and Man in 1811 he had attempted to collect the long-abandoned tithe of turnips, potatoes and green vegetables from his rural diocese after the failure of the 1817 harvest, an act of such arrant insensitivity that the aggrieved and hungry locals promptly took him to court. He won the legal battle but had learned nothing and again tried to enforce the tithe in 1825, at which five thousand angry men took up bludgeons and marched on his house. Murray grudgingly relented on the green vegetables but the local were in no mood for mealy-mouthed half measures and the Prime Minister had to remove him from the see to avoid bloodshed. Where to put him though? Rochester is about as far from the Isle of Man as it is possible to be, and he duly became its bishop in 1827, the year he was also installed at St John's. Certainly, Murray does call in from time to time; he takes the Easter Vestry meetings, for example, and he is often on hand for important events. But he does not live here, which is perhaps just as well.

In these men's absence, the curates did what they could. But this is a socially stratified time, a snobbish time, and often the curate will not do, however good he is. Pity poor Robert Cottam, curate in 1810. He was obviously one those energetic men who made the mistake of thinking that his congregation wanted to be challenged and involved in their faith, an "enthusiast", in the language of the time. You can't blame him for trying, at least. He had the audacity, for example, to run a series of evening lectures in church, annoying Thomas Rose, who had to buy extra lamp oil.

---

[158] Before pluralism was abolished by the Cathedrals Measure of 1839 five vicars of Bromsgrove had also been Deans of Worcester, including Henry Holbeach, Thomas Warmestry, John Waugh, St Andrew St John and George Murray, of whom Holbeach and Murray were additionally Bishops of Rochester. Some form of preference was in operation but its exact nature is unclear.

CHAPTER 6: THE SLEEPING CHURCH

[Picture 19] The Hon. George Murray, Bishop of Rochester and vicar of St John's, photographed in 1859

FAIRLY MOUNTED ON A HILL

He removed the pulpit sounding board and its comical dove, no doubt the better to engage in his *"Calvinistic and extempory"* sermons with their unreasonable injunctions against drinking and swearing.[159] He went and removed the font (very Calvinist) but he also dared to replace the psalms with hymns on the new organ (not at all Calvinist). And – horrors – he had a boy read the lesson, when children properly belonged in Sunday School.

He does seem to have been popular with the lower orders, though. John Crane, a strict churchman and local poet, complained in one of his doggerel verses that the congregation had been turned *"religion mad"* and *"we moneyed men have all withdrawn"*, while *"the poor who learn at such a rate, can lay no shilling on the plate"*. Pointless teaching the poor, wasn't it, if they couldn't pay their way. Cottam had to go. A petition was got up, and nineteen of the most offended signed it. They make an interesting group: eight farmers and three nail masters comprise the upper echelons, while trade is represented by two victuallers, a skinner, a currier, a baker, a tailor and a blacksmith – not all "moneyed men" after all. There is also a solitary "no payer", presumably a genteel non-contributor to the collection. Even an absent vicar was better than a flesh-and-blood curate; and, faced with that level of opposition, poor enthusiastic Mr Cottam had little chance.[160]

This lack of respect for junior clergy could go to extremes, as the Revd Thomas Moore found out to his cost one day in 1839. Just six weeks into his curacy at St

---

[159] His style, apparently, was to preach without notes, looking round at his congregation and catching their eye, rather than reading a printed sermon. This was most unfair on the distracted and the slumberers.

[160] The curate John Goodwin had a similar experience under a later (resident) vicar. One day in the mid 1850s, the young George Fletcher overheard a lady discussing Goodwin's errors and omissions with his mother, who had made the mistake of praising the curate. *"Oh yes, Mrs Fletcher"*, the critic remarked, *"it is all very well to admire his preaching and his work. He is all very well for the afternoon service, for maidservants, shop girls and children. He may do for them, but to save the souls of the chief of the congregation and the upper classes, we must have the vicar"*. This may account for Goodwin's willingness to take up the post of vicar at the new church built at Lickey in 1856.

CHAPTER 6: THE SLEEPING CHURCH

John's under the absentee George Murray and with his predecessor curate's wife and furniture still in the vicarage, Moore was asked to chair a vestry meeting on 14th February to vote on a proposed church rate. Church rates were an archaic tax that church officials could impose on parish ratepayers to raise funds for church repairs and day to day church expenses. This arbitrary levy was calculated to annoy just about everyone: Anglican parishioners, who already contributed through service collections, Nonconformists, who had no reason to support a church they did not attend, and Catholics, who felt the Church of England had made their lives difficult enough without taxing them for the privilege. Together with the equally loathed tithes, these financial hangovers from the days of a single protestant church were now a source of bitter resentment to all but the most die-hard traditionalists.

Just after 10AM Moore strolled across to the church accompanied by the elderly Captain John Adams of Perry Hall. Although half an hour was normally allowed for the meeting to convene, Moore was surprised to find it already in progress and some 200 people crammed into or outside the small vestry. Fighting his way through the throng he heard the self-appointed chairman, a Mr Greening, propose adjourning to the much larger town hall, and a mass of people then left. Moore took the chair and adjourned the meeting proper to the new school, accompanied by the remaining sixty or seventy people and the four churchwardens. The chairman's desk was set up on the stepped staging of the main classroom and the motion was put to levy a church rate of one penny in the pound.

But the town hall meeting - illegal as it was - had built up a head of steam, and it had a spy in the other camp. Back at the school Nicholas Hill, churchwarden and publican, looked at a note he had just been passed and proposed an amendment. The vote was taken and the motion rejected.[161] Moore requested a show of hands

---

[161] A majority vote was legally necessary following the Braintree case of 1837, where a Church Rate had been set by a minority vote of the Braintree Vestry in Essex. After a long legal fight it was eventually declared illegal by the House of Lords.

on whether any rate should be set at all - and then everything seemed to happen at once. The room suddenly filled with four or five hundred people *"generally of the lower orders"* from the town hall meeting; Hill and another man, Joshua Crane, raised their hand as a signal and about fifty men rushed the chairman's desk. Crane shouted *"we will show you what physical force is"* and for the next eight minutes the room was in complete uproar. Hill lunged for the Minute book but Moore clung to it for dear life until Hill forced the curate's hand against the sharp edge of the desk and Moore released his grip. Henry Ellins, the senior churchwarden, piled in and he and Hill tumbled to the floor in a sprawl of flailing arms and legs. Ellins regained and lost the book – twice – at the cost of a repeated kicking and punches to his face. But they made churchwardens of tough stuff in those days and a battered Ellins finally got the book back and passed it into safe hands, although his coat had been ripped from his back in shreds.

Others fared no better. After unsuccessfully trying to strangle Moore, Samuel Taylor, a labourer, picked up poor old Captain Adams and threw him bodily over the crowd and down the staging. He was afterwards heard to say that he had ripped the old man's shirt but that *"he wished he could have ripped the b*****r's heart"*. Samuel Jones was dragged round the room and repeatedly kicked by twenty to thirty people before Thomas Smith, another churchwarden, pulled him free. Jones's legs were so badly swollen that he needed medical attention. Order was only restored when Constable Kings waded into the melee and slapped his handcuffs on Taylor, bringing St John's least successful St Valentine's Day to a blood-spattered close.

Moore had no option but to prosecute. Taylor, Hill, Crane and five others were hauled before the Summer Assize court at Worcester on a charge of riot, Hill and Taylor additionally being charged with assault on the curate. It did not take long to hear the testimony and everyone corroborated Moore's account. Hill, Crane,

CHAPTER 6: THE SLEEPING CHURCH

[Picture 20] St John's over the smoky rooftops of Worcester Street, some time in the early 20th century. The view in 1840 would have been little different

Taylor and three others were all found guilty of riot, Hill was also was found guilty of assault and all were sent up to the Queen's Bench for sentencing.

FAIRLY MOUNTED ON A HILL

Vestries all over the country were turning against church rates, often after pressure from Nonconformists, but a full-blown riot was in a different league altogether.[162] The defence Counsel made some unconvincing argument about Moore's ineligibility to chair the meeting - as he had yet to move into the vicarage - but the real reason for all the violence lay below the surface of the case. It was that word "riot"; for in the 1830s the English working class found its voice and began to flex its muscles. Six Dorset labourers had gained national fame in 1834 after being tried for combining in an illegal union at Tolpuddle; and in 1838 the Chartist movement produced a People's Charter with six basic political rights, backed by a massive petition. The Black Country was a Chartist stronghold and Birmingham's Bullring would see a major Chartist riot in July 1839. The country was awash with panicky rumours of insurrection, secret stocks of arms, factory burnings and other lawlessness. When Counsel for the prosecution asked Moore how many "black hands" had been raised for the vote, everyone knew what he meant, for only working men had black hands. To the average Bromsgrove parishioner this little altercation in the schoolroom was the very edge of revolution itself.

If any further excuse for a punch-up was needed the Birmingham and Gloucester Railway was building past Bromsgrove that year and the town's pubs were full of thirsty navvies. Just two months earlier a needle maker had been killed in a fight with navvies outside the Malt Shovel public house in Worcester Street. There were plenty of spare fists around if a mob was needed and church rates were a perfect excuse to give the Establishment a bloody nose – in this case, literally.[163] Moore may not have thought so but he was lucky to escape with his life.

---

[162] By 1859, 1525 parishes had voted against setting a Church Rate and it was effectively dead as a compulsory tax. After various unsuccessful attempts to change the law, Parliament finally abolished Church Rates in 1868.

[163] At a celebratory dinner for the Birmingham and Gloucester Railway workers on the bowling green of the Bell Inn in July 1840, the main speech included a sharp denunciation of church rates.

CHAPTER 6: THE SLEEPING CHURCH

There was one final insult to come. After defending his employer's livelihood so courageously Thomas Moore might have thought that the Revd George Murray would be suitably grateful – and he would have been wrong. Costs of the case were paid from a subscription led by a number of parishioners, but His Lordship the Bishop of Rochester and Perpetual Vicar of St John's Parish Church refused to subscribe.

[Picture 21] St John's on the eve of restoration, around 1840. Battlements have been added to the chancel and vestry since the 1812 view.

A Monument of Shame

Perhaps vicar and congregation deserved each other, for here we must face an uncomfortable truth. By the middle of the nineteenth century St John's had the entirely justified reputation as one of the least friendly churches in the district. Indeed, newcomers to the town were often warned away from it and advised to go to Tardebigge, three miles away across country. In the absence of strong leadership from the vicar, the churchwardens ruled the roost. They were legally responsible for seating the congregation by rank and station, and the early Victorian interior of St John's was laid out for the benefit of those who could pay most. Nearly all the decent seats were now either appropriated by individuals or families and were jealously guarded. One pew in the south aisle was permanently held by Townsend Farm, another by Boldings Farm and several by local inns, including the Dragon, Golden Lion and Crown. Other seats were rented out annually for a typical sum of 15s although the rate varied considerably according to location and comfort. The few that came up for sale were usually bought up by the same small circle of owner-occupiers. Mr Dunn was typical. Owning Pew No. 24 in the old south gallery, he was entitled to a seat in its 1824 replacement and duly took up Pew No. 16 on virtually the same spot. In 1838 he sold it to Luke Minshall. Minshall in turn sold or leased it in 1841 to John Pearce but had it back again by 1857. All these reserved pews considerably reduced the number of freely available seats. As most people only attended two services at most on a Sunday these seats stood empty for at least one service: family pews were especially bad in this respect. Although in theory all seats became free after the bell had been rung just before the start of the service, the public humiliation of being turned from a pew by the sexton as his paying customer arrived at the last minute was enough to dissuade most people from trying this hazardous manoeuvre.

It was certainly enough to dissuade John Noake. Researching his 1848 book, "The Rambler in Worcestershire", he happened upon a service at St John's and thought he'd join it.

CHAPTER 6: THE SLEEPING CHURCH

"I entered the church by the south door a few minutes after the commencement of divine service. No person having been appointed to attend to the accommodation of strangers – the church, bye the bye, not seeming to anticipate the entertainment of angels unawares – I stood, hat in hand, until the footman and housemaid of some genteel family, taking compassion on me, opened their seat, which was near the entrance door, and I took my place between them".

Noake draws a veil over the service itself, but then delivers his coup de grace:

"Now, let me ask, why is there so much hoggishness and discourtesy in churchmen, distaining even to share with a stranger a seat in the house of God – that place where all distinctions should cease in the presence of our common Father".

But Noake was in a minority. Hoggishness and discourtesy are not a good advertisement for any church and by the late 1840s St John's was really in a poor state - spiritually, socially and physically. Bashed about in pursuit of ever more pew space, its now-venerable fabric patched and re-patched against decay *"by the barbarous hands of vandal churchwardens"*, it was literally creaking at the seams. Pressing home his attack Noake thundered:

"The horrid barbarisms which have...been inflicted on this noble edifice by the hands of those to whose conservation it has been entrusted are a monument of shame to the perpetrators and, in my wrath, I had almost said a disgrace to the whole parish".[164]

With the 1840s we find St John's at its lowest ebb. Something Had To Be Done, and The Reverend Dr John Day Collis was the man to do it - but not just yet.

---

[164] Noake had a very low opinion of the regime at St John's although his informant was Joseph Rose, who did rather emphasise his own part in keeping the old place standing.

FAIRLY MOUNTED ON A HILL

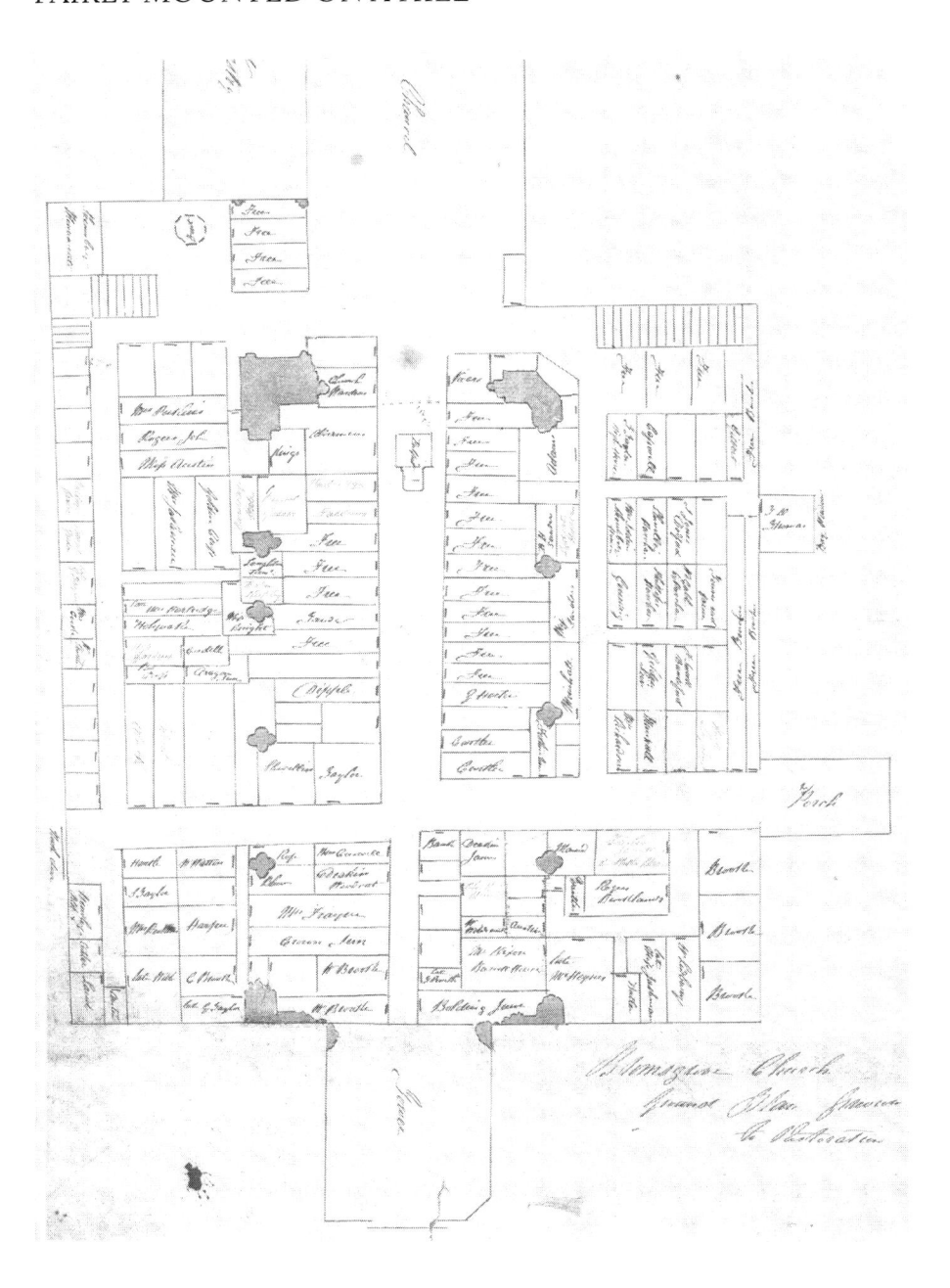

CHAPTER 6: THE SLEEPING CHURCH

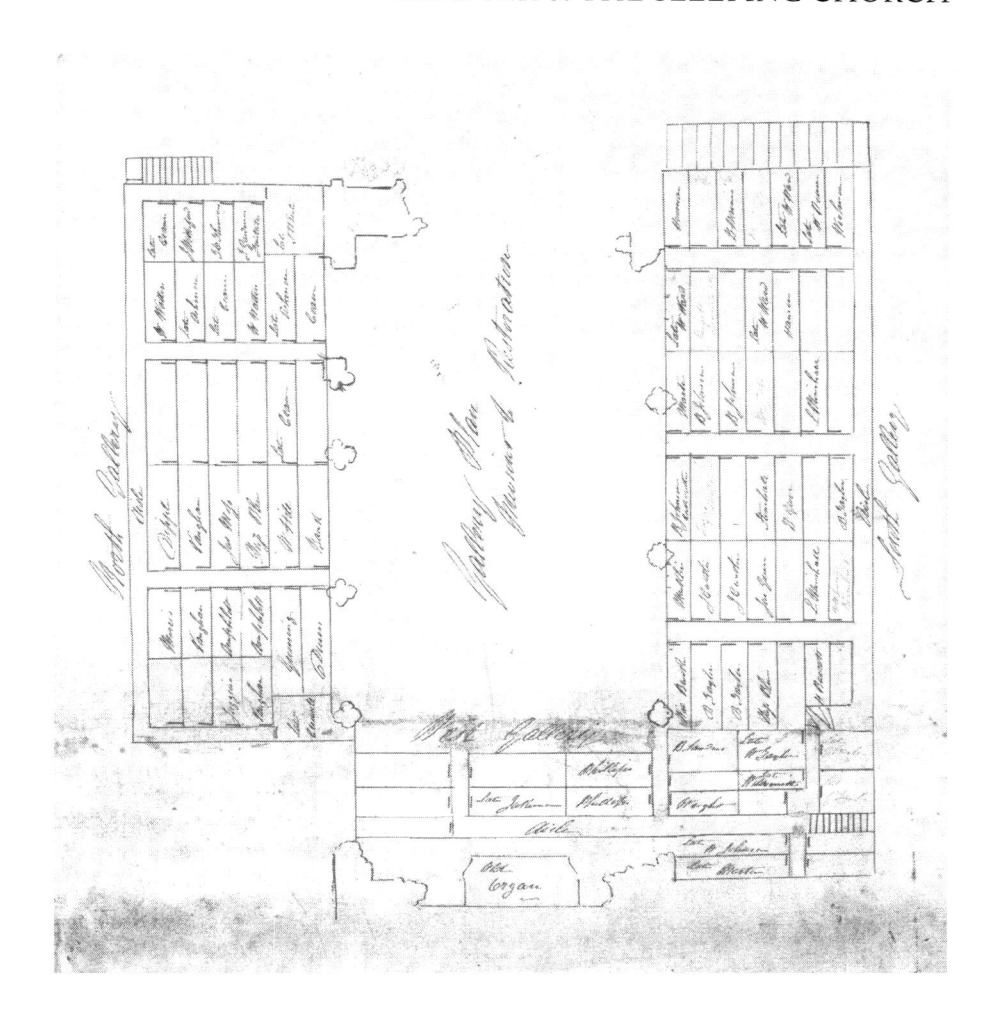

[Plans g and h] Pew rent plans from 1857, showing occupiers immediately before the 1858 restoration: east is at the top. Left – ground floor; Right - galleries

CHAPTER 7: A CHURCH RESTORED
The latter 19th Century

First Attempts

It is a cold January day in 1844 and the parish Vestry is gathered in the warmth of the rambling old vicarage at the foot of the church hill, its coats piled in the hallway and its snow-covered boots dripping in the porch. His Lordship, the Revd. George Murray, is presiding over a meeting, specially called to discuss the seating arrangements in the church. There is a problem. Despite the various improvements to the galleries, the old building still cannot accommodate the growing population of the town, as the Christmas services have just found. With so many of the good seats sold or rented out, there is now simply not enough room for all the nailer families and other parishioners too poor to secure a snug box pew and too loyal to succumb to the allure of Methodism.

The situation is not helped by the haphazard alterations to the pews in the main body of the church. Unlike the galleries, these pews have never been reordered. Instead, the old 1720 layout has been cut about, divided up and tunnelled into to form narrow alleyways leading to remote family enclaves that make a mockery of the ordered plan. Every inch of space is occupied, including Mr Thomas tucked into a snug little den in the monument bay. Like all problems at St John's, it generates a committee.

The church has some money, but it is not prepared to be too generous in such a utilitarian cause. A plain plan is called for and Henry Day, architect from Worcester,[165] provides it in unadorned deal panelling, at £800 all in. Two loans

CHAPTER 7: A CHURCH RESTORED

are applied for, £180 from the Diocesan Church Building Society and £100 from the Incorporated Church Building Society.[166] Not everyone likes the idea though. It is mean-spirited for a start, and it does not address the larger problems of the ramshackle old building. The faculty, the all-important diocesan planning permission, is opposed and the project grinds to a halt. George Murray loses interest. He has more important things to do and heads back down to Rochester.

Time passes. William Villers is a different kind of vicar, and the church he belongs to is itself changing. The rise of the Oxford Movement in the 1830s, with its emphasis on eucharistic liturgy, ornament and other supposedly lost traditions of the reformed church created a new interest in medieval church layouts. Whatever Viller's own leanings are to start with he sees the battered shell of St John's as a challenge.[167] Villers moves into the vicarage on 20th July 1846 - the first vicar to do so for 68 years - and almost immediately sets about changing things. He starts at home, for the rambling old building is on its last legs. Size notwithstanding, its age and bucolic appearance is unsuited to a modern man with reforming ideals.[168] So Henry Day is called in again, down comes the old building in 1848 and a rather handsome Tudor-style villa rises on the hill behind it, with a neat double frontage enlivened by Dutch-gabled bays and a pretty leaded glass oriel window over the front door.

---

[165] Day was also the architect for the new church of Holy Trinity, Lickey, built in 1856.

[166] They rejected it, as they were to do with several subsequent applications.

[167] It would be surprising if Villers were a rabid Ecclesiologist as he was appointed by Bishop Pepys, a rigid Evangelical who was open in his condemnation of everything the Oxford Movement stood for. One suspects that Villers was leant on by others, as we shall see.

[168] This was not untypical of the county's parsonages, and it may account for the reluctance of previous vicars to reside here. After visiting Worcestershire in 1826 the irascible William Cobbett observed that *"more than one half of the parishes have either no parsonage-houses at all, or have not one that a parson thinks fit for him to live in.... Is not this a monstrous shame? The parsons get the tithes and the rent of the glebe lands, and the parsonage-houses are left to tumble down, and nettles and brambles to hide the spot where they stood."*

FAIRLY MOUNTED ON A HILL

[Picture 22] William Villers' new vicarage, photographed c1910

Cheap pine may do for the church but the vicar needs solid oak. At the same time, Parson's Hill is diverted north through Crown Close, reuniting the vicarage with its now-private garden. There is a price to pay for all this elegance, of course. Most of the £1800 cost must be borrowed from the Queen Anne's Bounty[169] and succeeding vicars will have to pay it back in instalments over the next thirty years.

At the same time, Villers starts thinking about the church itself. With the vicarage under way, he forms a new committee, this time to make the church fit for modern worship. Henry Day is brought in yet again and a more ambitious plan emerges. This time, the whole ground floor will be re-pewed, the north gallery will be extended into the chantry chapel and the late 12th century north transept arch in the north arcade will be entirely reconstructed over a wider span incorporating

---
[169] An Anglican central fund for supporting poor clergy, set up by Queen Anne in 1704 out of the former papal taxes on parishes, the so-called *"first fruits and tenths"*.

CHAPTER 7: A CHURCH RESTORED

the adjacent solid pier, in order to improve sightlines from the lengthened gallery.[170]

[Picture 23] The rather dashing William Villers

---
[170] The Incorporated Church Building Society did not like this proposal either, and refused a grant.

FAIRLY MOUNTED ON A HILL

But down the Worcester Road a separate problem is converging on St John's. Bromsgrove School, founded out of the residue of Alianora Stafford's old chantry, has traditionally used St John's as its chapel and at times contributes a sizeable percentage of the congregation, overwhelming the free seats. Just three years later, the National Census of Religious Worship will record an attendance at morning worship on 30th March of an enormous 850 adults and 470 scholars. Afternoon worship is even more evenly balanced; 500 adults and 505 scholars. The only respite is Evening Prayer, attracting a mere 750 adults (a low estimate, apparently) and no scholars at all - perhaps Bromsgrove School is at tea.

Enter John Day Collis, an energetic and forceful Irishman, ordained clergyman and Headmaster of Bromsgrove School from 1847. Collis is no stranger to church building projects. A founder member of the Oxford Architectural Society in 1838 he has cut his teeth overseeing the design and construction of a new church for his father's parish in Kilconnell, Co. Galway, in 1842, and he will later help to set up the Worcester Diocesan Architectural Society in 1854.[171] His Ecclesiology is practical as well as spiritual, scholarly as well as emotional. As far as St John's is concerned however, his most pressing need is more space for his pupils. He therefore proposes a radical solution: an entirely new aisle, extending the existing south aisle eastwards almost the length of the chancel, to which it will be joined by an arcade. Seating a hundred boys and masters, it is to be called the King Edward Chapel and will be appropriated to the school. This is too much for some of the regulars. St John's is already a big, difficult church in which to conduct services and sermons are barely audible in the further recesses, sounding board or no. Assigning a special part of the church to grammar school boys who will not be

---

[171] The predecessor of the present Diocesan Advisory Committee, who oversee all alterations to church buildings.

[172] Collis had already funded the replacement of the font in August 1847, although he had to be content with leaving it in the gloom of the chantry chapel. It was restored to a more liturgically sound location near the nave crossing during the restoration, and then to the west end of the north aisle baptistery, where it remains.

CHAPTER 7: A CHURCH RESTORED

contributing to the general upkeep is anathema to certain sections of the congregation. Notwithstanding Collis's offer to raise £500 towards the cost, the Faculty is never lodged and the idea is dropped.[172]

Spurned by St John's, Collis goes it alone. *"In May 1850, despairing of any immediate prospect of an improvement in the church"*, he tells us, *"I commenced collecting funds for building a Chapel for the Grammar School"*. He works fast. The first stone is laid on the 19th June and the first service is held on the 22nd November the same year. The whole building costs £1100. Piqued or not, Collis shows just what he can do if given free rein.

Third Time Lucky

Time passes, churchwardens change and a new spirit enters the church. Perhaps William Villers feels more sure of himself now and able to stand up to the pessimists and the pew renters. In September 1856, Collis learns that the vicar and churchwardens are seriously thinking of a proper restoration of the church - as opposed to merely a reordering - and he drops them a line, *"touching upon the various points which seemed to require alteration and amendment in the Church"*. From what we know of previous reactions to Collis' proposals, we can imagine its authoritative, if not authoritarian, tone.

But Collis knows his church architecture. He has a vision of a church restored to the condition at its medieval apogee in 1500 - chaste, Gothic and Eucharistic. He advocates *"a conservative restoration"*, one which preserves its historic features of St John's, and he knows just who to use. Collis recommends George Gilbert Scott, probably the most famous and prolific Victorian architect, champion of the Gothic revival and designer and restorer of countless churches. Scott is currently working on the Home and Colonial Offices in Whitehall and will go on to design the Albert Memorial, St Pancras Station and Glasgow University, as

217

well as restore Worcester Cathedral and Pershore Abbey. But his bread and butter is parish churches. His large drawing office can handle numerous projects at the same time, each of which will bear his professional and scholarly, if rather well scrubbed, stamp. He has the same Ecclesiological vision as Collis; indeed, they probably already know each other.

The inevitable committee is inaugurated in the town hall on 4th December, chaired by the vicar, with Collis as co-secretary and a membership comprising the big names of mid-19th century Bromsgrove; Horton, Day, Housman, Maund and Sanders among them. Scott inspects the church on the 17th of the month and submits his report, together with his proposals for restoring it, although this very rapid action hints that Collis may have jumped the gun and tipped the architect off in advance. The committee approve the plan on the 15th April 1857, albeit with some omissions. Scott wants to remove all the galleries and reinstate the medieval openness of the aisles. The committee are more concerned at the apparent loss of seating than the purity of restored Gothic architecture and wish to keep Rickman's south gallery, the best of the three and the proposed location for the free seating. Scott accedes to their wishes but keeps his powder dry, for his experienced eye can see what the committee cannot.

Scott in Action

The contract is let to William Cooper, of Normanton Works, Derby in August 1857 at a cost of £2,800, with Scott's able Clerk of Works, Mr W. Prosser, on hand to check that the quality is to his master's satisfaction. To avoid having the church out of use over Christmas, Cooper starts work on Monday, 28th December. The parishioners move into Collis' new Bromsgrove School Chapel[173] and Cooper

---

[173] For the main services. The early and weekday services were held on the upper floor of the National School. Weddings by law had to be held in the church and the foreman sounded a gong for silence during the solemnisation of vows. The no- doubt relieved couple then signed the register in the vestry and left by the vestry door, while work resumed in the church.

CHAPTER 7: A CHURCH RESTORED

starts by ripping out the box pews and taking down the tattered old north gallery. The church immediately looks better. Scott's earlier advice is proved right, as he always knew, and a meeting is hastily convened on the 4th February to agree the removal of the south gallery as well: the free seats can go in the cold, dark north aisle instead. A similar effect is produced when Cooper pulls the plaster ceiling off the nave roof and exposes the 15th century timber trusses, complete with traces of coloured decoration on the easternmost. The thick layers of whitewash and plaster are stripped from the walls with metal scrapers, exposing the last vestiges of the old Doom painting, albeit too fragmentary to keep.

But all this pulling down has a less welcome aspect, for it exposes just how poor the underlying condition of the church actually is. So severely have the column capitals been cut back to take the gallery beams that the north arcade is barely standing. The chancel arch north pier, weakened by the medieval insertion of the rood loft staircase, is subsiding, the south wall stonework is crumbling and there are no foundations to speak off anywhere, apart from the tower. Collis shows his powers of persuasion. He convinces the committee to increase their fundraising rather than cut back the restoration, work proceeds and the nave floor rapidly becomes one great masons' shed.

The whole church must first be stabilised. Eighteen inch deep concrete underpinning is inserted to all the external walls at an extra cost of £100 and the external ground level is lowered round the church, to reduce the ingress of damp and restore the original wall height. The rood loft stairway is filled solid with mortared stone rubble to stabilise the pier and the top and bottom doors are re-opened, although now unusable. Other original features can then be reinstated. The medieval roof and its decorations are restored; rotted rafters are replaced and new bosses, spandrel brackets and corbels carved, using fragments of the original as a pattern.

FAIRLY MOUNTED ON A HILL

The butchered north transept arch is carefully propped and its lost inner order of stonework and corbels are replaced,[174] as are the capitals and mouldings to all the other arches in the arcade, complete with rather pious carved heads for label stops, carved by a Mr Irving. The two semi-circular openings in the adjacent solid pier are replaced with one of Scott's few conceits at St John's, a pretty little cusped Gothic arch of a type more akin to window tracery. The north aisle windows are taken back to their supposed original condition, pointed to either side of the north door and square in the Stafford Chantry, using the surviving easternmost window as a template. The south aisle windows are built up to their original cill height and the horrid doorway to the south gallery is infilled, as is the circular window over the north door. The window tracery is restored and all the windows are reglazed with Hartley's Rolled Cathedral Glass in diamond quarries.

The lowered belfry platform is taken out, exposing at last the full beauty of the great west window, and is reinstated at its medieval level on a beamed oak floor. New ceilings of stained and varnished red fir replace their plain plaster predecessors in both aisles and a panelled and planked oak ceiling in the chancel follows the line of the east window. The floor also receives attention, as centuries of family vaults are hygienically sealed below a concrete slab, while the vaults under the 14th century chantry chapel are rebuilt to suit the more mundane function of boiler room.[175] In the process, some of the medieval encaustic tiles are found and Collis pockets one as a souvenir.

The walls themselves need patching, inside and out. Much of the north arcade walling at the east end has to be refaced and other areas are individually pieced in.

---

[174] Scott preserved three courses of old masonry in the eastern respond of this arch to affirm the original profile.

[175] George Fletcher remembered an internment below the north aisle floor in the 1850s, directly outside the door to the family pew. The hazard to health was well acknowledged at the time. Only three floor slabs were left exposed at the foot of the chancel steps, commemorating Samuel Smart (died 19th March 1732), Peter Capelin (died 17th July 1700) and a third now indecipherable stone.

CHAPTER 7: A CHURCH RESTORED

[Picture 24] The restored church, looking west from the Chancel. The choir stalls were later altered. A corner of the new organ is just visible in the Chantry Chapel

FAIRLY MOUNTED ON A HILL

Those anachronistic battlements are removed from the chancel and vestry and the original eaves line reinstated, while pinnacles are replaced on the parapets and two gargoyles renewed on the tower. The medieval priest's door in the chancel south wall is replaced with something rather more Gothic. Finally, the old lime mortar is raked out and the soft sandstone walls are re-pointed in hard Portland cement, a mistake that has cost St John's dear ever since.

Once restoration is complete, the beautification can begin. Handsome oak pews with chestnut seats fill the floor space, naturalistic foliage individually carved into every pew end. Two rows of choir seats to a more elaborate pattern line the chancel. A panelled oak screen keeps the draughts from the reinstated west door off the rather more spartan children's seats under the tower, while blue and red Staffordshire quarry tiles enliven the aisle floors. New oak doors are fitted to every opening except, curiously, the north door, which remains blocked. More oak goes into the new altar, pulpit and reading desk, while a rather dour Ancaster stone reredos with marble shafts and alabaster panels featuring yet more pious heads replaces the old oak reredos, which Collis purchases as an honours board for his school library.[176] Oak and iron altar rails, and an altar cloth donated by Collis, complete the sanctuary.

Stained glass will appear in instalments over the next forty years but Collis starts the process by donating the north aisle east window (since moved to the clerestory) and Benjamin Maund funds two windows by Clayton and Bell in the chancel, in memory of members of his family. Scott reinstates the fragmentary decorations on the two easternmost roof trusses, adding a verse from Matthew's Gospel on the first to reflect the stark choice illustrated by the old Doom painting: *"Come ye blessed of my Father"* it reads; *"depart from me ye accursed"*. And on the second beam Scott (or is it Collis?) adds what might be the Ecclesiologists motto: *"Worship the*

---

[176] One of Scott's few mistakes, the new screen was too high and obscured the bottom of the east window. It was cut down early in the 20th Century.

222

CHAPTER 7: A CHURCH RESTORED

Lord in the beauty of Holiness", for a beautiful church was a holy church. The old organ goes out with its gallery and the table monuments in the chantry chapel are moved yet again to accommodate a fine new instrument by John Nicholson of Worcester costing £335. Nicholson, a Rochdale man, is building up what will rapidly become a major business and a Nicholson organ is a sign that the church is bang up to date.

For this is the 19th century, a modern, technological time, and candlepower will not light the now cavernous interior, nor will coal stoves heat it. This is the age of the engineer, and Francis Skidmore from Coventry supplies very elegant brass gas lighting standards for the nave and chancel, with 24 and 16 jets each respectively.[177] Mr Harper from Birmingham fits a clever heating system that generates hot air from a boiler in the vestry basement and blows it the length of the nave and aisles, before releasing it through cast iron floor grates. Clever it may be, but it never works properly and it will claim a man's life before long.

For the moment, however, Collis's dream is fulfilled. He has brought a church back from the brink of disintegration at a total cost of £5,396, and the town is grateful to him.[178] All but £678 has been raised by the time the church is reopened for Divine Service on Thursday, the 27th January 1859, when 68 clergy process in full vestments into the church and the bishop of Worcester preaches the first sermon. Seven further dedicatory services follow, each with a different preacher. Collis is fourth, taking the morning service on the following Sunday, two ahead of the vicar. He uses the opportunity for a theological explanation of dedication ceremonies, a highly selective romp through English history, an advertisement

---

[177] Francis Skidmore was a noted craft metalworker and longstanding collaborator with Scott, as might be expected from his membership of both the Ecclesiological Society and the Oxford Architectural Society. Skidmore also produced gas lighting standards for several churches in Coventry, as well as elaborate chancel screens for Lichfield and Hereford cathedrals.

[178] Unlike the former incumbent. Collis failed to get a penny from the Bishop of Rochester, who refused even to reply to Collis's letters.

for the Oxford Movement, a financial breakdown of the restoration costs, an appeal for more money and a rather pointed plea in favour of 10% alms-giving. Laced with Biblical references and rounded off with a poem, this is a fine compendium of High Church beliefs and leaves little else to be said.[179] Alfred Palmer, one of the churchwardens on the committee and Bromsgrove's printer, publishes the sermon and sells it in aid of the restoration. The diocese is also pleased. Scott's involvement has saved the day, as the Worcestershire Diocesan Architectural Society notes at its 1858 Annual General Meeting. And as the Worcestershire Diocesan Architectural Society now has the bishop's remit to vet all proposed church building plans, this is an official imprimatur of Ecclesiological correctness, a Victorian vision of the perfect medieval church.

The Past Described

John Day Collis starts something else too, for the description of the church's physical development appended to his printed sermon is the first proper analysis of the building as a work of architecture. Despite his Victorian penchant for ascribing strict dates to architectural styles, he puts the various parts of the church in order and shows its development from Early English roots to a Tudor completion. Previous histories had concentrated largely on "antiquities", tombs or charters. Collis shows the merits of the building itself. His short description is effectively the first guidebook, catering for the interested tourist and setting the scene for numerous successors.[180]

---

[179] Collis's obituary in the Messenger commented; *"as a preacher he was forceful and plainly spoken; too plainly spoken in fact, we may say, to suit the tastes of many of his congregation"*.

[180] William Cotton uses Collis's description of the restoration almost verbatim in his account of the church in 1881.

CHAPTER 7: A CHURCH RESTORED

[Picture 25] The restored church looking east. Note the painted roof trusses and relocated font. This and the previous view were produced as coloured prints for sale to support the restoration

And the church Collis describes is one we can now recognise, for it differs very little from the present day. St John's earlier incarnations may seem strange to us – incense-smoked and brightly painted, or stripped and whitewashed – but we are on reassuringly familiar ground now. Our image of St John's is John Day Collis', William Villers' and George Gilbert Scott's - which is fine, as long as we do not forget that it is just an image, created to meet the needs and fashions of its own time. It is no more "authentic" than John Spilsbury's or Richard Harforde's or William of Avignon's St John's, and it challenges us to ask what image of this ancient building best suits the present day.

The Challenge

Collis could restore the church but he found it rather more difficult restoring the congregation to match it. The Ecclesiologists assumed that Gothic architecture and eucharistic ceremony would induce *"true religion"* in its participants but it would take more than a few pointed arches to overcome two centuries of entrenched low churchmanship in Bromsgrove. For this was still a church divided, and its divisions did no more than reflect the polarisation of Victorian society in general - rich or poor, High or Low, Whig or Tory, establishment or dissenter, reformer or reactionary. The Established Church was merely one of many arenas in which the clash of cultures was played out, but the divisions were hardly clear cut. It was quite possible to be a social radical and a High Churchman, or a Tory and a dissenter, and the challenges faced by the congregation of St John's as the century advanced challenged both individual consciences and the very purpose of this ancient hilltop church.

If the congregation thought that William Villers was a High Churchman, it received a nasty shock when a new curate arrived to support the elderly and increasingly unwell vicar early in 1860. Charles Jenner was a strong-minded Oxford Movement man, and he immediately set about imposing his own

CHAPTER 7: A CHURCH RESTORED

uncompromising version of High Churchmanship on a forewarned and wary congregation. Jenner started by abolishing the mixed choir and substituting one composed solely of men and boys.[181] The bridgehead established, he next put them all in surplices and made them chant – rather than say – the psalms and prayers. The congregation were next. They now had to stand when the clergy entered, bow every time the name of Jesus was mentioned and face east at all times. And as a final touch Jenner donned a white surplice himself, covering the traditional protestant black Geneva gown with a tauntingly Catholic mantle. This was just too much. But a hastily convened meeting of parishioners in the town hall degenerated into an undignified hurling of sectarian taunts - *"No Popery... Jesuits in disguise... Pope of Rome"* and so on - interspersed with various cries of *"shut up"* and *"sit down"*; and failed actually to decide anything. Others voted with their feet. Churchwarden Thomas White got up, took his hat and books and walked slowly and deliberately down the centre aisle whenever Jenner got up to preach. He eventually refused to attend St John's at all while Villers remained vicar. Mr White notwithstanding, Charles Jenner seems to have been popular with many, *"a thoroughly kind-hearted gentleman, rather inclined to be stout, very fair and...a pleasant smile"*, as George Fletcher recalled.[182]

If Popish curates weren't bad enough, the old bugbear of pew rents reared its ugly head again. Anxious not to lose their established privileges, the pew owners had insisted on a plan of the existing arrangement being made before the church was restored. These two drawings show just how difficult it was going to be to accommodate the inhabitants of the coveted galleries in those shiny new oak

---

[181] This may have been a mercy. In 1848 John Noake observed that Bromsgrove's choir had once been famous but *"times are changed and singers, like other mortals, change with them. A more efficient musical corps is amongst the 150 things I have to recommend to the worthy vicar for adoption."*

[182] The reaction against the Oxford Movement reached its low point with the Public Worship Regulation Act of 1874, which made it an offence to use proscribed ornament, vesture or ritual. Five clergy were imprisoned under the Act, including Richard Enraght, vicar of Holy Trinity, Bordesley, Birmingham, in 1880. It was only repealed in 1965, although prosecutions ceased in 1906.

benches on the ground floor, with nothing to separate them from the unwashed masses in the adjacent free seats. The old church could hold 1350 parishioners, although the family pews were often half empty. The restorers reasoned that by allowing one seat per person in the new pews, the overall number of seats could be reduced to 1050 and the galleries could therefore be removed.

However reasonable an assumption it did not account for the sheer cussedness of certain sections of the congregation. Although removal of the box pews allowed outright ownership to be abolished, parishioners could still rent a pew for themselves or their family on an annual, renewable basis, allocated by the rentals committee. Pew owners like Thomas White had simply swapped their appropriated pews for the same number of rented seats, in his case three of each. Despite the allocation of the entire north aisle to free seating the demand for rented pews was so great that incursions were made, and the number of free seats actually dropped from 630 before the restoration to 350 in 1861.

There was outcry on both sides. George Fletcher's grandfather refused to contribute to the restoration appeal on the grounds that he had lost a pew worth £50 without any compensation. Another traditionalist threatened to take the churchwardens to court for disturbing him in the use of *"his"* pew, while the more progressive members of the congregation simply stayed away in protest. *"The church is totally inadequate to the spiritual wants of the parish"*, noted John Noake on a second visit in 1868; *"and yet it has scarcely ever a crowded or even moderately full congregation. This arises from absenteeism occasioned by the objectors to the allotment of seats"*. Collis and Villers saw their vision of a free and open church crumble before their eyes. Villers even resorted to printing a leaflet pleading for free seating, but to little avail. He died a year later and his successor, the Revd G.W.Murray – a relative of the absentee George Murray – blocked further freeing of seats. Bearing in mind that the same man also refused to support the local nail-

CHAPTER 7: A CHURCH RESTORED

makers when they struck for decent wages in 1863 it is hardly surprising that regular congregations dwindled to three or four hundred over the following years.[183] It was even claimed that the new nonconformist Hephzibah Chapel then being built in Birmingham Road was necessitated by the dissent in the parish church, and St John's unwelcoming reputation put down strong new roots.

St John's in the 1860s was an perhaps an extreme example of a common problem, as reforming clergy tried to overcome centuries of established practice by bringing rich and poor together in common worship. Rich and poor had so far kept themselves decently apart, preserving a social order that depended for its survival on both sides knowing their places in life and not transcending them. But not everyone was content to sit back. The Free and Open Church Association formally entered the fray in 1865, backed by no less than thirty-three bishops throughout the world-wide Anglican Communion[184] with a radical agenda to promote free seating, weekly plate offerings and all-week opening. Determined to root out *"class distinctions in the House of God"*, the "Free and Open" provided leaflets, newsletters, financial grants and guidance on every aspect of its aims - including how to influence the election of sympathetic churchwardens - and it acted as a catalyst for change in churches up and down the land.

The wave broke over Bromsgrove the very next year, when the town's young newspaper became the battleground in a vigorous debate between the free-seaters and the pew renters, with no holds barred. John Day Collis was in there, of course, fighting for his vision of a church free for all, but he had some stiff opposition. *"Paterfamilias Indignans"*, a furious and wisely anonymous pew renter, lambasted one poor supporter of free seating with a particularly vitriolic response

---

[183] He told them that he was more interested in their immortal souls than their bodily needs. Nonetheless George Fletcher considered G.W.Murray *"as near perfection as a human being could be as Vicar of a parish... [with] a heart full of Christian feeling"*. Good or bad, it all depended where one stood on churchmanship.

[184] But not, alas, the Bishop of Worcester.

FAIRLY MOUNTED ON A HILL

that inadvertently betrayed every Establishment fear. *"The rich have souls as well as those below them"*, he thundered:

"...and if your correspondent thinks he will drive us, by his ill-written and ungrammatical letter out of church to make room for a pack of labourers in smock frocks or artisans in fustian jackets, all I can say is that he is very much mistaken. Does he mean to say that the bettermost classes, wives, daughters and all, are to be thrust into holes and corners to make room for a rabble? I should like to know if the clergy would wish to see all the respectable people driven from the church, or if they would like to minister exclusively to the poor and ignorant and never see a decent bonnet, or a lady's face in front of them."

A bonnet-less church packed with the poor and ignorant may seem the very place most in need of Christian ministry but not, apparently, in Bromsgrove. The Revd G.W.Murray thought so too. The debate raged for most of the year but the vicar blocked any further action and St John's returned to its well-upholstered slumber. Visitors continued to be ejected rudely from allotted seats, *"right and left"*, according to one account. Stories abounded. Mr Lewis was thrown out of a free seat by a lady who insisted it was hers by right, the vicar's own cousin, on a rare visit to St John's, was asked to move after only five minutes; and another visiting clergyman was apparently turned from his pew by a little girl. It's a wonder that the church had any congregation at all.[185]

And these deep divisions persisted beyond death itself. The old churchyard had been filled to rather more than its limit for a number of years and the expanding town desperately needed a large new site for its departed souls. The town's local board purchased an open site immediately opposite the churchyard across Church Lane, laid out an expansive sward of paths and trees in 1857 and closed the church and churchyard to all new burials. But however attractive it was,

---

[185] Collis left Bromsgrove in 1867 to take up the incumbency of Holy Trinity, Stratford.

CHAPTER 7: A CHURCH RESTORED

some of the longer-established families insisted on keeping their link with the past. When George Fletcher's grandfather died not long after the new cemetery opened his body was interred in the new cemetery, rather than with his wife and daughters in the churchyard as the family had wished. Fletcher told his uncle, who remembered that a churchwarden's daughter had been buried in the family vault two years after the old yard had been closed. Incensed at this double standard, he fought the authorities up to Home Office level for permission to transfer the body. He eventually won his case and the old man was discreetly reburied one midnight.

Filthy Lucre

The diocese was no better. Since Saxon days, bishops had carried out annual visitations of the parishes in their diocese to assess how well each parish was being managed by its incumbent. As the number of parishes grew through the Middle Ages, this task was transferred to archdeacons, each of whom had a share of the diocese under their care. Churchwardens were responsible for presenting a report on the parish in a standard format drawn up by the bishop, the so-called articles of enquiry. To save the archdeacon and his entourage from having to travel to every last country church, the visitations were usually held in a conveniently central parish. When the archdeacon's annual visitation for 1859 was held at St John's, the diocesan registrar set himself up in the Shoulder of Mutton inn at the bottom of the church steps and attempted to extract a customary but totally illegal fee for each presentment from the churchwardens. The St John's wardens apparently acquiesced but William Wigginton and James Millward from St Edmund's, Dudley were made of sterner stuff. To Wigginton, an architect by profession, these fees were just *"the getting together of filthy lucre to enrich the pockets of the Bishop's followers"*. They had already challenged the registrar the previous year and were now prepared to fight. Asked to pay £1 13s 7½d, they proffered the correct nominal fee of 4d, and exhorted the other churchwardens present to do likewise, threatening the registrar with *"a perfect tornado of fourpenny pieces"*. The registrar confiscated Wigginton and Millward's Presentment documents but then sprinted up the church steps to inform the archdeacon before the rebels could bend his ear. Wigginton and the other wardens arrived to find the service to which they had been invited in full swing, and no mention of the incident in the archdeacon's address. When business resumed back at the inn after the service, Wigginton found the archdeacon sitting alongside the registrar, ineffectually trying to find a compromise that the now-furious churchwarden would accept. Wigginton held his ground, cited canon law, case law, natural law, precedent, practice and any other legal bludgeon he could lay his hands on and simply wore them all down. He knew his rights, rights that had been upheld successfully by other churchwardens in other parishes, and he went into print – at some considerable length – to make sure that no-one missed the point. It looks as if the diocese capitulated, for we hear no more about visitation fees at Bromsgrove.

A Voice From The Grave

In removing the galleries Scott's restoration had one entirely unexpected consequence in which another ordinary Bromsgrove citizen – and an old tomb - played a pivotal part. In 1856 the direct line of the Talbot family had become extinct on the death of Bertram Arthur, Earl of Shrewsbury and several claimants came forward to contest the title as well as the considerable estate that went with it. Strongest by far was the Right Honourable Henry John Chetwynd, Earl Talbot, a descendent of old Sir John Talbot's second wife, Elizabeth Wrottesley - or so he claimed. His task however lay in finding conclusive proof of a Wrottesley link and on the 13th July 1857 the case came before the Parliamentary Committee of Privileges, Lord Redesdale presiding. Lined up against Chetwynd was an exotic assembly of hopeful counter-claimants, including William Talbot of County Wexford, Lord Edmund Bernard Fitzalan Howard, the Duke and Duchess of Sora and the exotically titled Prince and Princess Doria Pamphili.[186] None however

CHAPTER 7: A CHURCH RESTORED

could wield the knighted legal clout that Chetwynd mustered - a four-man team led by Sir Frederick Thesiger and Sir FitzRoy Kelly - although they put up a good fight, as anyone hoping to acquire one of the richest titles in England might well do.

The court sat through days and days of interminable and ancient wills, indentures, parish records and family trees, all read out in full and frequently in dense legal Latin. A search through the places where Talbots had lived over the centuries led eventually to Bromsgrove, and to Sir John Talbot's tomb in the chantry chapel of St John's church. The court knew that Thomas Habington's mid 17th century description of the Talbot monument recorded both a Latin and an English inscription round its perimeter but although the latter included a unique reference to Elizabeth Wrottesley, Habington's handwritten account was considered inadmissible in court. First hand evidence was needed and Henry Barrett of Minshall and Sanders, solicitors of Bromsgrove, was dispatched to the church with orders to see what he could decipher. Barratt soon found a problem. In the two hundred years since Habington's visit someone had quite deliberately ground off the English inscription and painted over its former place, erasing it from sight and memory. Who could have done so? The court never found out but someone had obviously wanted to muddy the ancestral waters at some time, most probably in the mid 18th century. To compound the problem the monument was now crammed against the north gallery stairs, making it impossible even to see where the inscription had started.

Enter Samuel Clarkson, painter and gilder of Bromsgrove. Under Barrett's direction, Clarkson very, very carefully applied a potent solution of American potash and quicklime to the caked-on paint, quickly washing it off the delicate alabaster as soon as the paint came loose. Underneath lay the ghost of an

---

[186] The palazzo Doria Pamphili is on the southern outskirts of Rome. Their connection with the Talbots is unclear.

233

inscription, very faint but just discernible if the painter tilted his candle at the right angle. Clarkson was enough of an artist to sketch out the tomb and as much of the inscription as was visible, and he travelled to London with Barrett to present this to the court. Tantalising as it was, the court needed more, and the removal of the north gallery later that year provided it. With the end of the Talbot monument free of obstruction Clarkson returned to his task, copied out the remainder and in May 1858 he again took the train south. Poor man: Samuel Clarkson was just an ordinary tradesman, no doubt skilled at his job but hardly a verbal foil for knighted barristers. They pulled him every which way, casting doubt on his drawing ability, criticising his choice of paint-stripper, tripping him up over the minutiae of his earlier evidence, questioning his memory and snapping – *"give me an Answer to my Question"* – when the painter stumbled over their convoluted and repetitive lines of enquiry.

Clarkson held his own though, answering as truthfully as he could, and in the end his simple straightforward statements of fact were enough. The court accepted that the inscription was genuine and Chetwynd won his title, proving yet again that blood was rather thicker than water - or paint.

A People's Church

If our picture of late Victorian St John's seems rather mixed, this is perhaps more a reflection of a vocal minority than the congregation as a whole. And for these die-hard reactionaries time, like the century, was running out. Under the surface, good things were happening. We can now see through eyes other than the churchwardens, for in 1866 St John's started publishing a monthly parish magazine that painted a far more rounded picture of the Victorian church. Like most early parish magazines this consisted of a commercially available core, round which the local church could add pages specific to the parish. Modern tastes would find the mixture of uplifting adventure stories, Bible tales, stirring illustrations, mini-

CHAPTER 7: A CHURCH RESTORED

[Picture 26] The Chantry Chapel before restoration. Note the North Gallery stairs blocking the end of the Talbot monument. The old lectern, chest and font are still in the church

sermons and ephemera rather cloying but, at a penny-ha'penny for 24 pages, such magazines provided much needed reading material in many modest homes. The content of the local pages was equally fixed: news articles, *"parish intelligence"*, reports and accounts, the month's hymns, marriages, baptisms and burials, and a general calendar - in fact, not that different from any modern parish magazine. These now-yellowing pages show a rather livelier church than you might imagine from the row over pews, as a look at some of the stories from 1868 and 1869 shows.

No less than eighty people had sat down to the Sunday School teachers' tea in December 1868, teachers and friends. The Sunday School itself was running morning and afternoon sessions in the National School building, while a night school for older children ran on three nights a week, for a modest annual subscription of 2s 6d. The main day school, with nearly two hundred pupils, mixed book learning – history and scripture in particular – with more practical arts: the March magazine, for example, advertised that *"any lady in the parish or neighbourhood may have plain sewing done at the school at a moderate charge"*. The night school had a harder task in bringing some basic education to children who had missed out on an education in their earlier years, and the October 1869 magazine had to announce that *"two nights a week is as much as most of the scholars ...can give up for the present"*. The School Inspector had found its standards very elementary compared with the day school that year, although at least the girls were *"orderly and attentive"*.

Universal education, however modest, was both an agent for social improvement and a method of social control amongst a working population that might otherwise find alternative outlets for its frustrations. As the vicar remarked in the April edition, education *"not only awakens kindly feelings in the children towards their superiors but it sheds an influence for good not otherwise attainable"*. However

CHAPTER 7: A CHURCH RESTORED

modest it was, schooling was still a luxury to a working family and the day school headmistress had to remind everyone via the July magazine that the day school did not break up for holidays until the corn harvest was ready for gathering. To round off the school year, the annual school treat was held in July, when nearly seven hundred children, led by the clergy, marched out along the Kidderminster Road behind the local yeomanry band to a field by Monsieur's Hall, lent by Thomas Parkes. Games, food, drink, races and prizes filled the afternoon - sunny in 1868 but *"very unfavourable"* the following year - after which this enormous gathering trooped no doubt wearily back into town.

Affordable schooling for the poor was a typical Victorian response to the challenge of poverty; paternalistic, certainly, but practical, direct and by all accounts effective. A similar ethos underlay the establishment of the clothing and shoe club in February 1869, running every Monday between 12 noon and 1pm at the school. A working man's club was started in March the previous year and gained 186 members in the first six months, tempered only by an alcohol policy of no more than two pints a night. *"There are few who will say that this small amount can do harm"*, the May 1868 magazine observed rather sanctimoniously; *"We have always considered it an insult to the working man to accuse him of being unable to restrict himself to one or two glasses.......If properly treated he is as capable of moderation as anyone else"*.

The same year a temporary soup kitchen had been set up over the winter months in the Institute, providing *"well and carefully made.....warm and nourishing food"* for a heavily subsidised penny a quart. A team of ladies under the direction of the vicar's wife distributed 240 quarts a week throughout January and February, in exchange for tickets obtainable from the district visitors. The cost was defrayed by subscriptions, primarily from the vicar and his wife. In the church itself, eight large print Bibles and prayer books were donated in November, specifically for the use of the poor. A hundred and forty years later, most churches are just getting round to doing the same thing.

G.W.Murray and his family had been holidaying in Naples since December 1868 and Murray sent the March 1869 magazine a chatty letter extolling the virtues of this *"most salubrious"* region. He wasn't sure whether he would be back for Easter but *"wherever I am, I shall think of the Confirmation on the 1st of April"*. It would, he said *"be suicidal ….to go back to England during this bitterly cold month of March"*. April and May apparently proved equally dangerous, as our pleasure-loving vicar did not reappear in Bromsgrove until mid-June, after a six-month break. Adolphus Waller, Senior curate at Kidderminster had been drafted in to hold the fort in Murray's absence and judging by the flurry of activity over the following six months he and the regular curate, the Revd Llywellyn Jones, more than rose to the occasion.[187]

Church missions were an essential component of the British Empire and St John's was no stranger to visiting preachers, some of whom were distinctly exotic. The bishop of Honolulu preached the evening sermon on 17th January 1869 and St John's contributed £7 to his Hawaiian mission. Keeping up the theme, the Revd C.H.Prance illustrated a lecture on his travels in the Holy Land the following month by donning *"the dresses worn in those parts"*. It is perhaps as well that the two events were not combined. Even at the height of empire, however, the effectiveness of such missions was open to question. *"What enormous sums of money have been spent,"* commented Waller in the January 1869 magazine; *"is the END worthy of a lavish outlay? Are we justified in believing, on the whole, that the money is spent conscientiously and not in vain?"* There again, *"all the money spent on Missions by the Church of England since the Reformation might amount to one year's duty on spirits, wine, malt, hops and tobacco"*, a thought that has occurred to many a mission committee chairman since.

---

[187] Llewellyn Jones later became Bishop of Newfoundland, a post he held for 40 years.

CHAPTER 7: A CHURCH RESTORED

[Picture 27] George W. Murray

The growth of Bromsgrove town through the 19th century put pressure on the parish to provide churches nearer the new centres of population. The northern outlying village of Catshill had been created a separate parish in 1837 but had to wait until 1868 to get its own vicar. The following year it was holding three services every Sunday, together with churchings (a service for women who had just given birth), litany and baptisms on Tuesdays and Fridays. The bishop preached the sermon on 27th June in aid of the new Catshill church school but despite a large congregation the collection was less than expected because of a local strike by workmen - perhaps unsurprising in the light of Murray's lack of support. Further afield Kings Norton finally became a separate parish in 1848, Moseley in 1853 and Wythall the same year.

Several other new parishes were hewn out of the sprawling medieval parish in the following years to cater for an ever expanding Birmingham, including Balsall Heath in 1853, the Lickey in 1856 and Kings Heath in 1863. In Bromsgrove itself the expansion of the town northwards up the Birmingham Road split the urban portion of the parish in two with the construction of All Saint's church in 1874, to a rather severe design by the local architect John Cotton. Within the remaining parish of St John's a mission church was established in the poor working district of Sidemoor as an unsuccessful counter to the new Baptist Church in Broad Street, and another - more successfully - at Dodford in 1863, to serve the struggling Chartist settlement in the remote hilly country to the west of town. A concert was held in Dodford Priory house in January 1869 to raise funds for a new tea service for use at harvest festivals; this was duly inaugurated at a special tea on 26th April, accompanied by a musical concert by the church choir. Dodford would become a separate parish in 1908 with a very beautiful Arts and Crafts church of its own, but for now at least the timber and corrugated iron mission hall had to suffice.

The introduction of regular weekly plate offerings at evening - and later, morning – services was one of the principal objectives of the "Free and Open", and totals were assiduously published each month. The collections for 1868 raised a total of

CHAPTER 7: A CHURCH RESTORED

£305 12s 3¼d, almost half of which went to defray the churchwardens' expenses in the day-to-day running of the church - coal, gas and a hundred and one other payments. Just over £52 – a sixth – went to the sick and needy; around £16 went to foreign missions; a further £12 15s 2d augmented the curates' meagre salaries and the rest supported the Church Choral Association, school, choir and Church Extension Society funds. However, it was still necessary to remind everyone that these collections were freewill offerings and not payments. Churching of women was particularly singled out, perhaps because its ancient origins perpetuated a superstitious need for some kind of propitiatory offering. The August 1869 magazine had to point out that *"there is NO FEE whatsoever to be paid for the Churching Service. A thank-offering is directed to be given but this may be sufficiently complied with by poor women by putting a penny or even a halfpenny into the poor's (sic) box before leaving the church"*.

Births and deaths, baptisms and burials, form a constant record at the end of each magazine and serve as a crude indicator of the health of mid-Victorian Bromsgrove - or at least its Anglican inhabitants. 1869 started with a high number of both births and deaths, but while births peaked sharply at 31 in March, the number of deaths fell steadily to a low in June before climbing, as we would expect, towards the end of the year. But within this declining trend the number of infant deaths is a stark reminder that 19th century Bromsgrove was an industrial town with a high level of poverty and disease. Of the fourteen deaths in February nine were infants under a year old and a further three were aged two or under.

Death And Resurrection

One death had a page to itself. The January 1869 Parish Magazine sadly reported the funeral of Joseph Rose, who had died on 27th December past, aged 75. Rose had been sexton for forty-five years until illness forced his retirement that May and confined him to his house. *"A few days ago he was seen to be sinking"*, the

241

magazine lamented, *"and on Sunday last, as the bells were calling us to the evening service, he passed away, apparently in sleep....The familiar form and features of "Sexton Rose" will not soon be forgotten in Bromsgrove."* Nor were they given a chance. On the 9th January next, his son John placed an advertisement in the Messenger recommending himself to the parish as successor. John had been assisting his infirm father for the past five years and his public announcement was considered an entirely acceptable way of advertising his willingness to take on the office. He was elected unopposed as sexton at a specially convened meeting two days later, for a church without a Rose was unthinkable and John had been schooled for the job from birth.

But fate - and an awkward heating system - was about to intervene in the record of this long-lived family. Despite modification in 1872, Mr Harper's hot air blower had never really worked well. The apparatus required a through-draught to draw the air along the under-floor ducts and out through the ornate cast-iron floor grilles in each aisle. Short of leaving all the doors open the only way of ensuring sufficient draught was to raise one flap of the bell hatch on each floor of the tower and let the hot air vent out through the belfry windows, which were left open for the purpose. It was dark in the tower, beyond the reach of Mr Skidmore's fine gasoliers, and darker still on Saturday evening, the 22nd March 1879, when the 38-year old John Rose climbed the belfry stairs to wind the clock just after 7pm. The tower windows and trap had been opened at 4.40pm by his 19-year old nephew, Joseph William, who lived with his uncle and aunt at the Cemetery Lodge and often helped John with his duties. Joseph was working late in the schoolroom, revising for an exam. He noticed his uncle heading up the hill to the tower and returned to his books, his mind on his studies.

What made him snap-to around 7.45pm? Was it a sudden, sickening prescience that John might not see the open hatch in the all-enveloping gloom of the clock

CHAPTER 7: A CHURCH RESTORED

chamber, might step back into terrifying thin air and fall a dizzying seventy feet to the tiled floor below, flailing at the ting-tang bell rope in a last desperate attempt to save himself? Others recalled hearing the bell give four or five sudden irregular clangs but Joseph only had the image of the open hatch in his mind as he burst through the west door and to his horror heard a voice groaning his name in the near-total gloom. Working by touch alone Joseph found his uncle lying mortally injured on the floor, the snapped bell-rope nearby. He put a match to the nearest gaslight and frantically tried to find out what had happened, although John's shattered right arm and multiple head wounds were evidence enough of a calamity. John refused to tell him but one glance up at the open trap door confirmed Joseph's worst fear. John complained of pain in his hips and asked Joseph to lift him onto the nearest pew. After denying it twice, John finally admitted that he had been up in the belfry (had Joseph told him not to go up there?) and then collapsed in the young man's arms. Thinking him dead Joseph ran for Dr Wood, who found John still alive and, amazingly, asking to be allowed to walk home. But he could not take the offered drink and after being propped up where he lay, he died.

This *"good-natured and kindly man, genial and pleasant to everyone"* [188] left a grieving wife and four children, the youngest only 2 weeks old. He was buried on the 27th March, and the muffled peal of bells to mark his funeral lasted an hour and fifteen minutes. The inquest three days later at the Horn and Trumpet inn returned a verdict of accidental death, and it recommended that the trap door either be left closed or a grating fixed over it. Too late for poor John Rose, one was duly fitted.

Like uncle, like nephew. Joseph William duly placed his advertisement in the 5th April edition of the Messenger advertising his willingness to continue the 150 years' service of Roses as sextons. The 10th April Vestry had some slight concern about Joseph's youthfulness – he was after all still only 19 – and Thomas White

---

[188] As the "Messenger" recorded.

243

FAIRLY MOUNTED ON A HILL

would have been happier with a twelve month probationary period. But the vicar and churchwardens knew their Roses and they backed him. Joseph was elected unopposed, and his subsequent sixty-year service was a fitting testimony to a family that made a duty to their church their life's work.

The Beauty of Holiness

Scott's restoration had cleared the church of its 18th century encumbrances but had generally steered clear of overt beautification for its own sake. True, there was new carved stonework to the arches, and the roofs and pews were a distinct improvement; but the place was, to be frank, rather bare. The scraped stonework felt cold and dark on winter days, the great width was difficult to heat and the clear glazing to most windows merely showed up the starkness of the interior.

Stained glass was the response. Victorian advances in glass pigmentation allowed a much greater depth of colour, and the stained glass studios that sprang up in the wake of the Victorian church revival made full use of new technology. Compared with the paler painted glass of the 18th century, the vivid Victorian blues and reds could be garish and crude. St John's was therefore lucky largely to escape the worst on offer, and a modern reappraisal of 19th century stained glass art allows us to look at these windows with new eyes.

With the chancel windows already filled as part of the restoration, the aisle windows were next in line. The 13th century east window in the south aisle came first with a Lavers and Barrauld design in 1867, installed in memory of Thomas Day, Clerk to the Board of Guardians of the Workhouse. In recognition of his championship of the town's poor its theme was Jesus's works of mercy.[189]

This pleasant enough design was soon followed by an absolutely stunning piece of

---

[189] This window was removed to the north aisle west window when the organ was installed in the south aisle in 1950.

CHAPTER 7: A CHURCH RESTORED

work in the great west window under the tower. Recognising that it would catch the full glare of the evening sun, Jean-Baptiste Capronnier of Brussels came up with a rich, deeply coloured composition depicting the five wise and five foolish virgins. The wise virgins, suitably demure, are arranged in various industrious poses to the left of the returning Jesus, while their lackadaisical companions on the right visibly demonstrate the emotions of remorse and regret. In common with much Victorian church art it is the faces that appear most dated: respectable maidens with the plain neat features of mid-19th Century England – with one noble exception. In a daring piece of participatory art, Capronnier turned just one foolish girl's face directly towards the audience. Her bright red dress and Latin countenance hinting at an immodest past, she defiantly confronts any departing worshipper with her irrevocable fate – she has missed the boat, as a stark warning that they should not. This is Capronnier's largest window in England, an enormous blaze of colour that still has the power to stop you in your tracks.

This window actually had a rather sad genesis. Olivia Murray, G.W.Murray's 20-year old daughter, married the Revd H.W.More-Molyneux, one of Murray's curates, on 14th July 1868. Her death less than a month later on the 10th August, was as unexpected as it was sudden. Grief-stricken at his loss, More-Molyneux commissioned the window in her memory, no doubt as one of the wise virgins. He left for another parish soon after.

Other windows followed over the years, although none had the quite the same impact. A rather anodyne product by Lavers, Westlake and Company filled the tower south window in 1882 in memory of John Day Collis, who had died of untreated diabetes three years earlier. Acknowledging Collis's forceful leadership the composition depicts Jesus commissioning Peter to lead the Disciples. In the opposite opening the first of several windows commemorating the town's doctors was installed the same year. George Harcourt Hornsby's hard work as a surgeon at Bromsgrove Hospital was appropriately remembered in a composition depicting Jesus healing the sick. Doctors were front-line troops in the Victorian war on poverty and disease, and the nobility of their calling was emphasised by biblical allusions.[190] Roger Prosser, a well-loved town GP, was commemorated in a north aisle window of 1887 showing Faith, Hope and Charity, while Mary, his wife, inspired the adjoining window in 1906. This (and possibly the other) was designed in a semi-grisaille style by Amy Walford, a decorative metalwork teacher at Bromsgrove's School of Art and Science and, with her sisters, heavily involved in local charitable work.[191] Rather later the local surgeon Sir Thomas Chevasse was commemorated in the south aisle west window, a gift of his wife in July 1913. Four patriarchs of the Old Testament are shown in their role as healers, accompanied by various medicinal plants with Biblical associations.[192]

Two further windows tell an oddly touching story. In 1883 Ward and Hughes were commissioned by the parish to produce a suite of windows for the little monument bay in the south aisle in memory of G.W.Murray's much-liked wife Marianne, who had died on 23rd August the previous year. The 60-year old Henry Hughes duly travelled north from London to present his design, a colourful and attractive composition on the appropriate theme of the resurrection with unusual attention to detail in its depiction of wild flowers and grasses. His sudden and unexpected death on 17th February during his stay was therefore an understandable shock to all concerned. The window was duly commissioned, but in memory of the man

---

[190] Several generations of Hortons, all surgeons, are commemorated on plaques at the west end of the North Aisle, moved from the north wall in 1920.

[191] Amy Walford became a founder member of the Bromsgrove Guild, an arts and crafts collective started in the late 1890s by Walter Gilbert, formerly head of the school's art department. She also designed the South African memorial in the south aisle.

[192] Sir Thomas's son and nephew, both doctors, were killed in First World War and are commemorated on the war memorial in the north aisle. Noel, the nephew, was awarded the VC twice, one of only three people to be so honoured. He is also believed to be commemorated on more war memorials in the UK than any other individual.

CHAPTER 7: A CHURCH RESTORED

himself a second window was also installed nearly opposite in the north aisle. Showing the baptism of Jesus, it also appears to be by Hughes's hand and may have been an earlier design adapted to its sombre new use.

Not all attempts at beautification were so generally acceptable. In 1893, Edward Vine Hall, vicar from 1890 to 1905, received a gift of £50 "to beautify your grand old church", in the words of its anonymous donor. Vine Hall initially thought of retiling the chancel floor but on consideration felt that a chancel screen was a more appropriate way of acknowledging the donor's generosity. A lacy Scott-type design in gilded wrought iron was prepared and shown to the donor, who liked it and generously offered to increase his gift by £25 to pay the additional cost. So far so good.

Then the Vestry got to hear of it. At a special meeting on 22nd April, the carping started. Benjamin H. Sanders sent a letter stating that he would vote in favour if the design was not too *"weak or weedy to accord with the general architecture of the church"*. John Green of nearby Whitford Hall, a persistent and vocal critic, let everybody know that the gift could actually be used for any item of beautification and that a screen was certainly not his preference. Indeed, he felt that the vicar had not been *"honest and straightforward"* in his dealings with the Vestry and was deliberately misrepresenting the donor's wishes in pursuit of his own agenda. William Lewis waded in. *"What was the original use and object of the screen?"* he demanded to know: *"Would it add to the sacredness of the building and would it inspire more devotion in the worshippers to look through the bars and have the music come to them through the bars? There were divisions enough in the church".*

FAIRLY MOUNTED ON A HILL

[Picture 28] Vine Hall's controversial chancel screen

CHAPTER 7: A CHURCH RESTORED

It was a tough point, and Vine Hall rather conceded it. His prime object, he freely admitted, was to increase the beauty of the church and he was extremely vexed that his private conversations with the donor had been aired in public. The screen was merely an architectural feature, a replacement for the lost medieval original, and had no doctrinal significance. Furthermore, it didn't need the Vestry's consent. With Vine Hall's temper up it took the calm and measured Dr Cameron Kidd, one of the Vicar's Wardens, to pacify the dissenters and regain some consensus. In the end John Green backed down and grudgingly accepted a screen, provided that it wasn't *"flimsy or gimcrack"*. The motion was passed and the screen was duly installed but Green's concerns proved right in the end. Like its predecessor, the new screen was always going divide the priest from the people and in the true spirit of old John Hall it was torn down in 1928.

Despite Scott's restoration the sheer age of the old building meant that further repairs were constantly being needed to maintain the heavily weathered exterior. One area of the church that Scott avoided was the spire. Exposed and inaccessible, this always caught the worst of the weather, and its slender and flexible construction made the stonework and mortar particularly vulnerable to erosion. Joseph Johnson of Lichfield botched one repair in 1825, so much so that it *"was all to pieces in two years"*, according to Joseph Rose. Robinson of Redditch carried out a more thorough (and expensive) job in September 1836 under the eye of the ever-watchful sexton. Costing £106 1s 5½d, this included replacing the 19 foot long iron rod and weights that hung down inside the spire from the cap and kept it in place. Rose left an inscription on the stone below the capstone recording his involvement. Despite this the spire needed attention again the year after Scott's restoration, the repairs being carried by Brown of Sheffield. These lasted until the end of October 1891 when a severe lightning strike dislodged a large lump of stonework from the very top of the spire and sent it plummeting 190 feet to the churchyard below. A public meeting was called to discuss what to do and Joseph Blackburn, a Nottingham steeplejack, was engaged to replace completely the top 25 feet of the spire, at a cost of around £300.

Free For All - At Last!

Before the coming 20th century ushers in an era of increasing social integration, we must finally sort out those troublesome and divisive pew rents. Although the churchwardens had not made any new allotments since 1867, their new policy - letting seats become free as and when the sittings became vacant - had failed to dislodge a hard core of about fifty traditionalists. The "Free and Open" had achieved considerable success around the country and by the 1890s many of the local churches were entirely free, including Alvechurch, Walsall, Stratford and Alcester. St John's was now in a shrinking minority.

Having cut his teeth with the chancel screen Edward Vine Hall now decided to tackle the pews. Pew rents were, he said, *"thoroughly selfish and a disgrace to our Christianity"* but he needed to find some way of speeding up the process of natural attrition favoured by his churchwardens. After some years of indecisive contemplation he found one. Edmund Hartland, his senior churchwarden, received a letter in April 1895 from the churchwarden of St Mary's, Kidderminster, asking him to fill in a questionnaire about free seating, which that church was rather nervously contemplating. While Hartland dutifully wrote back confirming St John's so-far unfulfilled intentions, Vine Hall dropped a line to his colleague, the Revd Walter Farr, who had pushed through free seating at St John's, Worcester a year or so before. Farr's very positive response extolled the virtues of an open church, including the increased numbers of working men and women attending and the maintenance of the collection, albeit with a larger number of smaller coins in the plate.

Vine Hall was still cautious. Several big local names still clung to their pews and

CHAPTER 7: A CHURCH RESTORED

he could not afford to alienate the Sanders, Corbetts, Inces or Prossers. Free seats would therefore be marked with a letter "F", as a sort of compromise, but nobody would be forced to move. The matter dragged on through the following two years but no-one was brave enough to sanction a public meeting and confront the small band of reactionaries who clung to their pews. Even Hartland baulked at talking to some of them, although Vine Hall claimed to know *"heaps of people who would never attend again"* for fear of being turned away from a pew – 40, 50 or even 60, he thought.

The 1898 Harvest Festival proved the final straw. The church was seriously overcrowded, many working class parishioners could not find a seat for a service that celebrated the fruits of labour and there were a number of complaints. Vine Hall again sought advice from Walter Farr and circulated Farr's again-encouraging response to the Churchwardens, urging action. The following year's Easter Vestry meeting (essentially the parish AGM) favoured free seats in principle but baulked at an imposed solution. Instead, the churchwardens were to ask the remaining pew renters to give their seats voluntarily, after which the Vestry would consider the next step at a special meeting in a month's time. Vine Hall and Hartland could see that this was not going to get them a free church in the foreseeable future. In a secretive flurry of action, Hartland drew up his own carefully neutral questionnaire and sent it out to a list of forty-two local and regional churches that he and Vine Hall had identified.

Responses dribbled back in over the next few weeks, ranging from the wildly enthusiastic to the downright dismissive, but Hartland had enough positive news to take to the meeting on 4th May. Vine Hall set the tone by reminding everyone present that it was *"more important to do what was right than to think of one's pocket"*, a pointed reference to the doom-mongers who saw free seats as the road to parochial penury. In fact, the meeting was almost entirely positive

251

and Dr Kidd's motion to declare the church totally free was carried by 28 votes. It took a few weeks to organise the change, but the church was finally declared free of allotments on Saturday, 24th June 1899 - the Feast of St John the Baptist. Vine Hall held his first service in a free and open church the following day, a fitting way to end the old century.

A Clash of Conductors

Edward Vine Hall's own interests extended well beyond the parish boundaries. A keen musician and singer he composed several popular and still available collections of church anthems, as well as singing in the Westminster Abbey choir at Edward VII's coronation in 1902. But as he demonstrated with the chancel screen, Vine Hall had strong, fixed opinions and a thin skin. Anything that did not fit his narrow High Church theology was anathema, to be resisted as a matter of principle. Within his own parish – and with a supportive churchwarden - this was just about feasible. But the wider world was rather less willing to cooperate, especially when his opponent had his own demons to fight.

Before coming to St John's Vine Hall had founded an amateur choral society, the Worcester Musical Union in the early 1880s, as an outlet for his musical interests. This group performed two choral and two orchestral concerts a year, but despite Vine Hall's personal enthusiasm its fortunes and standards were decidedly mixed. What might have been perfectly adequate in the average provincial town sounded decidedly inferior in the home of the Three Choirs Festival and its rising star, Edward Elgar. The Musical Union actually tried at least one early Elgar piece itself - the now-lost "Three Pieces for String Orchestra" in 1888 - but was hard pressed to do it justice. Lack of skill notwithstanding, relations between the Musical Union and the great man were initially cordial, for Elgar was a strong encourager of musical talent and made his work available for performance as widely as he could. Indeed, he even interceded (unsuccessfully, in the end) on behalf of Vine

CHAPTER 7: A CHURCH RESTORED

Hall's group when the publishers were tardy in printing his Part Songs for Ladies Voices in time for a Musical Union Concert in 1895.

[Pictures 29 and 30] A tale of two Edwards: Elgar (left) and Vine Hall (right)

But the Musical Union was hidebound and its members grew increasingly frustrated with Vine Hall's reluctance to take on more ambitious pieces. Moreover, Elgar's growing reputation and the lack of an adequate local vehicle for his work was threatening to lure him away from Worcestershire to more progressive climes. By autumn 1897 the musicians had had enough. Breaking away from the Musical Union they founded a new orchestra, the Worcester Philharmonic Society, and invited Elgar to lead it. He was naturally delighted and saw it as a chance to *"let young England whoop!"*, as he enthusiastically wrote to his publishers that year. Presumably Vine Hall was not inclined to whooping.

But by then Vine Hall had already fallen out with Elgar – not over music but theology. Attending the first performance of Elgar's choral work "The Light of

253

FAIRLY MOUNTED ON A HILL

Life" in Worcester Cathedral on 8th September 1896, Vine Hall was shocked at the words of one quatrain, in which the "blind man's mother" addresses "Christ" with the words:

"Had'st thou a son, O Lord, how could'st thou bear
To see him made thy curse, to love and yet to hate
Thy child, thy sin's own signature, a gift
Not given in love but as a sinner's fate"

Incensed at the (to his eyes) inference that Christ could have a son and that he was capable of sin, Vine Hall dashed off a critical review for the Worcester Herald and sent a copy of it to Novello, Elgar's publishers, with a tart note suggesting that *"I think Mr Elgar w[oul]d be well advised if he c[oul]d get the words...rewritten. They strike me as absolutely irreverent"*. Elgar dismissed the criticism with polite but carefully crafted distain: *"Mr Vine Hall, who was reporting for a small local paper, mentioned the matter in his notice but I w[oul]d prefer to have an opinion from some unbiased person whose ability to judge literary or artistic matters is not so much open to doubt"*. That put the vicar of Bromsgrove in his place. Although Novello agreed with Elgar that Vine Hall's criticism was ill-judged and over-sensitive, they took the cautious path and persuaded the now-furious librettist, the Revd Edward Capel-Cure, to replace the contentious lines with a blander alternative.

An uneasy truce hung over proceedings until rehearsals for Elgar's greatest choral work, *"The Dream of Gerontius"* started in the cathedral, in preparation for the Three Choirs Festival of 1902. Elgar, himself a Catholic, took as his libretto a poem from 1865 by the Anglican vicar-turned-Roman Catholic priest John Henry Newman, with its very Catholic references to Purgatory and Masses. Most people would have accepted these in the context of the whole piece - but not Vine Hall. Stung by Elgar's deft put-down, he was now on the warpath for any similar misdemeanours. Romanish words sung in an English cathedral fitted the bill and

CHAPTER 7: A CHURCH RESTORED

he promptly organised some of the cathedral clergy into a formal protest.

Elgar, as usual, was bemused by the whole affair. He was a musician, not a theologian, and took Newman's poem as a piece of literature. He would accept whatever changes were necessary to silence Vine Hall but the man was becoming an irritation. Writing to his great friend Alfred Jaeger, Elgar lamented; *"the whole objection now is manufactured by one man with the express purpose of (as he thinks) ruining my work"*. On a postcard of Worcester Cathedral which he sent to the editor of the Musical Times on 8th October that year Elgar drew several little devils aiming arrows at Vine Hall's old home in College Yard and annotated it *"Former abode of Bowdler"*, a pointed reference to the notoriously prudish early 19th century censor of Shakespeare's works. On the back of the card, Elgar added: *"I'm sorry my Demons are so unlike EVH"*. Demon or just nuisance, Vine Hall again won in the end. The offending words were excised and Gerontius, went on to lasting fame.[193]

When he wasn't arguing with great composers Vine Hall also found time to write two books, one a child's guide to the Prayer Book and the other a general explanation of church services. He eventually paid the price for such an active, contentious nature. While planning to add a temporary chaplaincy at Lucerne to his already heavy Bromsgrove workload Vine Hall fell ill in autumn 1903 and was ordered to take two months rest. Although he went abroad at the end of November to recuperate, this was only partially successful and after a further year of intermittent illness the 68-year old vicar felt compelled to resign at the 1905 Easter Vestry.

---

[193] The following year, Elgar took the precaution of suggesting that an Anglican clergyman friend write an explanation in the programme of his next work, "The Apostles", to avoid criticism by *"the gentleman who made mischief over The Light of Life & later over Gerontius at Worcester, who is only too anxious to pull it to pieces"*.

FAIRLY MOUNTED ON A HILL

Ring Out The Old, Ring In The New

Edmund Hartland retired in 1901 at the age of 60, having completed ten years' service. Hartland had shown just how effective the ancient office of churchwarden could be if enough time and effort was given to it. When the bell frames needed renewal in 1897 he offered to pay £250 for the entire operation in honour of Queen Victoria's jubilee, if the congregation would fund a replacement for the now-ailing mechanical chimes. Although the frames were replaced without a hitch, the new carillon by Joyce of Whitchurch proved problematic to rig and Sexton Rose had to finish the job after the original contractors proved unequal to the task.[194]

Even after stepping down as churchwarden Hartland filled his newfound leisure time with other church duties. He was one of the first group of sidesmen when that role was belatedly introduced at St John's in 1907, and he acted as deanery synod representative in 1908. Edmund Hartland died a year later on Christmas Day in his home at Rydal Mount, next to the church, after a lifetime of service to both church and town. His widow Frances left a £100 bequest on her own death in 1924, to pay for curates at St John's. In 1931 the diocese bought the Hartlands' old house for £2,400 as a new vicarage, and its predecessor then became the district council offices. A large photograph of this generous and public-spirited man hangs proudly in the tower ringing chamber.

---

[194] Joyce also provided the present clock mechanism in 1946, at a cost of £250, one of the last mechanical clocks made by this company. It replaced an 1884 clock by A. Baldwin and has since been converted to electric operation.

CHAPTER 8: MODERN TIMES

The early 20th Century

An Historic Monument

The era of religious strife is largely past, at least as far as the venerable fabric of St John's is concerned. No-one will now come to smash its stained glass windows with hammers; no-one will drive its vicar from the town; no-one will hack its battered stonework about in pursuit of the latest fashion. St John's is now a Monument, an Historic Building whose history is itself a source of interest. William Cotton, a local auctioneer and the brother of the architect John Cotton, writes a detailed and scholarly account of the church in 1881 using as many first-hand sources as he can find, together with the writings of earlier visitors such as Thomas Habington and Dr Treadway Russell Nash. An inveterate collector of local records, Cotton locates St John's in both the history of Bromsgrove and church building, and the church is now recognised as a fine example of late medieval ecclesiastical architecture.

St John's will acquire further guidebooks over the coming years, the first of which is a slim pamphlet by Mr G.W. Hastings in 1912 with a professed indebtedness to Messrs Habington, Nash and Cotton. At the Revd. Thomas de la Hay's request, the architect Sir Harold Brakspear contributes a more professional guide in 1926 that lasts until the Revd Frederick Shepherd's useful booklet of 1946, which he expands into a larger history in 1952.

FAIRLY MOUNTED ON A HILL

[Picture 35] "A glorious old church": a hand tinted souvenir postcard sent in 1905

And when in 1921 A.E.B. Barnard, a county historian, discovers the rotting remains of the rectory manor records in the old parish chest, now dumped in the basement of the vicarage, much of the missing earlier history of the parish begins to emerge. Aghast at the extent of their ill-treatment over the centuries, he carefully dries them out, catalogues and transcribes them line by line before boxing them up and placing them in the safe-keeping of the Worcester Records Office. Whoever carries out any work to this church will now do so in the full knowledge of its historic importance and under the watchful eye of both amateur and professional experts.

Other checks are imposed. The old parish Vestry gives way to the modern parochial church council in 1921 with a wider remit to manage the church's affairs, including some of the churchwardens' former responsibilities. Churchwardens can no longer bash the fabric about with impunity or show favouritism to the

CHAPTER 8: MODERN TIMES

highest payer, although they are still capable of turning a blind eye to bureaucratic niceties when needed. The PCC - and thus the parish - also acquires the unwelcome responsibility for chancel repairs from the vicar under the Ecclesiastical Dilapidations Measure of 1923. The House of Lords throws out attempted changes to the 1662 Prayer Book in 1928, sending a very clear signal that it does not want to change the historic essence of Anglican worship. Tithes are finally abolished in 1936 [195] and there is little incentive - or money - to alter a building whose inherent shape dictates how it will be used. And as we move into modern times there is a danger that this story will disintegrate into a dull list of debated, approved and budgeted minor repairs, alterations and adaptations, the plethora of routine work that occupies the bulk of any modern fabric committee's time. But our story from the beginning has been a human one, of priests and people in a common task of building, using and maintaining their place of worship according to their Christian convictions and the needs of their age, even if they occasionally disagreed about just where those convictions lay. The 20th Century is no different, and this story closes by seeing how a building erected in a time of knights in armour coped with the century of mechanised world wars.

The Gift of a Lifetime

Now nearing the end of a long and generous life Thomas White wanted to leave a lasting legacy of his lifetime connection with St John's. All those arguments about High Church practice were now in the past and he had even agreed – a little reluctantly – to the freeing of pews in 1899. What gift would best serve the needs of his church in the 20th century though?

---

[195] The Tithe Commutation Act of 1836 had converted tithes to cash payments, calculated on the basis of the average profitability of the land under different crops over seven years. However, tithes were still regarded as an archaic and inequitable tax by a body that no longer had any role in government or large-scale social welfare.

FAIRLY MOUNTED ON A HILL

[Picture 31] Church and town at the beginning of the 20th Century. St John's from Hanover Street

CHAPTER 8: MODERN TIMES

At the 1908 Easter Vestry the 88-year old White proposed a new church hall, to save the parish sharing the school premises.[196] But a suitable site could not be found near the church and the idea was shelved. After a couple of months further thought he suggested re-leading the church roof, which was now showings signs of age. Hill Parker, the diocesan surveyor, was summoned to inspect the roof in early June and duly confirmed its parlous condition. All the leadwork had been poorly laid to start with and the over-large sheets were now cracking. The nave and north aisle still had a few years in them but the south aisle had last been repaired in 1844 and needed immediate attention. White gladly donated £230 for a new covering of 7lb lead sheet.

Practical though it was, new leadwork was hardly the most visible of gifts and White had a second suggestion. Despite all the changes to the fabric no physical additions had been made to the old church since the Reformation, and its overall shape was much as Richard Harforde would have known it. While the nave and aisle were adequate for public worship the growing choir was now putting pressure on the limited space in the vestry. Clergy and choir all wanted to robe at the same time and the need for separate accommodation was now an urgent necessity. Partitioning off part of the congregational area was not an option and the organ occupied the only convenient space near the existing vestry. The best solution was to build outwards and Thomas White suggested an extension to the vestry specifically for the choir, as *"a thank offering to God"*. His offer was immediately taken up and barely a month later on 16th July the Vestry met to view the plans. The design, a neat 15th century pastiche by A.H. Parker, suitably battlemented and gargoyled, was approved, the contract was let that autumn and work progressed through the winter, delayed only by bad weather at the year end.[197]

---

[196] White had taught in the Sunday School for some years.

[197] No builder is recorded in the parish records, although they are likely to have been J&A Brazier. Albert Brazier was churchwarden from 1909 to 1913 and his expertise was much appreciated by the church.

FAIRLY MOUNTED ON A HILL

The completed building was dedicated by the Right Revd Francis Paget, Bishop of Oxford, on Sunday 25th July 1909. Paget had succeeded the popular G.W. Murray as vicar in March 1883, but his otherwise brief stay to August 1885 made a lasting impression on the tall, willowy and politely reserved Oxford academic. Hitherto a strident High Churchman, he had fallen foul of one of the many internal wrangles within the university over appointments and had gratefully accepted the offer of a distant living as a convenient bolt-hole while the row blew over.

[Picture 32] Francis Paget, later Bishop of Oxford

CHAPTER 8: MODERN TIMES

Bromsgrove impressed itself on him, however. The poverty and hard working life of many of its inhabitants was a world away from the refined atmosphere of Christ Church and he was forced to confront his own rather narrow view of both his Christian calling and his fellow man. Paget returned to Oxford determined to broaden the Church's appeal, and although Bromsgrove was his only parochial incumbency he remembered its lessons in his later more elevated career.

Gilding the Lily

As well as reviving the choir the 1858 restoration had returned the chancel to its medieval role as the focus of worship, and the desire of successive vicars to beautify it carried on unabated into the new century. Noel Patterson, Vine Hall's successor, started just outside the chancel by replacing Scott's pulpit with – oddly - a rather inferior one designed by a Mr Whitcombe.[198]

The repaving of the chancel in 1907 in memory of Geraldine Hall, Patterson's mother-in-law, was rather more successful. A stylised tree of life designed by Walter Gilbert of the Bromsgrove Guild rises from the chancel steps in beautifully laid mosaic, matched by the Holy Spirit in the form of a dove at the altar steps. The subtle variations in colour and restrained design still feel fresh a hundred years later. The following year Scott's gothic altar made way for a very attractive piece by the Bromsgrove Guild of Applied Arts in 1911, carved from light Austrian oak and contributed in memory of Catherine Brakeridge by her children. More oak was felled for the delicate chantry chapel screen in 1915, another Guild production and funded by an anonymous donor. With Britain now at war and so many men away at the Front it was dedicated in rather subdued circumstances on the Sunday after Easter, when Dr Moore Ede, the Dean of Worcester, preached on the soberly appropriate theme *"The Lord giveth and the Lord taketh away"*.

---

[198] This eventually proved unequal to the task and had to be replaced again in 1946 with a better pulpit carved by Pancheri and Hack.

FAIRLY MOUNTED ON A HILL

[Picture 33] All gas and gaiters. Noel Patterson (left) with a living history of clergy fashions over the previous half-century

The medieval church commemorated only those who could afford the luxury of a permanent monument. By definition this limited the scope to the great and good - the Talbots, Staffords and their fellow aristocracy. The common man or woman scarcely featured, other than as an occasional anonymous skeleton disturbed in the course of grave-digging. Humphrey Stafford merited best Derbyshire alabaster but any casualties amongst his retainers at Blackheath were probably dumped into a mass grave on the battlefield. They were their master's vassals, his to dispose of as he saw fit, and they lived or died in his name.

The age of mass warfare demanded a rather different form of memorial. Victorian reform had liberated the common man, improved his rights of representation, his quality of life, hygiene and sanitation, and they had officially surveyed and recorded his existence as an individual. The least it could now do was to record his death as an individual too. The South African – or Boer – War between

CHAPTER 8: MODERN TIMES

1899 and 1902 was Britain's first conflict in this new age of warfare, with its trenches and concentration camps. It killed twelve men from Bromsgrove, and notwithstanding the erection of a county memorial outside Worcester Cathedral Amy Walford was commissioned to make a local record of their sacrifice. Her sombre repoussé bronze panel on the south aisle wall is framed by Victory - as a Roman soldier - and the winged angel of death, laying respectively a wreath and a laurel branch on a shrouded recumbent figure stretched across the bottom of the frame. *"It is sweet and becoming to die for one's country"*, runs the old Roman tag across the top, but it was cold comfort to the new widows and orphans of Bromsgrove.

Twenty-two thousand British soldiers died in South Africa. But death on the scale experienced at the Western Front from 1914 to 1918 touched nearly every town in Britain, decimated homes, wiped out generations, stripped businesses, farms and factories of their workforce, widowed and orphaned countless families. It winnowed Bromsgrove of ten times the number of men killed on the veldt, and the sheer industrial scale of the horror could only be reflected by recording every individual life lost. While some towns placed war memorials outside in public spaces Bromsgrove decided on a church setting. Richard Goulden RA was commissioned in 1919 to design a suitable memorial and he produced a dignified bronze panel at a cost of £775 0s 11d.[199] It was fixed onto the north wall of the north aisle, the traditional location for memorials since medieval times. To clear a suitable space J.W. Rose, in his professional capacity as monumental mason, removed two of the Horton family memorials and replaced them on the west wall of the same aisle. He then prepared the wall and fixed the heavy bronze panel in place at the very beginning of November 1920, allowing it to be dedicated by the dean of Worcester on the 7th, just in time for Armistice Day. Victory - this time a barefooted girl - steps out of a hollow cross in the centre of the frame bearing an

---

[199] Richard Goulden (1877 – 1932) sculpted a number of bronze war memorials after the Great War in Britain and abroad.

emblematic palm leaf. Her laurel halo is both the Roman victor's crown and the wreath of death. A silent army marches west behind her, their tin helmets and rifles counter-pointing the shattered buildings and flayed trees silhouetted against a golden sky. *"Pax sanguine, caro redempta"* reads the motto on which she stands - a bloodstained peace indeed

Not every monument was acquired with such care. In the mid 1920s John Humphries, a prominent local historian, decided that a suitable memorial was needed for Benjamin Maund (1790-1864), one of Bromsgrove's more illustrious sons. A printer and stationer by trade Maund had played an active part in town life as well as occupying pew No. 11 in the old south gallery. His lasting contribution however was the *"Botanic Garden"*, produced between 1837 and 1846 in thirteen volumes and printed at his own press. The 312 plates of delicately engraved flowers in a four-to-a-page format were the finest botanical miniatures of the 19th century and were drawn by a largely female group of artists, including Maund's daughter. In a lecture given in June 1926 Humphries suggested that a memorial tablet should be placed in the church to honour Maund's memory. Not everyone shared his enthusiasm. Amongst others Thomas Cuthbert de la Hey, the vicar, felt that Maund's house was a far more suitable location for a memorial that had no direct connection with the church.

Unperturbed, Humphries enlisted the backing of Frederick Baxter, one of Maund's descendents, and progressively browbeat de la Hey into acquiescing. Installed in the chancel without a faculty (or even any correspondence with the diocese), the alabaster plaque generated a stiff letter (*"most irregular"* is about as stiff as it got in 1928) from the diocesan registrar to J.H.Henderson, the parish secretary, as soon as he found out about it. Although the bishop initially refused to consecrate the offending object Humphries was unrepentant. The church simply did not have the authority it once carried and he knew that a little pressure

CHAPTER 8: MODERN TIMES

would get the desired result. A retrospective faculty was submitted, incorporating a number of other minor internal alterations to the church, and the offending memorial was finally dedicated on 14th April 1928.[200]

[Picture 34] Thomas Cuthbert de la Hey

Like many Anglican clergy of the time de la Hey was something of an amateur antiquarian, and in 1927 he made a discovery that takes us back to the very first centuries of St John's church. At that time the church still possessed its venerable library of religious books, locked away in a cupboard in the vestry. It is not unusual for such books to conceal secrets, older documents reused as linings or binding, and de la Hey knew where to look. For hidden in the bindings of an 8-volume set

---

[200] These included the relocation of the two Murray family tablets and the removal of two front pews in the nave.

of writings by St John Chrysostom, he found several leaves from a 13th century illuminated gradual. Graduals contained the words and plainsong notation for the sacred music sung at the Mass and the ancient words of the Sarum Rite were found to be still perfectly legible after nearly 700 years.

Amid great excitement the Latin text was translated by Sister Laurentia McLachlan, abbess of Stanbrook Abbey at Malvern, and then sent to the Public Records Office for conservation.[201] But how they came to be in a book of 1612 remains a mystery. The book itself had been published in Eton, when the fragments may just have been convenient scrap paper with which to line the covers, but investigations were inconclusive. Even the great M.R. James, antiquarian, translator of the Apocrypha, ghost story writer extraordinary and Provost of Eton College, could shed no light on their origins and we are left with just the music itself, a faint, harmonic whisper of long lost worship and a precious insight into how St John's may actually have sounded in the late 13th century.

Keeping the Rain Out

Our story starts and finishes with building and builders. The south aisle had last been re-leaded in 1908 but the nave leads dated back to 1759. Scott's restoration of 1858 concentrated on exposing the medieval timbers and left most of this already time-expired covering in place. By early 1923 however, the patched and pieced-in leadwork was in terminal decline and on the advice of the Diocesan Advisory Committee the architect Harold Brakspear was called in to give an opinion. His preliminary investigation that autumn revealed severe decay to the nave battlements and pinnacles, as well as indications that water leaking through the old lead gutters was damaging the wall-heads and roof timbers. A more

---

[201] Laurentia McLachlan was a remarkable woman, a pioneer in the restoration of Gregorian chant in England and a leading authority on medieval music and manuscripts. She was also a tireless correspondent with several literary figures of her day, including George Bernard Shaw. She is commemorated in the Millennium Window in Worcester Cathedral.

CHAPTER 8: MODERN TIMES

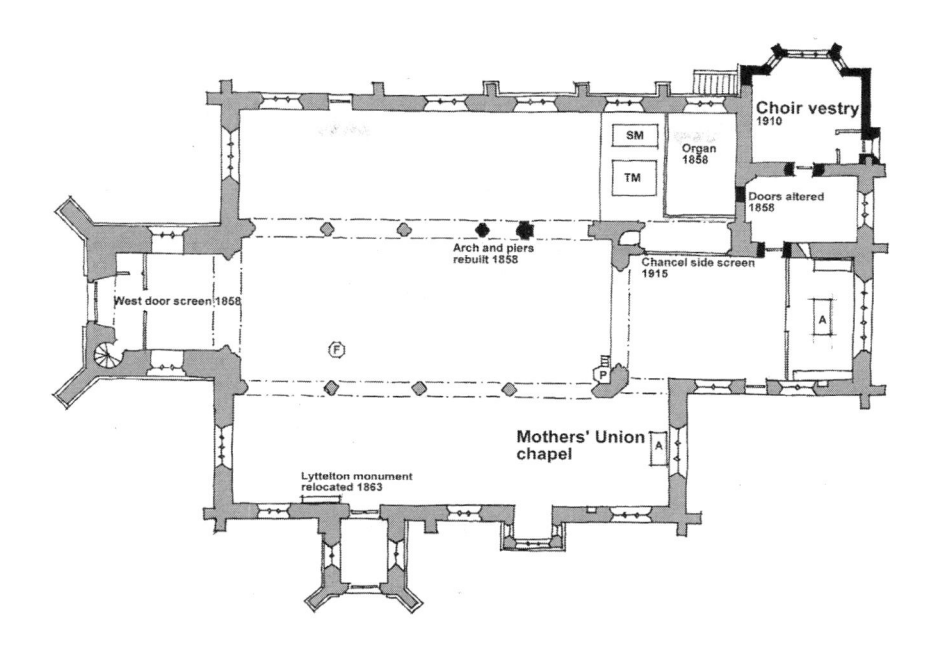

[Plan i] St John's c1928. The choir vestry of 1909 was the only substantive alteration to the footprint of the church since the Reformation. The organ was relocated to the former Mothers Union chapel in 1950, allowing the east end of the north aisle to be reordered as a chantry chapel with the 17th century communion table and lectern. The font and pulpit have also since moved.

detailed investigation the following February stripped back part of the roof to discover that several of the main roof beams no longer rested on the wall-heads at all and that a botched previous repair (Scott's?) had merely bolted timber extension pieces to the top of the main rafters, transferring the whole weight of the roof onto the bolts themselves and pushing the walls apart. To gain a closer look at the underside of the roof Brakspear ordered a steel platform to be slung across the nave at high level in August 1924. But the more he saw, the worse it got. Every single beam end had rotted away from the wall-heads and the rafter extension repairs were only taking part of the roof load. The rest was being transferred onto the decorative stone corbels below Scott's restored curved roof

269

brackets, two of which had now split. The north clerestory wall was well out of plumb and just to complete the bad news there was widespread beetle infection. Brakspear estimated that it would cost around £2000, a then-considerable sum, to put everything right.

Faced with a roof in imminent danger of collapse, bringing the nave walls with it, the November 1924 Parochial Church Council had no option but to approve Brakspear's report, but it carped at the cost. Harold Brakspear was a prominent and successful diocesan architect, his opinion was much sought after and his fees were pitched accordingly. Although he had initially told de la Hay that *"I can assure you that we shall not fall out over the amount"*, the PCC wanted good news for their money, not a spiralling litany of defects. When J.H.Henderson voiced the PCC's concerns in writing, Brakspear told him that he had only done what had been asked of him. *"Of course, I may be wrong"*, he added reproachfully, *"but after working on old churches for over 30 years one does gain a little expertise"*. That put them in their place.

J & A Brazier, the town's leading building contractors, had been asked to cost the work and submitted a tender to Brakspear on 7th November. Only the leadwork could be accurately priced, as the true extent of work needed to the timbers and pinnacles would only be known when the whole roof was accessible. The Brazier family had a long connection with both church and town, contributing several churchwardens to St John's, including Sydney Brazier from 1923 to 1927, and the church was therefore confident of a good job. Finding the funds was a different matter. This kind of money was well beyond the parish's resources and a local fundraising appeal was the only solution. A six-man restoration committee was quickly formed under John Green, the parish treasurer, and two public meetings were held early in the New Year, jointly chaired by the historian J.W. Willis Bund and the bishop of Worcester. Graphic leaflets warning of "St John's in danger!" were

CHAPTER 8: MODERN TIMES

printed and begging letters were sent in every direction, including grant-giving bodies and the local gentry. Neither was particularly forthcoming. The diocese – as ever - pleaded lack of funds, and the gentry were unwilling to give unless the diocese did, a neat and circular excuse. The money had to come from the town and the town, as ever, rose to the occasion. Taking a risk that income would keep pace with the builders the PCC appointed Braziers almost immediately. They set to work that spring, aiming to finish by Christmas.

A timber working platform was first constructed the full width and length of the church, level with the clerestory window cills and supported by tall posts onto the nave floor. This also protected the congregation below, for the church could not afford to be taken out of use during the work. The first news from this new vantage place was bad. The timber decay was even worse than Brakspear had anticipated, with half the main rafters rotted beyond repair and much of the roof boarding and plasterwork decayed. Damp had been seeping into the wall-heads for centuries through cracks in the parapet stonework caused by the rusting iron dowels that held each stone to its neighbour. To prevent this happening again, these dowels were replaced with slate pins, adding to the original cost and putting further pressure on the fundraising.

But now the main work could start. Each main beam was propped, the rotted ends cut out and new oak spliced in and reinforced with bolted steel channels. Five of the six beams were restored this way, although almost half the timber in each was new. The sixth beam, second from the chancel arch, could not be saved and had to be completely replaced. De la Hay watched anxiously from below as Brazier's men laboriously winched 1½ tons of Suffolk oak up through the clerestory with block and tackle, manoeuvred it through the roof space and lowered it carefully onto the wall-heads. The king post was knocked in and the principal rafters dropped onto it. Purlins, common rafters, boarding and lead were then re-laid, and new lead gutters formed. The timberwork was treated with *"Professor Lefroy's preparation"* against death-watch beetle and the plasterwork was painted out in an off-white colour, a better contrast to the newly restored timber than the previous blue.

The additional work pushed the contract completion date over the end of the year, a delay exacerbated by the appalling weather of 1925 which saw a succession of exceptionally wet and windy months and a white Christmas Day. The work was finally complete by 25th January 1926 and a great Service of Thanksgiving was held at 11am on Sunday 14th February, at which the bishop of Worcester preached, albeit rather unmemorably. It was left to de la Hay to set the appeal in context at the evening service, both as an event in St John's long history and as the work of the town's many skilled craftsmen.

Braziers' final account came in at £2,882 6s 11d, reflecting the greater amount of work necessary to the roof timbers and wall-heads. When the administrative costs of running the appeal were added, the total project cost £2,909 9s, every penny of which came from local people. The restoration committee had hoped to be able to reach the appeal target in time for the service but £200 remained outstanding on the day and the last few pounds took several months to come in. It was however an heroic effort at a time of depressed trade and union unrest, and in an increasingly secular town. Religion – of any denomination – was no longer uppermost in the lives of many people, and news of the appeal had to share the pages of the Messenger with long-running correspondence on *"Modernism and religion"* and *"The decay of Christianity"*, together with all the other trappings of the 20th century world from underwear adverts to motor car smashes. That it succeeded – as de la Hay acknowledged – was down to the underlying regard the people of Bromsgrove had for their shared heritage, the one building in town that nearly everyone had some link with, if only through generations long gone.

CHAPTER 8: MODERN TIMES

As you might expect, a photographer from the Bromsgrove Messenger was on hand to capture key moments in the work. But his pictures show us something more than just a 1920s building contract. The timber scaffolding, the simple ropes and pulleys and the workmen with their rough clothes, weathered faces and calloused hands would all be entirely familiar to the 15th century builders of the original roof. We have come a long way since sweating Saxon carpenters felled a corner of Brem's little wood to provide oak for their lord's chapel on the hill. Bromsgrove's church has grown and changed beyond all record over these last thousand years and it has taken many shapes - sprouted aisles, chapels, clerestory and tower; gained and lost windows, glass, galleries, screens, altars, fonts and pews. To the casual visitor the church is a fine example of medieval ecclesiastical architecture; to town planners a Grade 1 Listed Building; to the tourist board a local landmark, to many newly-weds a picturesque backdrop to their nuptials. But in the end St John's is the work of human hands, men and women who through the centuries have moulded and shaped stone, timber, glass, fabric and lead to meet the needs of their day. Its history is their history. Without them this church is just a series of architectural styles, another historic building and a rather inconvenient venue for modern worship.

Pause and listen a moment, as the Reverend Dr Treadway Russell Nash does one day in the late 18th century. Compiling his magisterial "History of Worcestershire" he calls in at St John's to update old Thomas Habington's manuscript account. Much is still as Habington saw it, and hidden amongst the jumbled box pews and galleries Nash finds the various alabaster monuments, the tombs and inscriptions, the few remaining pieces of stained glass in the battered windows. But he notices – or rather, hears - something else. St John's church, he says, has *"good echoes in the east and west corners"*. Echoes and whispers - voices from the past - reverberate around this ancient building. Through its cavernous interior marches a procession of real people - vicars, churchwardens and gentry; farmers, yeomen and shop-keepers; Alienora Stafford, John Spilsbury and "Paterfamilias Indignans"; you and me. The echoes of their voices tell a rather different tale and if we are wise we will listen to it.

Echoes and Whispers

Throughout this story I have dealt in the common currency of historians - records, account books, court rolls and the cold hard facts of stone and timber, none of which can dispute my occasionally personal interpretation of their evidence. But history has the habit of rushing away from us as we run to catch up with it, and the modern history of St John's lies as much in the hearts and minds of its parishioners as in the Worcestershire Records Office or the Cotton Collection. This story must stop somewhere. With the restoration of 1926 we enter the realm of the living, when history becomes that most elusive thing, a personal memory. Every age has a story to tell – the Sunday in 1936 when a party of Hitler Youth attended morning service at St John's is just one example – but it must wait for another time.

The church of the early 21st century has very different requirements from its predecessors, both in the forms of worship and the expectations of its users, and yet the building itself still largely reflects mid-Victorian high church practice. Are George Gilbert Scott's fine oak pews and stalls an ornament or a hindrance? Can a medieval church accommodate a kitchen and toilets? How comfortable or warm are worshippers entitled to be? Should children be seen and heard? What balance should be struck between access and security in a time of rising crime? How much of the scarce parochial finances should be spent on maintaining a public historic building rather than the Christian work of the church in the community? Attend any PCC meeting and you will hear these and similar questions being asked - and answers eventually found, for the life of the church must go on. If this story has shown anything it is that change is rarely unanimous, that personal

CHAPTER 8: MODERN TIMES

expressions of belief can divide as well as unite. But it is beyond the scope of this story to interpret the actions of those who now have to make these ancient stones serve today's needs. Our successors will judge whether the parish of the early 21st century was up to the task; whether it just thought for today or had an eye to the future, as well as a care for the past. Like those who have gone before we can only live in the present, and we must leave it for others to weave our everyday lives into the stuff of history.

FAIRLY MOUNTED ON A HILL

[Picture 36] The epitome of the country church. An idealised but nonetheless charming view of St John's from the late 1840s, carefully omitting the ugly iron window frames in the north aisle but clearly showing the gallery window over the north door. Joseph Rose entertains two visitors on the main path in his usual lively manner. Towering over them is William Chance's rather crude effigy of 1769, still railed and at its full height. The church paths are already heavily revetted with old gravestones and the fairly rough grass of the yard itself appears to be kept in order by sheep rather than scythes.

BIBLIOGRAPHY

Much of this story comes from first-hand accounts, either held by St John's PCC or lodged with the Worcester Records Office and the Public Records Office at Kew. These include the parish registers from 1590, the churchwardens account books and presentments, parish papers, wills and the various court records referred to. As they are numerous I have not listed them individually. The Cotton Collection of local papers in Birmingham City Library is a major source of information about St John's, and the Prattinton Collection at the London Society of Antiquaries library has a number of useful transcripts of historical documents. The Bromsgrove Messenger is a rich source of detail for all local events from 1860 and I have mined it freely.

In addition, I found the following books and articles useful in compiling this story.

References mentioning St John's Church, its incumbents or parishioners

Aitken, John (ed.)	*Census of Religious Worship, 1851. The Returns for Worcestershire* (WHS 2000)
Anon	*The life of the late Rev. Mr John Flavel, Minister of Dartmouth* (c1691)
Atkin, Malcolm	*Worcestershire under arms* (2004)
Baber, A.F.C.	*The Court Rolls of the Manor of Bromsgrove and Kings Norton 1494-1504* (WHS 1963)

Barnard, E.A.B.	*Old Bromsgrove 1649 -1721 (1926)*
Barnard, E.A.B.	*The Earliest Register of the Parish of Bromsgrove In TrWAS Vol 1 (1923)*
Barnard, E.A.B. and Wace, A.J.B.	
	The Sheldon Tapestry Weavers and their work (1928)
Baxter, Richard	*Reliquiæ Baxterianæ, or Mr Richard Baxter's narrative of the most important passages in his life and times, faithfully publish'd from his own manuscript by Matthew Sylvester (1696)*
Besse, Joseph	*A collection of the sufferings of the people called Quakers: Vol. II Worcestershire (1753)*
Bloore, Peter D. (ed.)	*The Poor Law Settlement Documents of the Parish Church of St John the Baptist, Bromsgrove, Worcestershire (1988)*
Bridges, Tim	*Churches of Worcestershire (2000)*
Brock, Susan	*Worcester Cathedral Library: Catalogue of Muniments (1981)*
Broomfield, Alan	*Bromsgrove and the Poll Tax of 1690 (n.d. transc. From Cotton, W.A. 1881)*
Burton, Revd. John R. (ed.)	*Bibliography of Worcestershire: Pt 2 (WHS 1903)*
Calamy, Edmund	*An Account of the Ministers, Lecturers, Masters and Fellows of Colleges and Schoolmasters who were Ejected of Silenced after the Restoration in 1660 by or before the Act for Uniformity, Vol. 2 (2nd ed. 1713)*
Bromsgrove Baptist Church and the Baptist Historical Society	
	Church Record Book Volume One 1670-1715 (1974)

BIBLIOGRAPHY

Brooks, Alan and Pevsner, Nikolaus
> *The Buildings of England; Worcestershire (2007)*

Cole, T.W.
> *Pre-reformation church accessories in the Diocese of Worcester (1933)*

Collis, Revd John Day
> *Historical and Architectural notes on the Parish Church of St John the Baptist with a Sermon preached on January 30, 1859 (1859)*

Cotton, William A.
> *Bromsgrove Church: its History and Antiquities (1881)*

Cotton, William A.
> *Extracts from the Calendar of State Papers having reference to the City and County of Worcester (1547-1667) (1886)*

Cotton, William A.
> *The Old Houses of Bromsgrove and Neighbourhood and their Associations (1881)*

Darlington, R.R. (ed.)
> *The Cartulary of Worcester Cathedral Priory: Register I (1968)*

Davenport, James
> *Worcester Diocesan Registry: presentations to livings, list and place index 1526 – 1602 (1916)*

Downing, M.
> *Medieval Military Effigies up to 1500 remaining in Worcestershire In TrWAS Vol.18 (2002)*

Dyer, Christopher
> *Bromsgrove; a small town in Worcestershire in the Middle Ages (WHS 2000)*

Eckells, John
> *The Funeral Sermon of John Spilsbury, Together with His Personal Confession of Faith (1699)*

Finberg, W.P.R.
> *The Early Charters of the West Midlands (1961)*

Fletcher, Dr George	*Bromsgrove 1852-72 In Bromsgrove Messenger (Jan-Jul 1930)*
Ford, James	*The Puritan Vicars of Bromsgrove and the rise of local Nonconformity in the 17th century (1909)*
Foster, Joseph (ed.)	*Alumni Oxonienses: the members of the University of Oxford 1500-1714 (1891)*
Gilbert, C.D.	*Magistracy and ministry in Cromwellian England; The case of Kings Norton, Worcestershire In Midland History Vol. XXIII (1998)*
Habington, Thomas	*Survey of Worcestershire (before 1647)*
Haines, R.M.	*A Calendar of the Register of Simon de Montacute, Bishop of Worcester 1334-1337 (1996)*
Haines R.M.	*A Calendar of the Register of Wolstan de Bransford, Bishop of Worcester 1339-49 (1966)*
Hodgson, Aileen M.	*The Chapel and Manor of Grafton Manor 1218-1874 In Worcestershire Recusant, Vol 8 (December 1966)*
Hoult, E.Anne, Irving, John and Townshend, Jenny	*The 17th Century Constables Accounts of Bromsgrove (nd)*
Humphries, John	*Bromsgrove Church and Grafton Manor In TrBAS Vol XLVII (1921)*
Humphries, John	*Bromsgrove Church and Harvington Hall In TrBAS Vol LIV (1929)*
Humphries, John	*Studies in Worcestershire History (1938)*
Humphries, John	*The Sheldon Tapestry Maps of Worcestershire In TrBAS Vol XLIII (1917)*

BIBLIOGRAPHY

Hunsworth, George	*Baxter's Nonconformist Descendents (1874)*
Icely, H.E.M.	*Bromsgrove School through four centuries (1953)*

Keeble, N.H. and Nuttall, Geoffrey F.
Calendar of the Correspondence of Richard Baxter, Vol. I: 1638-1660; Vol II: 1660-1696 (1991)

Kinney, Byron W. John Boweter (1629 – 1704),
His Life As A Quaker And His "Sermons From Prison" (self published 2010)

Lacy, John	*A Survey of Bromsgrove Parish (manuscript 1778)*
Laird, Mr [Frances Charles]	*Worcestershire; or original delineations, topographical, historical, and descriptive of that county; the result of personal survey (1818)*
Leadbetter, William G.	*The Story of Bromsgrove (1946)*
Lock, Arthur B.	*The History of Kings Norton and Northfield Wards (c.1910)*
Matthews, A.G.	*Calamy Revised, being a revision of Edmund Calamy's Account of minister and others ejected and silenced 1660-2 (1934)*

Matthew, H.C.G. and Harrison, Brian (ed.)
The Oxford Dictionary of National Biography (2004)

Metcalfe, Walter C.	*The Visitation of the County of Worcester: 1682 (WHS 1883)*

Minutes of Evidence taken before the Committee of Privileges, to whom were referred the Petition of the Right Honourable Henry John Chetwynd, Earl Talbot... (1858)

Moore, Jerrold Northrop	*Elgar and his publishers; letters of a creative life (1987)*

Morgan, Paul (ed.)	*Inspections of Churches and Parsonage Houses in the Diocese of Worcester in 1674, 1676, 1684 and 1687 (WHS 1986)*
Nash, Treadway R.	*History of Worcestershire (1781, 2ed. 1794)*
Noake, John	*Guide to Worcestershire (1868)*
Noake, John	*Notes and Queries for Worcestershire (1856)*
Noake, John	*The Rambler in Worcestershire (1848)*
Noake, John (writing as An Old Digger)	*Worcestershire Nuggets (1889)*

Nonarum Inquisitiones in Curia scaccarii: Temp. Edwardi III (1341: printed 1807 by command of Geo.III)

Notes and Queries for Bromsgrove Vols 1-5 (1909-1913)

Nuttall, Geoffrey F.	*The Worcestershire Association: Its Membership In JEH Vol. I (1950)*
Price, Clement (ed.)	*Liber Pensionem Prioratus Wigorn (WHS 1925)*
Richards, Alan	*Braziers, Builders of Bromsgrove 1850-1990 (1996)*
Richards, Alan	*Bromsgrove Now and Then (1988)*
Rose, Bob	*The Curfew Tolls the Knell of Parting Day (article, 1979)*
Salter, Mike	*The old parish churches of Worcestershire (1989)*
Shepherd, Revd. F.C.	*Bromsgrove Parish Church (1958)*
Skinner, R.F.	*Nonconformity in Shropshire 1662-1816 (1964)*
Smith, Revd. I. Gregory	*Diocesan Histories: Worcester (1883)*
Stanton, George K.	*Rambles and Researches in Worcestershire Churches (1881)*

BIBLIOGRAPHY

Sumner, Sir James and Coles, T.W.
: *Worcestershire Scratch Dials In TrWAS Vol IX (1932)*

Thorn, Frank and Caroline (ed.)
: *Domesday Book: Vol.16 - Worcestershire (1982)*

Townshend, Henry
: *Diary of Henry Townshend of Elmley Lovett 1640 – 1663 Ed J.W. Willis Bund for WHS (1920)*

Vaughan, J.A.
: *John Hall of Bromsgrove: a biographical note In TrWAS Vol XXXVIII (1961)*

Venn, J. and J.A.
: *Alumni Cantabrigienses (1922)*

Walker, John
: *An attempt towards recovering an account of the numbers and sufferings of the clergy of the Church of England who were sequester'd, harassed in the late times of the grand rebellion (1714)*

Walters, H.B.
: *Inventories of Worcestershire Church Goods (1552) Pt 1 In TrWAS Vol XVII (1940)*

Wigginton, William
: *The late Archidiaconal Visitation at Bromsgrove and the Injustice and Illegality of Visitation fees (1859)*

Willis Bund, J.W.
: *Episcopal Registers, Diocese of Worcester: Register of Bishop Godfrey Gifford, September 23rd 1268 to August 15th 1301, Vol. II (WHS 1902)*

Willis Bund J.W.
: *Register of the Diocese of Worcester during the Vacancy of the See 1301-1435 (WHS 1897)*

Willis Bund J.W. and Page, W. (ed.)
: *Victoria History of the County of Worcestershire: Vols II & III (1906)*

Yule, George
: *The Independents in the English Civil War (1958)*

FAIRLY MOUNTED ON A HILL
Background references

Addleshaw, G.W.O.	*Rectors, Vicars and Patrons in twelfth and early 13th century Canon Law (1956)*
Baxter, Richard	*Christian Concord: or the Agreement of the Associated Pastors and Churches of Worcestershire, with Rich. Baxter's Explication and Defence of it and his Exhortation to Unity (1653)*
Baxter, Richard	*One Sheet against the Quakers (1652)*
Baxter, Richard	*The Agreement of divers Ministers of Christ In the County of Worcester and some adjacent parts for Catechizing or Personally Instructing All in the several Parishes that will consent thereto (1656)*
Baxter, Richard	*The Humble Petition of many Thousands…of the County of Worcester to the Parliament of the Common-wealth of England in behalf of the Able, Faithful, Godly Ministry of this Nation (1652)*
Bettey, J.H.	*Church and Parish: a guide for local historians (1987)*
Cobbett, William	*Rural Rides (1830)*
Collins, Jeffery R.	*The Church Settlement of Oliver Cromwell In History, Vol 87 (2002)*
Cotton, William	*The Antiquities of Bromsgrove (Paper read to the Bromsgrove Institute 1879)*
Cressy, David	*Agnes Bowker's Cat: Travesties and Transgressions in Tudor and Stuart England (2000)*
Dearmer, Percy	*Everyman's History of the Prayer Book (1912)*

BIBLIOGRAPHY

Drew, Charles	*Early Parochial Organisation in England: The origins of the office of Churchwarden (1954)*
Duffy, Eamon	*The Stripping of the Altars (1992)*
Gardiner, Samuel R.	*The Constitutional Documents of the Puritan Revolution, 1625-1660 (1906)*
Gelling, Margaret	*Place Names in the Landscape (1984)*
Gwilliam, H.W	*Curiosities of the Church in Worcestershire (n.d.)*
Hill, Christopher	*The English Bible and the 17th Century Revolution (1997)*
Hill, Christopher	*Society and Puritanism in Pre-Revolutionary England (1964)*
Hill, Christopher	*The World Turned Upside Down (1972)*
Humphries, John	*The Forest of Feckenham (...)*
Hutton, Graham et al	*English Parish Churches (1976)*
Knowles, Nigel	*Kidderminster and Bewdley during the Civil War 1642-1651 (2002)*
Knowles, Nigel	*Richard Baxter of Kidderminster (2000)*
Leatherbarrow, Canon J.S.	*The Victorians look at their churches In TrWAS Vol .9 (1984)*
Leland, John	*The itinerary of John Leland in or about the years 1535-1543: Pts IV and V Ed Lucy Toulmin Smith (1964)*
Manning, Brian	*Aristocrats, Plebeians and revolution in England, 1640 - 1660 (1996)*
Morris, Richard	*Churches in the Landscape (1989)*

FAIRLY MOUNTED ON A HILL

Nicholson, W.F.H, Gelling, M. and Richards, M.	
	The Names of Towns and Cities in Britain (...)
Parsons, David	*Liturgy and architecture in the Middle Ages* (Third Deerhurst Lecture, 1986)
Phillimore, W.P.W.	*The Visitation of the County of Worcester made in the year 1569* (1888)
Sherwood, Roy	*The Civil War in the Midlands 1642-1651* (1992)
Stenton, Frank	*Anglo Saxon England* (1947)
Stansbury, Don	*The Lady who fought the Vikings* (1993)
Stephens, W.B. (ed.)	*Victoria History of the County of Warwickshire* (1964)
Terret, I.B. and Darby, H.C.	*The Domesday Geography of Middle England* (1971)
Willis Bund J.W.	*The Civil War in Worcestershire 1642-1646* (1905)
Willis Bund J.W.	*The Restored Churches of Worcestershire* (WHS 1908)
Zaluckyj, Sarah	*Mercia: the Anglo-Saxon Kingdom of Central England* (2002)

GENERAL INDEX

References in italic are pictures

Absentee vicars, 101, 107-9, 199-200
Accidents, 242-3
Acts of Parliament
  Burial in Woollen (1666), 156
  Corporation (1661), 142
  Conventicle (1664), 144
  Five Mile (1664), 144
  Public Worship Regulation (1874), 227
  Sectaries (1593), 96
  Second Conventicle (1670), 152
  Tithe Commutation Act (1836), 259
  Toleration (1689), 145
  Uniformity (1662), 132, 143, 144
Aisles
  North, 18, 30, *30*, 31, 41, 167-8, 174
  South, 20, 30, 31, 47, 173
All Saints' church, 240
Altars
  generally, 48, 60, 67, 77
  high, 67, 77, 177, 222, 263
  nave, 89*fn*, 134
  rails, 134, 172, 178, 222
Anabaptists, 95*fn*, 116
Appointment of clergy
  by Patron, 51, 119, 149, 152
  by King, 25, 102, 108, 152
  disputed, 51, 99,
  generally, 114,
Appropriation, 26, 28

Arcades, 30, 66
Attendance, surveys of, 76, 145, 216

Baptism, attitudes to, 115, 123, 132, 139
Baptists
  generally, 144,
  in Bewdley, 115-7, 124
  in Bromsgrove, 146-7
Barstardy records, 164
Battlements, 68
Beer, consumption of, 162, 185
Bellman, 133, 164-5
Bell, passing, 188
Bell ropes, 165, 179*fn*, 180
Bell ringers, 178-80
Bell ringing, 113, 179, 188, 208
Bells, 59, 82, 133, 179-80, 188,
Beoley, 43, 165*fn*
Bewdley, 114-6, 123
Bible, 77, 95, 96, 149, 237-8
Bishop Hall's Charity, 130-1
Bounds, beating of, 113
Bromsgrove
  boundary disputes, 33-4, 34*fn*
  development of town, 33-4, 37, 55
  Guild, 246*fn*
  High Street, 33-4
  Messenger (newspaper), 229, 243*fn*
Burh, 15-6
Burglary, in church, 191

Burial, right of, 16, 43, 148, 231
Callow Hill, 113
Carillon, 256
Catholics
  attitudes to, 89, 92-4, 145*fn*, 154-5
  recusant, 93-4, 106
Catshill, 240
Chadwich, chapel at, 24, 34-5, 166*fn*
Chancel, 20, 21, *21*, 29, 70, 176-8, 263
Chancel repairs, 55, 166-7
Chancel screen, 247-9, *248*
Chandelier, in nave, 184 & *fn*
Chapels
  Chantry, 42-3, 60, 63-5, *63*, 67, 77, 168
  Our Lady, 20, 67
  St John, 20, 67
  St Nicholas, 67
Chetton, church at, 114, 119
Children in church, 197, 202
Chimes, 181-2
Choir, *58*, 166, 173, 227 & *fn*
Church ales, 18*fn*, 60-1
Church house, 61-2
Church paths, 22, 37*fn*, 71-2, 158, 189, 214
Church rates, 203-4, 206 & *fn*
Church steps, 18, 22, 71, 72,
Church Street, 22
Churchwardens, 78, 110*fn*, 118, 151, 154, 161-2, 173-4, 178, 209, 227, 256
Churchyard
  closure of for burials, 230-1
  expansion of, 187
  gates, 71, 190

  generally, 22, 71, 186-90, *276*
  maintenance of, 189
  paths, 187, 189-90
  trees in, 49, 190
  wall, 71, 190
Civil War
  course of, 107-12
  events preceding, 105-7
  execution, evidence of, 142 & *fn*
  taxation for, 110
Clarendon Code, 142-3, 144
Classis system, 90, 109, 115 & *fn*
Cleaning, church, 184-5
Clerestorey, 66
Clergy, minor, 50-1, 79 & *fn*
Clock
  tower, *58*, 133, 181-2 & *fn*, *183*
  town hall, 182
  west gallery, 174
Clothing and shoe club, 237
Coffin, heart, 32
Commissioners
  Parliamentary, 113
  Royal, 83, 87
Common Prayer, Book of, 82, 143-4, 183
Communion table, 134
Compton survey (1676), see Attendance
Congregational Church, 145
Conventicle, seditious, 153
Courts
  Baron, 33
  Church, 53
  Leet, 194

GENERAL INDEX

Quarter Sessions, 94, 105, 118, 127
Crosses
   altar, 87
   nave (rood), 67, 82
   preaching, 22
   town, 23
Crown Close, 37, 140, 158
Crypts, see Vaults
Curates, 200, 202 & *fn*, 226-7, 238, 245
Curfew, 133

Decoration, 39, 82, 87, 139, 168, 219, 272
Diocesan Church Building Society, 213 & *fn*
Dissent, growth of, 94-8, 115, 144, 152, 156-7
Dodford, 50, 109 & *fn*, 240
Domesday Book, 14, 17
Doom painting, 39, 82, 219
Doors
   Chancel, 222
   north, 20, 31, 174, 222
   south, 20, 31, 69-70
   west, 20, 46
Dream of Gerontius, 254-5
Droitwich, 13, 48*fn*
Dust-hole, 188, 197

Ecclesiologists, 213 & *fn*, 216
Excommunication, 49, 149*fn*
Exhumation, 188-9

Familists, 95, 97-8 & *fn*
Flooring, 29, 220, 263

Font, 138, 139 & *fn*, 178, 216*fn*
Free and Open Church Association, 229, 240
Funerals, 130, 188

Galleries, 172-3, 174-6, 197, 218-9, 235
Glass, stained, 168-9, 222, 244-7
Glebe land, 28, 38
Grafton
   Chapel, 24, 35, 73*fn*, 92*fn*
   Manor, 43 & *fn*, 63, 72, 73
Graves, 22, 112, 128, 131, 177, see also Monuments
Grave digging, 165, 187
Grave robbing, 190-1, *192*
Gravestones, 71, 186-7
Green Men, 39
Guides, to church, 224, 257
Guilds, 60
Gunpowder plot, 74*fn*, 92

Hagioscope, 42
Hearth Tax, 159
Heating in church, 169, 184, 223, 242
Hedgehogs, 186
Histories, of church, 88, 273
Holy Lane, see Church Street
Holy water stoop, 69, 82
Homilies, Books of, see Sermons

Iconoclasm, evidence for, 139-40
Incorporated Church Building Society, 213, 215*fn*
Independent chapel, 128, 145

289

Independent Church, 91, 114, 118, 145
Jews, in Bromsgrove, 155-6
Kidderminster, 107, 111, *121*, 151
Kings Norton, 24, 103*fn*, 111, 121, *132*, 152, 240
Knights Templar, action against, 34

Lectern, 135
Lecturers, 107, 108*fn*, 117*fn*
Library, church, 136, 267-8
Lickey, Holy Trinity church, 202*fn*, 213*fn*
Lighting, of church, 183-4, 223 & *fn*
Lightning strike, 197
Lych gate, 71, 139-40, *140*

Magazine, parish, 234-30
Magistrates, 104, 126*fn*
Manor
  boundary disputes, 33-4 & *fn*
  rectory, 28-9, 33, 258
  royal, 13, 14, 17-8, 33
Manorial rights, disputed, 193 & *fn*
Marriage, during Commonwealth, 133-4
Market, 18, 33, 34*fn*
Market Hall, 18, 182, 196
Missal, 70
Missions, church, 238
Monuments, 31-2, 73-6, 86, 88, 131, 135, 232-4, 266-7
Monument bay, 66
Mortuaries, 26 & *fn*
Moseley, chapel at, 24, 111, 114, 119
Musicians, church, 68, 173 & *fn*

Nave, 20, 47, *84*, 168
Newfoundland, Bishop of, 238*fn*
Nun's Path, see Churchyard, paths

Offerings, 202, 240-1, 250
Ordinands, 50
Organ, 68, 82, 87, 173-4 & *fn*, 176, 223
Origins of church, 14-6
Oxford Movement, see Ecclesiologists

Paganism, supposed evidence for, 15
Parish
  boundaries of, 16
  boundaries, disputed, 27-8
  bounds, beating of, 133 & *fn*
  clerk, 133, 155*fn* 165
  chest, 80, 81, 193, 285
  origins of, 16
  records, 81*fn*, 193, 285
  registers, 80, 102*fn*, 109, 111, 116, 123
  division of in 19th C., 240
Parochial Church Council, 258
Parson's Hill, 36, 214
Patron, 17-8, 24, 25-6
Patronal day, 26
Perry Hall, 112-3, 203
Pews
  generally, 48, 139, 171, 212, 222
  payment for, 139, 171, 176, 208, 227-9, 250-2
Plague, 41, 48
Pluralism, 100-1, 148
Poor box, 137-8, 241
Poor, alms for, 136-8

GENERAL INDEX

Poor Law, 137, 164
Porch, 68-9, *69*
Presbyterian Church, 90-1, 105, 106, 111-4, 125, 130-1, 143, 144, 195
Presentments, churchwardens', 97, 156-7
Pulpit, 139, 170-1, 202, 263
Puritanism, rise of, 90, 98-9, 109, 125, 149

Quakers, 125-6 & *fn*, 147-8 & *fn*, 153-4 & *fn*, 155*fn*
Queen Anne's Bounty, 214

Railway, Birmingham & Gloucs, 206*fn*
Rack Close, 38
Ranters, local evidence for, 97-8 & *fn*
Rectors, lay, 20, 99
Redmarley D'Abitot, 128*fn*, 148*fn*
Reformation, 76-7
Registrar, 133-4, 213-2
Reputation, of church in 19th C, 207-9, 229
Reredos, 178, 222
Restoration
  of the monarchy, 127
  of St John's, 214-6, 2017-23, *221*, 225
Riot, in church, 203-7
Rogation day, 113
Roman road, 12
Roman coin, 12*fn*
Rood
  screen, 67-8, 82, 138-9
  loft, 68, 82, 219

Roof
  construction of, 47, 65
  repairs to, 167-8, 219, 222, 268-72
  chantry chapel, 68, 124
Royal arms, 82
Rydal Mount, see Vicarage

Sacramental certificate, 106, 155
Savoy Conference, 143
School house, 197-8, *198*
Schoolmaster, 77, 148*fn*, 109*fn*, 216
Schools
  Church (National), 196, 198, 203, 218*fn*, 236-7
  Bromsgrove (grammar), 77, 109*fn*, 216-7, 222
  Sunday, 196-7, 236, 261*fn*
Scratch dials, see sun dials
Sermons, 50 & *fn*, 83, 87 & *fn*, 129, 202 & *fn*, 223-4 & *fn*
Services, in church, 23, 170
Sextons, 164-6, 187-8, 214-4
Sexual misdemeanours, 49-50, 53-4, 127, 162-4
Sidesmen, creation of, 256
Sidnals, 27*fn*
Silver, church, 82, 87
Slander against clergy, 126-7, 148-9
Soup kitchen, 237
Spadesbourne, River, 12, 33, 36
Spire, 56-7, 249-50
Sports, cruel, in 18th C, 195*fn*
Statues, medieval, 46
Stoke Prior, 14, 28*fn*, 100, 164*fn*

291

Stratford, Holy Trinity church, 230*fn*
Sundials, 59-60
Superstition, 22-3, 39

Tapestry maps, Sheldon, 43-4, *44*
Tardebigge, 27, 208
Taxation, 29*fn*, 36, 55, 77*fn*
Ting-tang, 166 & *fn*, 181*fn*, 243
Tithe Barn, 32
Tithes, 26-7, 55, 112, 154, 259 & *fn*
Toleration, attitudes to, 114 & *fn*, 157
Tower
   early evidence for, 21-2, 43-4
   generally, 43-7, *45*, 56-7, *58*, 178-81
Town Hall, see Market Hall
Transepts, traces of, 19, 31, 47-8, 220
Triers, 118-9
Turks, 151*fn*

Umbrella, vicar's, 188
Upton Warren, 27-8

Vaults, 74, 76, 220 & *fn*
Vestments, 82, 166, 227
Vestry, 166, 169-70
Vestry, choir, 261-2
Vestry meetings, 169, 200, 247, 251

Vicarage, 26, 36-7, 80, 158-9, 213-4, *214*, 256
Vicars, see under Index of Names
Visitations, diocesan, 48-9, 166, 231-2

Wall paintings, 38-9, 219
Wands, churchwardens, 172
War memorials, see Monuments
Wills, 74*fn*, 76*fn*, 88-90, 113, 129, 137, 145*fn*
Windows
   aisle, 64, 67, *177*, 220
   east, 21, 29
   generally, 20, 41, 168-9, 220
   west, 46, 165
Wine, communion, 183
Working men's club, 237
Wythall, chapel at, 24, 111
Worcester
   cathedral or priory, 25, 114, 254
   dean and chapter of, 78, 114, 150
   Diocesan Advisory Committee, 162*fn*
   Diocesan Architectural Society, 216, 224
   in Civil War, 150
Worcestershire Agreement, 122, 150
Worcestershire Association, 120-3, 125, 131

INDEX OF NAMES

(v) denotes vicar of St John's　　(c) denotes curate at St John's

Adams, Capt John, 203-4
Æthelflaed, 15
Æthelmund, 13
Æthelric, 13
Ainge, Joseph (v), 114,117-8,119, 144
Ainge, Samuel, 119*fn*
Aldworth, John (v?), 101,102*fn*, 158
ap Davies, Robert (c), 87
Archbold, John (v), 101-2, 103
Arden, Robert, 99-100
Asmore, John, 154
Astmore, Richard, 26*fn*
Astmore, William, 153*fn*
Athersitch, Mary (widow), 163
atte Lake, Richard (v), 55
Avys, Robert (v), 45*fn*, 100

Bache, Edward, 89
Bache, Elizabeth, 148-9, 153*fn*
Bache, Margaret, 149*fn*
Badger, Mary, 105
Badger, Rebecca, 164
Badger, Thomas, 100
Baggeley, William, 119
Baggott, Elizabeth, 163
Baldwin, A, 256*fn*
Bard, Col. Sir Henry, 110
Baldwin, Thomas, 130
Banyster, Edward, 97, 98*fn*

Bardulf, Hugh, 18
Barnard, A.E.B, 258
Barnes, Henry, 112*fn*
Barnesley, family of Barnesley Hall, 88, 112*fn*, 177
Barrett, Henry (solicitor), 233-4
Baxter, – (widow), 163
Baxter, Frederick, 266
Baxter, Richard, 105*fn*, 107, 108*fn*, 111, 117*fn*, 120-7, *120*, 130, 131*fn*, 143, 144, 150, 151
Baylis, William, 138
Bayliss, -, 195
Benson, George, 114,
Biddle, John, 110*fn*
Bigg, Jane, 97, 98*fn*
Bishops
　Cobham (Worcs). 54
　Cranmer, Archbishop Thomas, 82
　de Bransford, Wulstan (Worcs), 51
　de Montacute, Simon (Worcs), 51
　Hall, John (Bristol), 104,112,117,130-1
　Heaberht (Worcs), 13
　Jewel, John, 135
　John (Llandaff), 50
　Laud, William, Archb. of Canterbury, 98, 106, 134
　Morley (Worcs), 127
　Pepys (Worcs), 213*fn*

293

Bishops (cont.)
  Prideaux, John (Worcs), 108
  Sanderson, 143*fn*
  Sandys (Worcs), 95, 99*fn*
  Skinner (Worcs), 152
  Thornborough (Worcs), 102, 103*fn*
  Wakefield (Worcs), 55
  Whitgift (Worcs), 93, 96
  William de Blois (Worcs), 25
Blackburn, Joseph (steeplejack), 250
Blick, Alice, 145
Blick, John, 155*fn*
Blick, Martin, 155*fn*
Blick, Nicholas, 127, 145, 155
Blundell, Edward, 66
Blundell, Margery, 66
Bodle, William, 90
Bonner, John, 109
Boraston, John, 117*fn*
Boulton, Thomas, 167
Bowers, Ralph, 110*fn*
Boweter, John, 153-4
Bradley, Walter and Anne, 155
Brakspear, Sir Harold, 257, 268-71
Brakeridge, Catherine, 263
Brazier, Albert, 261*fn*
Brazier, Jonathan, 184*fn*
Brazier, J&A, 261*fn*, 270-2
Brazier, Sydney, 270
Brem, 13
Brigge, Edward, 52
Brook, - (builder), 185
Brook, William, 196
Brooke, Edward, 91

Brookes, Henry, 138
Broughton, William (c), 151
Brown, - (builder), 249
Burton, John Boulton, 162, 186
Butler, Elizabeth (later Eckells), 147*fn*

Cade, Jack, 64
Calamy, Edmund, 123, 129, 131
Calvin, John, 90
Capelin, Peter, 220*fn*
Capel-Cure, Edward, 254
Capronnier, Jean-Baptiste, 245
Carpenter, - (widow), 163
Carrington, Gervas (v), 80, 100-2
Carrington, Elizabeth, 101*fn*
Carter, Edward, 181, 184
Cartwright, John, 163*fn*
Cartwright, Matthew, 153*fn*
Chance, Thomas, 45*fn*
Chance, William, 177, 276
Chandler, John, 153*fn*
Chaunce, Richard, 89
Chetle, Mr, 167
Chetwynd, Henry, Earl Talbot, 232-4
Chevasse, Sir Thomas, 246
Chevasse, Noel, 246*fn*
Christopher, Sarah, 154
Clarkson, Samuel (painter), 233-4
Clare, William (c), 79
Clayton & Bell, 220
Cobbett, William, 213*fn*
Cokes, family, 112, see also Cookes
Cokes, Charles, of Cleeve, 112*fn*
Cokes, Charles, of Norton, 167

INDEX OF NAMES

Cokes, Sir Thomas, of Bromsgrove, 81
Cole, Anthony, 148
Collis, John Day, 209, 216-20, 222-4, 226, 228-9, 230*fn*, 245
Colyar, William, 179*fn*
Conway, Edward, 102
Cookes, John, 149
Cookes, Sweet-my-footsteps, 149
Cooper, Joseph, 120, 144
Cooper, William (builder), 218-9
Cottam, Robert (c), 200, 202
Cotton, John, 240, 257
Cotton, William, 224*fn*, 257
Crane, John, 202
Crane, Joshua, 204
Crane, Simon, 173
Cromwell, Oliver, 107, 111, 114, 118, 155*fn*, 156
Cromwell, Thomas, 76, 77, 78, 80
Crowe, Ann, 163
Crowe, John, 153*fn*, 155*fn*
Crowe, Mary, 163
Crowe, Roger, 89

Davis, William (whitesmith), 193
Day, Henry (architect), 212-4
Day, Thomas, 218, 244
d'Abitot, Urso, 18, 43
d'Anjou, Margaret, 64
d'Avignon, William (v), 24, 226
de Belne, Robert (v), 37, 80
de Bromsgrove, John, 55
de Bromsgrove, Richard, 50
de Bromsgrove, Robert, 50

de Catshill, John, 35
de Chadwich, Sir Ralph, 34, 35
de Furnell, William (v), 25
de Grafton, John, 35
de Hampton, William (v), 51
de la Hey, Thomas Cuthbert (v), 257, 266, *267*, 270-2
de la Lynde, Richard, 42
de Longespeé, William, 18
de Mortimer, Joan, 53
de Mortimer, John, 52,
de Mortimer, Roger, 53
Dennys, Walter, 97, 98*fn*
de Oxford, John (v), 52
de Pencrich, Richard, 50*fn*
de Prestford, Nicholas, 37
de Raggele, Henry, 52
de Southwood, John, 50
de Wych, Robert, of Alvechurch, 28
Dipple (family), 61, 187
Doria Pamphili, Prince & Princess, *186*
Dovey, - , 189
Dowdeswell, John, 162
Dracott, Edward, 182
Dugard, Henry, 109*fn*
Dugard, William, 109*fn*
Dunn, -, 208

Eckols, Jane, 147
Eckells (also Eckols, Echells) John, 117, 128-30, 146-7, 155
Ede, Dr Moore, Dean of Worcs, 263
Edwards, Thomas, 114*fn*
Edwin, Earl of Mercia, 13

295

Elgar, Edward, 252-5, *253*
Ellins, Henry, 204
Enraght, Revd Richard, 227*fn*

Fairbrother, William, 160
Farnworth, Richard, 126*fn*
Farr, Revd Walter, 250-1
Fawkner, Anthony, 108
Fielding, Sir John, 191
Field, John, 105
Flavell, Ann, 106
Flavell, Richard (c), 106, 144
Flavell, John, 106*fn*
Flavell, Thomas (c), 106, 155
Fletcher, George, 187-8, 202*fn*, 220*fn*, 227-8, 229*fn*, 231
Folyott, Roger, 99-100
Fountaine, Thomas (v), 199
Fowke, Henry, 89*fn*
Fownes, Ann (later Hall), 103
Fownes, John, 109*fn*
Fownes, William, 77, 78
Fox, George, 126*fn*, 147
Freeman, William, 162

Giles, Tobias (c), 105, 111
Glen, George (v), 152, 158, 159
Goode, Benjamin, 163
Goodsoul, Henry, 50
Goodwin, John (c), 202*fn*
Goulden, Richard, 265
Greaves, William, 162
Grosner, Issac (later Paul), 151*fn*
Green, – (builder), 185

Green, John, 247, 247, 270
Greening, -, 203
Habington, Thomas, 53, 66, 87-8, 92*fn*, 135, 138, 233, 257
Haden, Thomas, 153*fn*
Hall, Ann see Fownes, Ann
Hall, Edmund, 105*fn*, 111-2
Hall, Elizabeth, 104, 128*fn*, 148
Hall, Geraldine, 263
Hall, Henry, 50
Hall, Humphrey, 100
Hall, John (v), 103-13, 117, 125, 129, 134, 158, 160, 162
Hall, Bishop John see Bishops
Hall, Phebe, 104
Hall, Rebecca, 104
Hall, Richard (v), 99-100
Hall, Sarah, 104
Hall, Thomas, 111-2, 115*fn*, 119, 124*fn*, 125*fn*, 126, 131-2, 144, 165*fn*
Harding, Thomas (c), 64
Harforde, Richard (v), 82-3, 87, 99, 226
Harper, - (engineer), 223, 242
Hartland, Edmund, 250-1, 256
Hartland, Frances, 256
Hartle, Samuel, 198
Harward, John Netherton (c), 198, 199*fn*
Hastings, Catherine, 43
Hastings, Maud, 43
Hastings, Sir John, 43
Hastings, G.W., 257
Heale, Thomas (v), 100
Heath, Edward, 163

INDEX OF NAMES

Heeks, Jane, 126, 148
Heeks, Richard, 45*fn*
Henderson, J.H., 266, 270
Hepworth and Davis (builders), 175
Hickman, Henry, 124
Higgs, Daniel, 119*fn*
Hill, Edward, 119*fn*
Higgs, John, 162
Hill, John, 165
Hill, Nicholas (1654), 118
Hill, Nicholas (1839), 203-5
Hill, Robert, 152
Hill, Thomas, 163
Hill/Hyll, Thomas (c), 79, 89
Holbeach, Henry (v), 78-9, 200
Holme, Henry see Ulm
Hornsby, George Harcourt, 246
Horton family, 218, 246
Horwood, William (c), 79
Housman, -, 218
Howard, Ld Edmund Bernard, 232
Howe, Sir Scrope, 193
Howle, Ann, Mary and Hanna, 163
Hucheinn, Agnes, 49
Hughes, Henry, 246-7
Humphries, John, 266
Hunniott, John and Mary, 156

Irving, - , 220

Jaeger, Alfred, 255
James, Francis, 169
James, M.R., 268
James, Thomas (c), 77, 89

Jenner, Charles.H., 226-7
Johnson, Joseph (builder), 249
Jolliffe, -, JP, 155
Jones, Llewellyn (c), 238
Jones, Samuel, 204
Joyce of Whitchurch (clockmaker), 256

Kelly, Sir FitzRoy (barrister), 233
Kidd, Dr Cameron, 249, 252
Kimberley, William, 128, 148
Kings
  Alfred, 15
  Ceolwulf, 13
  Charles I, 98, 107, 108, 11, 113*fn*, 115
  Charles II, 130, 142, 144, 160
  Edward I, 51
  Edward II, 53
  Edward III, 53, 55
  Edward VI, 89, 92, 179*fn*
  Edward VII, 252
  George III, 199
  Henry III, 25, 53
  Henry VI, 63
  Henry VII, 65, 72
  Henry VIII, 76, 89, 95
  James I, 93, 98, 102-3
  James II, 194
  John, 25
  Richard III, 72
  William I, 14, 17, 43
  William III, 145
Kings -, police constable, 204
Knight, Stephen, 97, 98*fn*, 179
Lacy, John, 139*fn*, 147, 193, 195

Laird, Francis, 178
Lavers & Barrauld, 244
Lavers, Westlake & Co., 245
le Coke, Adam, 53
Lewis, William, 230, 247
le Yonge, Philip, 51-2
Lidford, - , 188
Lowe, Roger, 112-3
Lylly, Nicholas, 138
Lynall, James, 89, 137
Lyttelton, George, 86, 91, 135, 140

Martin, John, 180
Mallett, Sarah, 163
Malmsbury, William of, 23
Matts, William, 93
Maund, Benjamin, 218, 222, 266
McLachlin, Sr Laurentia, 268
Melewarde, Juliana, 53
Melewarde, Thomas, 53
Meers, Thomas, 180
Middlemore, -,81
Millward, James, 231-2
Milward, Thomas, JP. 126
Minshall, Luke, 208
Moore, Edward, 178, 195
Moore, Hannah, 177
Moore, Robert, 163
Moore, Simon, 114
Moore, Thomas (c), 203, 206-7
Moore, William, Prior of Worcs, 70
More-Molyneux, Revd H.W. (c) 245
Murray, George (v), 199-200, *201*, 203, 207, 212-3, 223*fn*

Murray, George W. (v), 228, 229*fn*, 230, 238, *239*, 240, 245, 262
Murray, Marianne, 246
Murray, Olivia, 245

Nash, Treadway Russell, 169, 257, 273
Newman, John Henry, 254
Nicholson, Benjamin, 126
Nicholson, John, 223
Noake, John, 197*fn*, 208-9, 227*fn*
Norton, William, 182
Notingham, Robert (v?), 100

Oasland, Henry, 117*fn*
Oldcorne, Fr Edward, 92
Owen, Mary, 127
Oxford, John de (v), 52

Paget, Rt Revd Francis (v), 262, *262*
Palmer - (butcher, of Alcester), 138
Palmer, Alfred, 224
Panchieri & Hack, 263*fn*
Parker, Hill, 261
Parkes, Thomas, 237
Patterson, Noel (v), 263, *264*
Paul, Thomas, 180
Payton, Henry, 182
Penne, Richard, 60
Pencrich, Richard, 50
Peake, Mary, 127
Pearce, John, 208
Pearks, John, 123
Perrott, William, 153*fn*
Persey, John (v), 99-100

INDEX OF NAMES

Phillips, William (v), 195
Pinfield, John (builder), 189
Pinock, Ann, 156
Potter, Humphrey, 118, 126*fn*, 146,
Prance, Revd C.H., 238
Prattington, Peter, 71, 177
Prentice, Thomas, 64
Prosser, Mary, 246
Prosser, Dr Roger, 246
Prosser, W., 218

Queens
　Elizabeth I, 87*fn*, 90, 92, 109
　Mary (Tudor), 89, 100

Reynolds, William, 106
Rickman, Thomas, 174-6
Robinson, - (builder), 249
Roger (v), 49
Rose, John (fl 1651), 165*fn*
Rose, John, 165, 242-3
Rose, Joseph, 165-6
Rose, Joseph II, 165, 179, 182*fn*, 188-9, *189*, 197, 209*fn*, 241-2, 249, 276
Rose, Joseph William, 165, 242-4, 256, 265
Rose, Thomas, 165-6, 181, 187, 190, 200
Rose, Walter, 165*fn*
Rose, William, 165
Rose, William II, 165, 180, 184
Rudhall, Abraham, 180
Rudhall, Thomas, 180
Russell, John, 87

Salvay, Nathaniel, 109*fn*
Sampson, of Bromsgrove, 28, 35*fn*
Sanders, Benjamin H., 218, 247
Sekestein (Sexton), John, 49
Scott, George Gilbert, 217-20, 222, 223*fn*, 224, 226, 249
Shayland, Ann, 163
Sheldon, Edward, 118, 171
Sheldon, William of Beoley, 43
Sheldon, William (1552), 87,
Sheldon, William (1651), 110*fn*, 138
Shenstone, William, 162
Shepherd, Frederick (v), 257
Shuard, Thomas, 90
Shurnford, Rachel, 163
Simms, Bishop, 173
Simms, James, 173*fn*
Simple, Richard, 50
Simpson, Leonard, JP, 153
Simson, William, 125*fn*
Sinfield, John, 185
Skidmore, Francis (metalworker), 223, 242
Smart, Samuel, 220*fn*
Smith, Elizabeth, 163
Smith, Thomas, 204
Sora, Duke and Duchess of, 232
Southall, John, 165
Spilsbery, John,116
Spilsbury, James, 127*fn*
Spilsbury, John (v), 114-20, 123-30, 134, 139, 144-6, 152, 159, 226
Spilsbury, John II, 128, 130-1

Spilsbury, Hannah (nee Hall), 104, 117, 128-9
Spilsbury, William and Anne, 114, 116
Spinstowe, John, 180
Stafford, Alienora (nee Burdett), 63-5, 73, 168
Stafford, Sir Humphrey, 63-5, 135, 140, 264
Stafford, Sir Humphrey II, 65, 72
Stafford, Sir Humphrey (nephew), 65
Stafford, Sir Ralph, 43
Staples, John, 154
Steedman -, 193
Steele – (alias Fraser), 153*fn*
St John, St Andrew (v), 199, 200*fn*
Suthwell, William, 133
Sutton, Robert, 64

Talbot, Anna (nee Paston), 74*fn*
Talbot, Anne, 76
Talbot, Audrey (or Ethelreda), 73
Talbot, Bertram Arthur, 232
Talbot, Bridget, 76, 135
Talbot, Elizabeth (nee Greystock), 73
Talbot, Elizabeth (nee Wrottesley), 74, 232-3
Talbot, Elizabeth (nee Wynter), 74
Talbot, Sir Gilbert of Grafton, 72-3, 75
Talbot, Sir Gilbert II of Grafton, 73*fn*, 74
Talbot, John of Grafton, 73*fn*, 74-5, 77, 93, 140, 233
Talbot, Humphrey of Grafton, 73, 76

Talbot, Margaret (nee Troutbeck), 74
Talbot, Margaret, 76, 135
Talbot, William, of Co. Wexford, 232
Taylor, Ralph and Ann, 93
Taylor, Samuel, 204-5
Taylor, William, 181
Thesiger, Sir Frederick (barrister), 233
Thomas, William, 162
Thomas, -, 212
Tidman, John, 179-80
Tilsley, Mary, 126*fn*
Tirbutt, John B, 173*fn*
Tombes, John, 115-7, 119, 123, 124*fn*, 127*fn*
Twitty and Bell (solicitors), 193
Tybson, Richard, 138
Tylt, William, 119*fn*

Ulm Henry, 57

Vine Hall, Edward (v), 247, 249-55, *253*
Villers, William (v), 213-7, *215*, 226-8

Waldron, Henry, 147
Waldron, Humphrey, 115*fn*
Walford, Amy, 246, 265
Wall, Elizabeth, 163
Wall, George, 87
Waller, Adolphus (c), 238
Waller, Sir William, 142
Wallis, John, 154-5
Wannerton, Abel, 71*fn*
Ward & Hughes, 246

INDEX OF NAMES

Warmestry, William, 99
Warmstry, Thomas (v), 150-1, 160, 200*fn*
Waters, Margery, Clement and Catherine, 93
Waugh, John (v), 177, 199, 200*fn*
Weaver, Peter (v), 99-100
Westwood, John, 109, 110*fn*, 113*fn*
Whitcombe, - (builder), 263
White, Thomas, 227-8, 244, 259-61
Wigginton, William, 231-2
Wilkes, Richard, 162
Williamson, family, 93
Willis Bund, J.W., 270
Willmott, Johusha, 158-9
Willmott, Thomas (v), 147, 152-9
Wilmot, Thomas (v), 155*fn*, 162
Winchcombe, Richard of (v), 25, 26
Windsor, Other Hickman, 3rd Earl of Plymouth, 193
Windsor, Thomas Hickman, 1st Earl of Plymouth, 193
Wood, Dr -, 243
Woodhouse - (builder), 169, 198
Wooley, -, 190
Woolley, John (v), 149-50, 159
Worman, Joseph, 163
Wulfhaerd of Inkberrow, 13
Wyatt, Ralph, 99

Friends of ST. JOHN'S

The Friends of St John's exist to raise funds for the ongoing maintenance and restoration needs at the church. We invite people who feel a connection to St John's to join the Friends of St John's for a small annual donation and to attend our organised events.

Keep up to date with Friends and get more information:

Email *friends.stjohns.church@gmail.com*
www.facebook.com/FriendsStJohnsBromsgrove
Twitter *@FriendsStJohns*
Website *stjohns.bromsgrove.church* (within groups)

Visitors to St John's are always welcome.

The church is open daily and on a Saturday where possible. Each year the church opens as part of the Heritage Open Day weekend in September when it is possible for visitors to climb the tower. Sunday services are held at 10.45am.

St John's can be viewed by appointment and it is advisable to call before making a long journey to ensure the church is open on the day of your planned visit.

St John's Church
14 Kidderminster Road
Bromsgrove, Worcestershire, B61 7JW

Parish Office 01527 878801